T0291412

The Creative Wealth of Nations

Development seen from a more holistic perspective looks beyond the expansion of material means and considers the enrichment of people's lives. The arts are an indispensable asset in taking a comprehensive approach toward the improvement of lives. Incorporating aspects of international trade, education, sustainability, gender, mental health, and social inclusion, *The Creative Wealth of Nations* demonstrates the diverse impact of applying the arts in development to promote meaningful economic and social progress. Patrick Kabanda explores a counterintuitive and largely invisible creative economy: whilst many artists struggle to make ends meet, the arts can also be a promising engine for economic growth. If nations can fully engage their creative wealth manifested in the arts, they are likely to reap major monetary and nonmonetary benefits from their cultural sector. Drawing from his own experience of the support music provided growing up amidst political and economic turmoil in Uganda, Kabanda shows us the benefits of an arts-inclusive approach to development in Africa, and beyond.

PATRICK KABANDA is a Juilliard-trained organist and a Fletcher-trained international affairs professional. He received Juilliard's William Schuman Prize for outstanding achievement and leadership in music in 2003, and from 2012 to 2013 he was a Charles Francis Adams Scholar at The Fletcher School. Besides concertizing and lecturing worldwide, he has taught at Phillips Academy, consulted for the World Bank's Office of the Senior Vice President and Chief Economist, and contributed to the *World Development Report 2016* and UNDP's *Human Development Report 2015*. He was awarded the 2013 Presidential Award for Citizenship and Public Service from Tufts.

The Creative Wealth of Nations

Can the Arts Advance Development?

PATRICK KABANDA

Foreword by

AMARTYA SEN

CAMBRIDGE
UNIVERSITY PRESS

CAMBRIDGE
UNIVERSITY PRESS

University Printing House, Cambridge CB2 8BS, United Kingdom

One Liberty Plaza, 20th Floor, New York, NY 10006, USA

477 Williamstown Road, Port Melbourne, VIC 3207, Australia

314–321, 3rd Floor, Plot 3, Splendor Forum, Jasola District Centre,
New Delhi – 110025, India

79 Anson Road, #06–04/06, Singapore 079906

Cambridge University Press is part of the University of Cambridge.

It furthers the University's mission by disseminating knowledge in the pursuit of education, learning, and research at the highest international levels of excellence.

www.cambridge.org
Information on this title: www.cambridge.org/9781108423571
DOI: 10.1017/9781108528832

First published 2018

Printed in the United Kingdom by Clays, St Ives plc

A catalogue record for this publication is available from the British Library.

Library of Congress Cataloging-in-Publication Data
Names: Kabanda, Patrick, author.
Title: The creative wealth of nations : can the arts advance development? / Patrick Kabanda, Dr.
Description: New York : Cambridge University Press, 2018. | Includes bibliographical references and index.
Identifiers: LCCN 2017055355 | ISBN 9781108423571 (hardback)
Subjects: LCSH: Economics – Sociological aspects. | Creative ability in business. | Cultural industries.
Classification: LCC HM548 .K33 2018 | DDC 650.1–dc23
LC record available at https://lccn.loc.gov/2017055355

ISBN 978-1-108-42357-1 Hardback
ISBN 978-1-108-43768-4 Paperback

For my mother

Contents

Foreword

How can the arts promote development? At one level, the answer is absolutely obvious. Development seen in a human perspective, rather than grossly in terms of the expansion of material means, must take note of the enrichment of people's lives. The arts cannot but have a major role in making our lives richer and finer. In this sense, the creative wealth represented by the tradition and practice of the arts is constitutively a part of the process of development.

Despite the obviousness, this basic point is worth stressing, since the temptation to impoverish the understanding of the inclusive nature of development by an exclusive concentration on material objects or convenience, rather than the quality of human lives, is distressingly common in the literature of growth and development.

This, however, is only the beginning of a complex story, and it is the larger account with which Patrick Kabanda is concerned in his brilliant analysis of the arts and how they can promote development in many different ways. If the poorer countries of the world, thoroughly challenged as they are with many economic, social, political, and medical problems, have to search rationally for channels of progress and enrichment of human lives, the role of music, drama, dance, and other such activities has to be seen *also* in terms of their economic contributions, among the other benefits they provide.

Kabanda brings out how the arts can enrich the economies of the world, even when they are stricken by material poverty: Through generating saleable commodities from which the world can benefit and for which the rest of humanity would be ready to make a material contribution, thereby enriching the economic life of people in poorer nations. The complementarity between the economic and the cultural is a major theme of this book, and Kabanda has brought out beautifully how the two could be viewed together in understanding the role of the arts in *The Creative Wealth of Nations*.

Kabanda writes with great facility and clarity. I am impressed to see how his well-known skills as a musician – and Patrick Kabanda has exceptional musical talents with tremendous creativity – can easily be combined with his proficiency in describing difficult problems and their solutions in a lucid and powerfully communicable form.

This is a lovely book on a very important subject. It is fun to read and to reflect on, but it is also an immensely important contribution to the broadening of the understanding of the process of development and human progress. The battle to eradicate poverty need not be seen as an exercise of blood, sweat, and tears. Julius Caesar complained about Cassius, "He hears no music; seldom he smiles." Music and smiling are important not only for a livable human life, but also as a part of a creative process, which has profound economic and social implications, even as it enhances cultural lives. The celebration of creativity in the arts can work hand in hand with the appreciation of the diverse sources of economic progress.

Amartya Sen

Prelude

When I was a child, I lived in two worlds. The first world was a creative one, filled with music, a teeming treasure of sounds that stretched from church to nature. It included thunderous organ chords, melodious tube fiddles, and raspy frog choruses. My second world, meanwhile, was more sober in nature, marked with political instability, hardships, and poverty. These two worlds came together in a loud cacophony that is my home country, Uganda.

Like many so-called developing countries, Uganda is no stranger to strife. As the story often goes, many of us grew up wearing imported second-hand clothes, which some say crashed our textile industry. Many of us walked to school for miles barefoot, only to be spanked for lateness or poor grades. Potholes ruled the roads (they still do), turning some streets into muddy swimming pools after heavy rains.

The list of problems goes on and on, frequently overshadowing the reality and progress of developing countries, and detracting from the visibility of their creative wealth. As a musician, the arts world helped me understand how culture can enrich our lives. When HIV/AIDS descended on Uganda, infecting even fellow classmates who where just coming of age, a Ugandan singer, Philly Lutaaya, took it upon himself to sing messages raising awareness of the disease across the country. When artillery rocked my home city of Kampala, escaping to sing in a choir kept my spirits high. When I was hungry, I bought food using income from playing and teaching music. Simply put, my first world guarded me; it overrode my second world.

I was fortunate to escape my second world and to continue my education in the United States. After studying music at The Juilliard School in New York and teaching at Phillips Academy in Massachusetts, intrigued by my "two-world" experience, I began to consider the possibility of mobilizing the arts behind development, in Africa and elsewhere. And so, I decided to complement my music vocation with studies in international affairs. The idea was to explore how creative output promotes development. The outcome was a thesis on music and international trade and more recently, a working paper that became the basis for this book.

The Creative Wealth of Nations considers both monetary and nonmonetary contributions of the arts to development. Drawing on examples from around the world, it touches on such areas as arts education, environmental stewardship, intellectual property, nation branding, digital technology, tourism, gender equality, mental health, social healing, urban renewal, and creative data collection.

Heeding advice from my writing guru, William Zinsser, I more or less pivot on the performing arts just to bite off one corner of the subject I can chew over now to sustain my zest. By the performing arts, I mean generally dance, drama, and music. Although most examples in this book center on music, examples from dance, theater, and movies are also provided. For the sake of readers unfamiliar with some musical terms, I provide a glossary for those used here.

The book, however, has a comprehensive purpose. It takes a broader perspective – namely, it deals with the performing arts as an exemplar of the wider contribution of the arts to human welfare. After all, from architecture to dance, painting to poetry, the arts tend to feed off each other. This is true, whether they inspire us to innovate, deal with the inevitable, or push us to not only ask questions, but also critically assess the answers we get.

The message of this book rings loud and clear: the importance of the arts is undervalued. As someone whose life has been enriched by music, I must join those challenging this undervaluation, building a case for a strategy that captures the diverse contributions of culture to human welfare. Such creative wealth can unleash all sorts of possibilities – possibilities that harmonize with what meaningful development is all about. That what motivated me to focus on this subject was fueled by personal conviction is to concur with Robert and Michèle Root-Bernstein that feeling and intuition are not impediments to rational thought. They lie at the heart of its foundation.

Acknowledgments

This book draws on my working paper called "The Creative Wealth of Nations" and other related research. I am grateful for the support from former World Bank Senior Vice President and Chief Economist Kaushik Basu, whose intellect and compassion I much admire.

Many investigations that led me to work with Basu germinated at The Fletcher School, where, under Carsten Kowalczyk, I wrote my thesis "Where Culture Leads, Trade Follows," a work on advancing Ugandan music in international trade in services. I recall our debates on the lack of data and what to include and what to exclude. Of particular note is the fact that Amartya Sen encouraged me to engage with the World Bank on this rather unusual subject matter in the field of modern economic thought. As we joked, he wanted to make sure that I sit at the right hand of the chief economist. I have very much learned from Sen, whose book *Development as Freedom* greatly anchored my thinking, and whose intellectual guidance and kindness I admire – he could easily write another book called *Development as Kindness* or *Development as Compassion*. And, speaking of Sen, his faculty assistant, Chie Ri, who dealt with countless emails and assisted in a variety of matters, remains as helpful as ever.

I have had the great luck of having people – some friends, some strangers – who have provided useful comments. These include Karole Armitage, Jessica Hoffmann Davis, Alicia Hammond, Sunil Iyengar, Anna Langdell, Sheila Braka Musiime, Elly Oloo Nyamwaya, Blair A. Ruble, Nandana Sen, Craig Whitney, whose editing prowess no doubt improved the readability of the book, and Daniel Willingham. Many thanks also to the anonymous reviewers. Their comments greatly enabled me to improve the manuscript.

My research for the United Nations Development Programme's *Human Development Report 2015* pushed me to examine the question of women in creative work. Many thanks to Astra Bonini, Selim Jahan, and Shantanu Mukherjee for the opportunity to work with their team and for their comments. Uwe Deichmann gave me an opportunity to contribute to the *World Development Report 2016* and also commented on my background paper on music for development in the digital age.

Many thanks to Laurie Carter, the former vice president for Arts Education at the New Jersey Performing Arts Center (NJPAC) for inviting me to write reports for the Center's arts education digital strategy. Also, thanks to Alison Scott-Williams, the current vice president for Arts Education, and to John Schreiber, the Center's president and CEO, for reviewing my discussion on NJPAC's contribution to Newark's renewal.

I am grateful to all whose insights and comments enriched my analysis. They include: former World Bank president James D. Wolfensohn, Abdul-Rahman B. Akande, Trine Bille, William Caruso, Diane Coyle, Maitreyi B. Das, Sylvie Debomy, Shanta Devarajan, Makthar Diop, Morten Jerven, Joost de Laat, Neil Fantom, Benny Gandy, Colum Garrity, Bodel A. Gnintedem, Phillip J. Hay, Jeremy Andrew Hillman, Samali Kajubi, Laurent Kemoe, Guido Licciardi, Shiva S. Makki, Gerardo Martinez-Freyssinier, Peter G. Moll, Edward Mountfield, Josses Mugabi, Maelle Noe, Fabio Pittaluga, Vijayendra Rao, Dilip Ratha, Felipe Buitrago Restrepo, Natalie Schorr, Joseph Senyonjo, Sally Torbert, Giorgio Valentini, and Albert G. Zeufack; and Professors Miguel E. Basáñez, Diana Chigas, Jeanne Fromer, John Hammock, the late Gerre Hancock, Alan K. Henrikson, Karen Jacobsen, Ian Johnstone, the late Calestous Juma, Harjeet Khosla, Lawrence Krohn, Nathalie Laidler-Kylander, the late William Martel, Greg Morris, Robert Nakosteen, the late Marilyn Neeley, Peter M. Rojcewicz, Jeswald W. Salacuse, Julie Schaffner, Bernard L. Simonin, Charlie W. Steele, Joel P. Trachtman, Christopher Tunnard, John Weaver, Michael Woolcock, and Samuel Zyman.

While at Phillips Academy, Temba and Vuyelwa Maqubela encouraged me to research the role of music as social action in southern Africa. I am equally indebted to the musicians I interviewed, especially J. S. Mzilikazi Khumalo and Richard Cock. Berklee College of Music President Roger H. Brown and Juilliard President Joseph W. Polisi accepted my invitation to speak at Fletcher via the Charles Francis Adams Lecture series. Their ideas on the arts and international affairs strengthened my thoughts on why this topic matters. Also, thanks Paulett Folkins and Karen Mollung for arranging these lectures, and to Dean Gerard F. Sheehan, whose office made these visits possible. I had brief but useful discussions with Harvard's Howard Gardner and Joseph Nye, and I wish to acknowledge their interest in my ideas.

At the World Bank, and Stephen MacGroarty and David Rosenblatt considered my initial draft. I received logistical support from several people, including Dipankar M. Bhanot, Laverne L. Cook, Saida D. Gall, Gabriela E. Calderon Motta, Mikael Ello Reventar, Mihaela Stangu, Jason Victor, and Roula I. Yazigi. Meanwhile, Nancy Morrison edited my previous draft and worked way more than she was contracted to do.

At Cambridge University Press, I am grateful to the team, including the commissioning editor Phil Good and his assistants, Toby Ginsberg and James Gregory, for their contribution to this project. Many thanks also to the content manager, Bethany Johnson, for working swiftly on getting the book through the press, and to the commissioning editor, Maria Marsh, my initial contact at the Press. A word of thanks must also go to Arc Indexing, Inc. and others whose services were invaluable, including the copy-editor, Matthew Bastock, and the production manager, Saranya Jeeva Nath Singh of Integra. Also, a number of organizations and scholars, from Geneva to Tokyo, Nashville to Varna, granted me permission to use their research, including illustrations and excerpts. Long live their generous gestures.

Many people have helped this book move from strength to strength. Since our memory is bounded, as Hebert Simon said, I apologize to anyone I have missed, but I am thankful to the following individuals: the Hon. Arthur Bagunywa, Barnard Birungi, the late Saulo B. Bulega, Mary Belanger, Christy Scott Cashman, Charlie Clements, Nick Danforth, Karen L. Dean, Susu Durst, Neil and Hannah Fairbairn, Haishan Fu, Ellen M. Greenberg, Johanna Grüssner, Lillemor Grüssner Sarah Jackson-Han, Jim Hellinger, Helen T. Herpel, Yuko Hori, Elizabeth Joseph, the late Senteza Kajubi, Fred E. Kirumira, Jim and Louise Kamihachi, David Katuramu, Gregory Kee, Claudia Krimsky, Margo Lamb, Patty Lemmerman, Henry Lippincott, Glenn Little, Ellen E. Mashiko, Maria Matovu, Nancy Miller, Derek and Linda Mithaug, Tariq Muhammad, Budala Mukasa, James Mulondo, Angela Musoke, the late Frank Mwine, Don and Sarah Myracle, Fr. Francisco Nahoe, Fatuma Nalubwama, Dale and Connie Nash, Deborah Nash, George and Mary Neureither, Tony Newman, Takemichi Okui, Carroll Perry, Pete and Ronnie Peterman, Gerard Pierce, Wayne and Barbro Pollock, the late Nathaniel E. Porter, Bertie and Natalie Ray III, Catherine Rielly, Brad Rockwell, Pete Sauerbrey, Andrew Scott, Patrick Scott, Miriam Seltzer, Kanthan Shankar, Doug and Linda Sjostrom, Dirk ten Brink, Philip Theruvakattil, Robert and Elizabeth Torregrossa, Jonathan Vickery, the late Bishop Orris G. Walker, Nathaniel Waxman, Carol Weisel, Dale and Dorothy Whetter, Greg Williams, the late Ralph C. and Barbara T. Williams, Craig and Heidi Whitney, James Wolford, Jean P. Young, and members of the English Chapel, St. Mary Anne's Episcopal Church, and Trinity Episcopal Arlington.

I dedicate this book to my mother, Gladys Nalwoga, who dealt with a kid who wanted to do nothing but play music. Ugandan music geniuses Samuel Kimuli and Michaiah Mukiibi inspired my artistic aspirations, causing one spectator to comment: "It is as if their fingers itch if they do not play music!" My fingers have yet to itch from playing music. But they might have itched from writing this book. I will therefore have reason to feel well rewarded if readers will find this discussion meaningful and act on advancing the arts in development.

Overture

From Sustainable to Meaningful Development: The Role of the Arts

> Preserving and promoting cultural heritage and cultural products can help reduce extreme poverty in those developing countries that are economically poor but endowed with a rich and diverse heritage.
>
> The World Bank[1]

There was once a country we shall call Creativeria, which had natural resources beyond measure – gold and oil, lakes and rivers, forests and soil. But the problem was all too familiar: These resources benefitted the very few. Although Creativeria's gross domestic product (GDP)[2] was growing at an impressive pace, its riches failed to trickle down to those at the bottom. As wealth for the haves was increasing, poverty for the have-nots was also increasing. The situation puzzled "experts" so much that development agencies started to talk about promoting shared prosperity.

As development summits cropped up here and there, the leaders of Creativeria decided to call a summit of their own. Unlike models shaped by the Bretton Woods agenda, theirs was a summit attended by people from diverse walks of life – from artists to economists, from teachers to rural workers, and from the young to the old. The idea of diversifying the economy and integrating the Sustainable Development Goals in Creativeria's new development strategy was much discussed. Some participants decided to even simply call the targets Good Development Goals.[3]

At this event, various stratagems – including taking on tax evasion, dubious development programs, and military spending – were deliberated. On the last day of the summit, Creativeria made a remarkable move: It pledged to decrease its military spending and increase its spending on health care, education, and creative industries. For security is not only a military issue, Creativeria reckoned; it is also a human one. There is health security as well as education security. There is speech security. There is climate security as well as food security. There is cultural security. And so on.[4]

Creativeria recognized that it had not only a rich natural resource base, but abundant cultural riches as well. Many art forms lay untapped. In a notable move, Creativeria's leaders avoided the trap of going to important summits and meeting important people who say important things but then do nothing. They pledged to act on promoting culture in development. Soon other countries decided to follow Creativeria's example.

Why? Because new approaches to development are badly needed. Although impressive gains have been made, as we now know too well, all too often development experts have failed to meet their clients' needs. Around the world, many people remain trapped in extreme poverty and other deprivations. In fact, new challenges, including frequent natural disasters, violent extremism, and forced displacement of people threaten to reverse the progress that has been made.[5] In charting the path forward, one key area is often neglected: culture.

"Things are to be tried," as one Zimbabwean Proverb puts it. "An old lady cooked stones and they produced soup." Since there is no magic formula to achieve development,[6] trying new things also means shifting ideological preferences and embracing a far-reaching question: How can the creative wealth abundant even in the poorest of nations be utilized to promote meaningful economic and social progress?

The country called Creativeria does not actually exist.[7] Imagining it nevertheless invites us to consider this: If developing countries can promote their creative resources, they are likely to see gains they have not even thought about before.

THE CREATIVE WEALTH OF NATIONS

This book argues that the arts and culture are not "luxuries," but are essential to the central task of development: improving people's lives.

If nations can fully engage their creative wealth, they are likely to reap major monetary and nonmonetary benefits. But the conversation between an arts advocate and a development expert – at a development organization like the World Bank – is likely to go like this:

ARTS ADVOCATE: You know, countries like Jamaica and the Congo have great music. But the music sector there is largely untapped. The Bank could help develop this area.

DEVELOPMENT EXPERT: Oh, I see what you mean. But what is the comparative advantage for the Bank?

Another typical answer: I see what you mean, I see, I see. But what is the economic argument for this?

There are clear and ringing answers to these questions. Culture contributes to development in many ways. Here are just three: First, by generating direct economic activity through performances and trade in cultural goods and services. Second, through the arts' ability to emancipate or foster human imagination. Third, by cultivating community solidarity, inclusion, and collaboration.[8] The arts have a compelling role, both directly and indirectly.

I will expand on the three examples above throughout this book. Meanwhile, consider the following points: *economic diversification, international trade, creativity and innovation,*[9] *job creation, youth employment, social inclusion*, and *cultural democracy*. In the interrelated structure of culture in development it is not difficult to see that creativity and innovation can lead to job creation, for example, while also contributing to the quality of people's lives. With that in mind, let me comment a little on these points.

Much-needed economic diversification. Developing countries with a restricted range of exports and job-creating arrangements are often advised to diversify. So, if they have a comparative advantage in the cultural sector, there is a compelling reason for them to augment their arts resources; this work could be done under a broad framework of developing cultural industries.

International trade. International trade in cultural items is likely to promote trade in other sectors and give nations a distinctive and positive "brand." "[R]aising the profile of a country's culture in foreign lands may also be an element in a wider trade agenda, in pursuit of the old adage 'where culture leads, trade follows.' Thus sending a symphony orchestra or a dance troupe or an art exhibition to a potential trading partner may increase mutual understanding between countries and facilitate trade deals in commodities far removed from the arts and culture."[10] Trade in cultural products from low-income countries can help them integrate in global trade, an area where they especially lag.

Creativity and innovation. Modern economic growth is driven by creativity and innovation. For this, we are told. Since the arts are custodians of creativity and imagination, there is much reason to court them in areas such as education, entrepreneurship, and business, as well as research and development.[11] While the arts do not have a monopoly on inducing new ways of thinking, they can push us to expand our thinking. They challenge us to attack difficult problems, work in teams, concede failure, learn from mistakes, overcome self-doubt, observe, indulge in curiosity, develop patience – and yes, even cultivate "constructive impatience." These attributes may not be "creative" as such, but they encourage a culture that celebrates direct and indirect learning, open mindedness, adapting, execution, and so on – aspects in steady courtship with creativity and innovation.

Job creation. "As a basis for an effective employment policy, the cultural industries offer governments a particularly attractive target for investment, since the labour content of cultural output is typically higher than in other sectors."[12] Apart from direct artistic jobs, various jobs spin off from staging a performance, conducting tours, and so on, ranging from food services to arts management, from dry cleaning to legal services.

Youth employment. The problem of youth unemployment is huge and growing. It is clear that the traditional systems of employment are not sufficient to address the problem of unemployment – and indeed that of underemployment. Countries need to consider strategies that link youth employment to the economic benefits the arts can bring (creativity and innovation, international trade, and job creation). Although the problem of ageism deserves much attention, as does the question of older people's contribution and access to cultural employment, many young people may gravitate toward artistic jobs. For these jobs tend to "provide greater levels of employee satisfaction than more routine occupations because of the commitment and sense of cultural involvement engendered among participants in a creative endeavor."[13]

Social inclusion. As social creatures, human beings need one another. Indeed, the problem of social exclusion may be among the reasons that fuel some forms of inequality and intolerance. The arts, as widely acknowledged, can be a circuit-breaker of human isolation.[14] For example, "[t]he arts can nurture social capital by strengthening friendships, helping communities to understand and celebrate their heritage, and providing a safe way to discuss and solve difficult social problems."[15] From South Africa, where music helped dismantle apartheid, to India, where participatory theater is giving the oppressed a voice, the arts exhibit a promising role in advancing social inclusion.

Cultural democracy. The words "culture" and "democracy" can take on diverse meanings.[16] But it can be argued that cultural democracy mirrors UNESCO's Universal Declaration on Cultural Diversity. The following Articles from the Declaration are worthy of note:

> **Article 2:** From cultural diversity to cultural pluralism: In our increasingly diverse societies, it is essential to ensure harmonious interaction among people and groups with plural, varied and dynamic cultural identities as well as their willingness to live together. Policies for the inclusion and participation of all citizens are guarantees of social cohesion, the

> vitality of civil society and peace. Thus defined, cultural pluralism gives policy expression to the reality of cultural diversity. Indissociable from a democratic framework, cultural pluralism is conducive to cultural exchange and to the flourishing of creative capacities that sustain public life.
>
> **Article 3:** Cultural diversity as a factor in development: Cultural diversity widens the range of options open to everyone; it is one of the roots of development, understood not simply in terms of economic growth, but also as a means to achieve a more satisfactory intellectual, emotional, moral and spiritual existence.[17]

In many ways, the arts can contribute to social progress and economic growth. Across the so-called "developing world," this cultural diversity is astonishingly developed and rich. Acknowledging this is critical. It can unleash all sorts of possibilities in a world of limited resources. As we try to fund dams and roads, we should also seek ways to promote trade in music and films. As we try to attack the tyranny of gender bias or reform the judiciary and governance, we should seek ways to use culture to promote social progress. As we invite finance ministers to places like the World Bank, we should also invite cultural ministers to discuss the promotion of creative output in the modern economy.

By overlooking the cultural wealth of developing countries, we miss the bigger picture. There are no easy answers, but we need to ask how the arts can be a part of sound economic strategies to make lives better.

Most fundamentally, culture and the arts are part of what gives development and growth meaning, as leaders in Creativeria reckoned. So what this book is advocating is not just sustainable development, but meaningful development.

The arts cannot do it alone, but they can be part of the solution. Supporting creativity in developing countries could play a notable role in reducing extreme poverty and sharing prosperity – but only if we care to actively consider such wealth in our thinking. And if that thinking is to translate into effective action, then that good old phrase "leadership" comes up. But since leadership seminars are all over the place these days, what qualities of leadership are we talking about?

The Art of Leadership: Lessons from a Master Pianist

Noel Tichy and Warren Bennis attempt to answer that question in their book *Judgment: How Winning Leaders Make Great Calls*: "Like a master pianist, a gifted leader knows which chords to strike hard and how to strike them, at certain times fortissimo, at others a subtle pianissimo. That's called *touch*."[18] Since anyone involved in development is somehow a leader, directly or indirectly, what can the arts teach us about "*touch*" in development?

That question is particularly pertinent because development tends to draw heavily on economic theory. Research in modern economic theory, however, is largely driven by mathematical economists. "This has meant that ideas that might have been important, but were not mathematically hard enough, got left by the wayside. This is understandable (not to be confused with commendable)," as Kaushik Basu has argued in his book *Beyond the Invisible Hand*. "This quest for complication has hurt the discipline of economics. Simple truths escape our attention in the stampede to discover complicated truths or, worse, complicate truths."[19] I sometimes wonder what Adam Smith would have said about dismissing *touch* just because we cannot baptize it in math.

Do we not need to rethink the over-application of mathematical economics in driving development?[20] "Public policy, like politics, is the art of the possible, and this is important to bear in mind in combining theoretical insights with realistic readings of practical feasibility."[21] Should we not recall that insight? *Touch* is not easy to quantify. But it has never been more important in the realistic application of what is practically feasible.

And talking of practical feasibility, the art of the possible, let me use this moment to signal what I shall comment on again at end of this book. Economics is much better at describing the *consequences* of the paths we may take than it is at predicting the exact paths we will elect to follow.[22] That is why a holistic approach that considers varied touches is badly needed. Here, Robert L. Heilbroner, who foreshadows the need for holistic knowledge noted in Chapter 2, notes: "What we lack, in a word, is a unifying theory of social change in which the distinctions of 'economics' and 'sociology' and 'political science' would yield to a new 'holistic' science of society."[23] A master pianist may know about the math in the music, but she draws on holistic view as she applies *touch* in performance. Even as she strikes chord by chord, that is case. That is her unifying theory. So, practically speaking, the touch metaphor can guide leadership in development, precisely because it expresses the diverse techniques needed to achieve meaningful progress.

The Arts Are Not a Luxury

Many of us would like to see a world free of poverty, where every human being can live a life of meaning, where all people can achieve their fullest potential. In assessing the diverse contribution of the arts, regardless of their monetary impact, the first task is to recognize that the arts are not a luxury – a nice "add-on" after basic necessities have been met. In many places where needless hardship rules people's lives, the arts often provide much-needed life support.

In the Democratic Republic of the Congo, where natural resources flow like gifts from heaven, but often do nothing but carry problems from hell, the Director of National Institute of the Arts, Yoka Lye, told writer Alexis Okeowo: "Art and music in our country are another way of breathing for people – another way of resisting."[24]

In Paraguay, a place with blazing inequality, deprived young children started making music instruments out of garbage to make their lives a little better (see Chapter 3): As Favio Chávez, the director of the Recycled Orchestra of Cateura, put it, the world sends them garbage, they send back music.

In Taiwan, a place that has not escaped the idea that the "dominant value" is "to be successful,"[25] from 1990 to 2010, common mental disorders in the population rose from 11.5 percent to 23.8 percent.[26] "Efforts have been stepped up in recent years to improve care and treatment for people with mental health issues," the BBC reports. "The island is at the forefront of a trend in some Asian societies to openly confront the issue." Besides employing strategies such as providing job skills, recovering patients also compete at an annual arts talent show. Despite the common misconception, this artistic effort is not a luxury, but a movement to help those in mental distress regain their confidence as dignified contributors to society.[27]

Indeed, marginalized people across the world can understand what Voltaire meant: "Life is a shipwreck, but we must not forget to sing in the lifeboats."

A Long Tradition: The Links between Culture, Economics, and Development

The centrality of culture to economics and development is not a new idea. Some early names that shed light on the link between culture and the operation of societies include Adam Smith, John Stuart Mill, Alfred Marshall,[28] John Maynard Keynes,[29] and Lionel Robbins. Contemporary economists, including José Antonio Abreu, Kaushik Basu, Amartya Sen, and David Throsby, have also explored the role of culture in development.

This book draws on that tradition, and many ideas in it have been discussed in the Creative Economy Reports of the United Nations, which provide "a robust framework for identifying and understanding the functioning of the creative economy as a cross-cutting economic sector…"[30] On such issues as innovation, international trade, cultural heritage, dignity, and job creation, youth employment, sustainability, and social inclusion, readers can learn many things from this body of work.

The Time Is Ripe

With the current interest in ending extreme poverty, there has never been a better time to fully engage cultural activities in development.

The world has made a major advance. Although the United Nations Sustainable Development Goals (SDGs) fall short of fully acknowledging culture's potential role in development, they mention the "appreciation of cultural diversity, and of culture's contribution to sustainable development." Consider the following targets: 8.9: "By 2030, devise and implement policies to promote sustainable tourism that creates jobs and promotes local culture and products". 12.b: "Develop and implement tools to monitor sustainable development impacts for sustainable tourism that creates jobs and promotes local culture and products."[31]

Moreover, as the United Nations put it, global interconnectedness and new technologies have the potential to accelerate human progress.[32] In a cultural dimension, cultural activities are increasingly becoming recognized as drivers of meaningful development.[33] This approach is welcome. For the utility of the arts is strikingly in line with development that advances wellbeing in full dimensions. Indeed, development programs, whatever their means of delivery, should seek to enhance the quality of people's lives. If that is the case, then it bears remembering not to confuse fat bank accounts with the quality of life.[34] I would summarize this way:

Development that is consistent with reducing "extreme poverty and sharing prosperity is ultimately about enriching the life and enabling the potential of every human being," as the World Bank put it. The arts can help in this process of enrichment: specifically in the tasks of developing human capability, gender equality, "voice and participation, and freedom from violence."[35]

Although developing countries are poor in terms of GDP, they have rich cultural assets. Lifting their poorest citizens out of extreme poverty is a multidimensional task that requires applying a number of tools. So, the menu of options should include further systematic understanding of how cultural activities can be part of the solution, fostering social inclusion, climate action, and income-generating activities.[36] This reflects the World Bank's document on cultural heritage and poverty reduction: "Preserving and promoting cultural heritage and cultural products can help reduce extreme poverty in those developing countries that are economically poor but endowed with a rich and diverse heritage."[37] But also, as widely understood, cultural activities can foster nation-building, bridge social differences, and much more.

As South African singer Lucky Dube said during one of his performances in Uganda in the early '90s, dismantling apartheid from South Africa's legal codes did not automatically guarantee the removal of apartheid from people's minds. In keeping the candle of reconciliation burning, South African artists have organized choral festivals (some of them showcasing as many as 3,000 singers) in an attempt to bring whites and blacks together.[38] "[S]everal white South African composers have intentionally juxtaposed, borrowed, imitated, and quoted indigenous African music to bring attention to the issues of race relations within their country," as Allyss Angela Haecker wrote in 2012: "The results of this synthesis are not only innovative musical compositions, but may also reflect an endeavor to unify a divided nation."[39]

More recently, the European Commission's Library and e-Resources Centre assembled a list of selected "publications on the inclusion [and] integration of refugees and migrants in European societies through" the arts and culture.[40]

Such examples show that while its instrumental value is compelling, culture is not restricted to monetary reward. The social contribution of culture deserves closer scrutiny in building foundations of human and sustainable development, even as these ideas evolve. Cultural activities are vehicles for collective voice, gender equality, social capital, mental health, education, environmental promotion, national identity, cultural heritage, and so on. To acknowledge this is to move beyond relegating them to the basket of simplemindedness.[41] Along those lines, to build on the opening example of Creativeria, this book seeks to exhibit development beyond GDP growth. "Development," as Amartya Sen reminds us, "requires the removal of major sources of unfreedom: poverty as well as tyranny, poor economic opportunities as well as systematic social deprivation, neglect of public facilities as well as intolerance or overactivity of repressive states."[42]

The arts have a vital role to play in achieving a world free of poverty, where every human being can live a life of meaning, and where all people can achieve their fullest potential.

PART I The Arts, the Economy, and Development

1 An Untapped and Unmeasured Economy

On the Value of the Arts

The contributions to the richness of human lives made by the creative arts – often available free or at little cost – does not figure much in the gross national product (GNP), or for that matter in the Human Development Index (HDI). But that is a problem for the GNP and the HDI, not a reason for the neglect of the creative arts.

Amartya Sen[1]

THE SYMPHONY OF "CHICKEN VERSUS EGG"

What comes first? Is it the arts and then development, or is it development and then the arts? The discussion often goes off in both directions, like a symphony full of "deceptive cadences" that take the harmony off in unexpected directions. The debate can be passionate, but it conceals as much as it reveals, because what drives progress is a complex mix of things. While some believe economic expansion comes first, there is reason to consider why others say "No, no, no. Culture comes first because we make progress by building on the past." This chapter, the opening measures of this opus, attempts to demonstrate the instrumental and non-instrumental value of the arts (pun intended).[2] Movement I begins by citing the United States and Nigeria to show the latest developments in figuring out ways to count the value of the creative sector's contribution to the economy. A countersubject to this theme is how the arts have contributed to innovation even in seemingly unrelated sectors of the economy. Movement II, meanwhile, weaves together the themes of the arts, social inclusion, and social capital, with the counterpoint of the costs of social exclusion and cultural confusion. It ends with a coda foreshadowing the later theme of creative trade, which will be picked up in Chapters 4, 5, and 6.

***

MOVEMENT I

ON THE INSTRUMENTAL CONTRIBUTION OF THE CREATIVE SECTOR TO THE ECONOMY

An inquiry into the nature and causes of human progress tells us that in the beginning there was art, and art was life, and life was art.[3] That artistic life enriched people's lives and contributed to the wealth of nations. But it remained largely invisible. Fortunately, even in the narrow sense of economic accounting, things are changing. Not long ago, for example, the Bureau of Economic Analysis, an agency whose job is to help us better understand the economy of the United States, took a creative step: It started to record expenditures for research and development and "for entertainment, literary, and artistic originals as fixed investment." Grouped with software expenditures, these expenditures are now part of a new investment category called "intellectual property products."[4] This revision makes the US economy roughly "3 percent – or $400 billion – larger than thought."[5]

Nigeria undertook a similar exercise. With the adjustment of some statistical categories, its GDP grew 90 percent overnight, to overtake South Africa as the largest African economy. "Nigeria's statistician-general announced that his country's GDP for 2013 had been revised from 42.4 trillion naira to 80.2 trillion naira ($509 billion). The estimated income of the average Nigerian went from less than $1,500 a year to $2,688 in a trice" (of course, average Nigerians did not suddenly become richer). And whether or not Nigeria keeps the top spot as Africa's crown economy, the priority should be to ensure how all this works to improve the lives of poor Nigerians. But how did this accounting come about? Primarily by recognizing that the old way of accounting "gave little or no weight to fast-growing parts of the economy such as mobile telephony or the movie industry."[6]

In Brazil, where cultural diversity flows like honey from heaven, the creative sector has employed more than eleven million people in recent years – although, needless to say, this figure may not say much, as it does not account for the direct and indirect jobs in the creative informal sector. All the same, the country is now one of the world's prominent cultural markets. No wonder the Brazilian government has recognized "the importance of the cultural industries by creating a permanent Secretariat for Creative Economy within the Ministry of Culture."[7]

That acknowledgment notwithstanding, Brazil's recent political turmoil cannot but invite comment. Not only did the turmoil lead to the impeachment of President Dilma Rousseff, it also led to the shutdown of a number of government ministries to cut costs. No sooner did Michel Temer become interim president in May 2016 than he subsumed the Ministry of Culture into that of education – because, we are told, this is where it was in the 1980s.[8] But while the cost-cutting exercise included axing the Ministry of Science and Technology, that move did not get as much attention as that which attacked culture. Brazilian artists took to the streets, demanding their ministry back.[9] And sure enough, shortly thereafter, the cultural ministry was reinstated.[10]

Now and again in the cost-benefit analyses, politicians forget that sometimes culture is not just about money – although that is of course important. Culture is also about people's identity and dignity, which they have reason to value. Having full-fledged representation of those values in the government is one assurance that leaders care about the heritage of their peoples.

Moreover, as Eric Weiner reminds us in his book *The Geography of Genius* – and this is a subtle but important point in understanding the diverse dimensions of the creative wealth of nations – it is difficult to move forward without knowing the past. From Athens to Hangzhou, history is replete with examples of this.[11] And if you take a leaf out of the books of Bach or jazz, for example, this is not difficult to see. In assessing the contribution of knowledge to development,[12] a leitmotif that will appear in this work, there is much reason to consider how learning from the past can inform the future. This is important to make progress, be it economic, political, or social.

Innovation is not just about making products. It is also about executing ideas. (I will highlight this later in this chapter with a case study on Nashville.) Moreover, learning from the past includes reflecting on how, for example, our legal frameworks or customs have worked before and how we might improve upon them. Many developing countries and their development partners, however, pay scarce attention to how culture might stimulate ideas for growth. The modus operandi for the most part is to exploit land and extractives. No wonder that, until recently, accounting practices in Nigeria and elsewhere were less concerned with considering the creative intangible aspects of the economy.

Countries, of course, should not wake up tomorrow and dump their extractive activities altogether. The question might be how extraction should be done in a more sustainable manner, how its benefits should trickle down to the poorest of the poor, and how to diversify so that the economy is not dependent on just a few items. All this requires cultivating diverse ideas. In fact, as Todd G. Buchholz notes is his book *New Ideas from Dead Economists*, countries that tend to prosper invest in ideas. Indeed, whether standard economics hides as much as it reveals, consider this question: "In the race for economic development, would you rather bet on a country with a million tons of endowed zinc or one with a couple of extra IQ points and a free flow of ideas?"[13]

The Republic of Korea, whose development was mostly industrial led, is often cited as an example of a country which has considered learning from its past as it seeks to build a new knowledge-based economy. Korea is not without its problems. (And telling is the recent political scandal, which, as in Brazil, engulfed a head of state, leading to the 2017 ouster of President Park Geun-hye.[14]) Nevertheless, in the cultural sector, which is very much part of the knowledge economy, there is reason to consider what other countries can learn from this East Asian republic. "South Korea, a country of less than fifty million, somehow figured out how to make pop hits for more than a billion and a half other Asians, contributing two billion dollars a year to Korea's economy, according to the BBC. K-pop concerts in Hong Kong and on mainland China are already lucrative, and no country is better positioned to sell recorded music in China, a potentially enormous market, should its endemic piracy be stamped out."[15]

And speaking of China, there is the Wanda Cultural Industry Group, which suggests that it is China's largest cultural enterprise – in the first half of 2017, it reported revenue of more than 30 billion yuan. The group, which is also active in the terrain of commercial properties, internet, and finance, ranked 380th on the 2016 Fortune Global 500 List.[16] In assessing Wanda's investments, of particular note is its Cultural Tourism Planning & Research Institute.

The Institute, we are told, is not only Wanda's cultural creativity center, but also its science and technology innovation center. It "brings together domestic and foreign top art masters" in addition to "science and technology talents." And "its business covers the theme-related entertainment businesses ... creative development, performing arts production, technology research and development, intellectual property licensing and service of the derivatives."[17] On top of that, when it comes to foreign cultural investments, Wanda's recent interest in investing billions in Hollywood suggests that the Wanda-Hollywood dance may just be getting started.[18]

As these examples show, the so-called creative economy is huge, under constant transformation, and hard to measure. Consider these direct and indirect contributions to the economy:

A Large and Growing Sector. Trade in the creative sector has enjoyed continuous growth even in the recent turbulent economic times, a 2010 United Nations report on the global creative economy suggests. It more than doubled from $267 billion in 2002 to $592 billion worldwide in 2008. But most of this commerce is realized in developed countries, which accounted for 83 percent of exports in creative services and 56 percent in creative goods. Developing countries could tap into this market and benefit from their own cultural production.[19] (There is also the possibility for regional growth through trade in the arts; see the recommendation at the end of this chapter.)

Substantial Multiplier Effects. Arts Council England estimates that every £1 of salary paid by the arts and culture industry generates an additional £2.01 in the wide economy by "attracting visitors; creating jobs and developing skills; attracting and retaining businesses revitalizing places; and developing talent."[20] The US Bureau of Economic Analysis, in partnership with the National Endowment for the Arts, found that for every dollar consumers spend on arts education, an additional 56 cents is generated elsewhere in the US economy.[21] There are few such estimates for developing regions, but arguably every additional pound or dollar is worth more to developing countries than it is to England or to the United States.

The Green Economy and Cultural Jobs. "[T]he types of jobs created in the cultural sector are greener, more enjoyable and deliver greater non-pecuniary rewards to workers than is the case for jobs in other sectors such as manufacturing."[22] What is more, as the Australian cultural economist David Throsby tells us, "the creative industries have a particular role to play, not just through exemplary environmental practice in their own operations, but also through the contribution that creative ideas in design, architecture," and so forth, "can make to the development of carbon-reducing technologies in other industries."[23] In promoting the green wealth of nations, there are also various ways in which the arts can shift behaviors and attitudes toward climate change (see Chapter 3).

Innovation. When Steve Jobs said that marrying technology with liberal arts and the humanities is what made Apple's heart sing, as Jonah Lehrer noted, he was not simply repeating platitudes common in Silicon Valley. Jobs believed that technology did not live by computer science alone, but by connecting with the arts and humanities.[24] In fact, although Steve Jobs was no saint by all accounts, and there is debate as to whether he was more of a marketing genius than a genuine artist,[25] it's difficult to gainsay Walter Isaacson's conclusion in his biography on the man: "Jobs stands as the ultimate icon of inventiveness, imagination, and sustained innovation. He knew that the best way to create value in the twenty-first century was to connect creativity with technology, so he built a company where leaps of the imagination were combined with remarkable feats of engineering."[26] The arts can lead to creativity that induces innovation in other areas, often with unanticipated payoffs. Those payoffs, as I signaled earlier, are not new as such; they are discoveries we make as we observe, become more curious, build on the past, embrace mistakes, and learn by doing. Consider the following episode, which involves a hymnal, science, and scrap paper.

THE ARTS AND INNOVATION

Arthur Fry, a scientist and inventor, had no idea that singing in a church choir could lead him to cocreate a billion-dollar product; he simply wanted reliable bookmarks that would not fall out of his hymnbook while singing. But that is what happened to him. This accidental invention – Post-it® Notes – became one of the top five best-selling office supply products in the world. Here is how these sticky notes became an office staple.

Some decades ago, when chemist Spencer Silver was working at the Minnesota Mining and Manufacturing Company (later renamed 3M) in the United States, he wanted to make super-strong adhesives that could be used to build airplanes. But his invention was far from super-strong: he accidentally created an "incredibly weak, pressure sensitive adhesive agent called Acrylate Copolymer Microspheres."[27]

Since the agent was seen as too weak to be useful, "no one, not even Silver himself, could think up a good marketable use for it. Thus, even with Silver promoting it for five years straight to various 3M employees, the adhesive was more or less shelved."[28]

But not all was lost. Silver had an idea. When Geoff Nicholson was made 3M's products laboratory manager in 1973, Silver approached him to sound out what he thought of the idea of creating a sticky "bulletin board with the adhesive sprayed on it." That sounded like a good idea. But since annual sales of bulletin boards are usually low, the idea was not seen as potentially profitable.

Then Arthur Fry entered the picture. A product development engineer at 3M, he knew of Silver's work. He also sang in a local church choir. Tired of having his song page markers fall out of his hymnal while singing, his mind flipped back to Silver's adhesive. Maybe it could "help keep the slips of paper in the hymnal. Fry then suggested to Nicholson and Silver that they were using the adhesive backwards. Instead of sticking the adhesive to the bulletin board, they should 'put it on a piece of paper and then we can stick it to anything.'"[29]

That "proved easier said than done, in terms of practical application." It took years of further experimentation, and since the management at 3M "still didn't think the product would be commercially successful," the product was shelved for three more years – even though the sticky notes were extremely popular at 3M labs during that time. Finally, in 1977, 3M began running test sales in four cities "to see if people would buy and use the product." (It was then named "Press 'n Peel.") "It turns out, no one much did, which confirmed in the minds of the executives that it wasn't a good commercial product."[30]

Luckily for offices the world over, Nicholson and Joe Ramey, Nicholson's boss, did not feel like giving up yet. They felt that people needed to see for themselves how useful the notes could be. So a year later, 3M reintroduced sticky notes, this time giving away huge amounts of samples for free in Boise, Idaho. "The re-order rate went from almost nothing, in the previous attempt, to 90 percent" – this was "double the best initial rate 3M had seen for any other product they'd introduced. Two years later, the Post-It note was released throughout the United States . . . Today it is a staple in homes, schools, and businesses the world over."[31]

The sticky-note episode is a remarkable story that speaks for itself. Let me nonetheless unpack some lessons we might draw from it.

First, we all know that there are many good ideas produced every day, but that few succeed. That, however, does not mean that we should not cultivate an environment that encourages creativity and innovation. But it also does not mean that arts education – or math and science education for that matter – automatically produces genius. As *The Geography of Genius* makes clear, creativity is holistic, it is interconnected, and it dances with constraints and the law of unintended consequences.[32] As if to warm the hearts of arts education advocates (more on this in Chapter 2), Arthur Fry was an inventor whose passion for singing stirred his creative buds. His interest in solving a problem that affected his choral experience made him see a connection with science. He is a smart guy, for sure. Nevertheless, what made him and his collaborators smarter was not just training in more music or more science. It was their ability to see a connection that ran from a church pew to a science lab. As if to remain true to theory of delight-induced innovation, these sticky notes have gone on to even inspire playful humor. I cannot help but marvel about the "Gone Chopin" and "Bach Soon" stickies that have cropped up, not to mention the "Chopin Liszt."

Second, in the framework of knowledge for development, economists have illustrated a learning curve that deserves scrutiny. For it "addresses the centrality of investment in the learning-by-doing model. More investment leads to more experience and unit costs will decrease as a result of more experience and knowledge," as Franz cites Mikic.[33] That is all well and good. But "this approach ignores the role of the individual, the team, and appropriability environment in the formation of new ideas. It focuses on the process of invention in the production of goods; but, not on conception of new goods."[34] Does the sticky-note story not show that conception is just as important? "Everyone knows the old saying 'Necessity is the mother of invention,'" as Steven Johnson writes in his book *Wonderland: How Play Made the Modern World*. If you observe carefully, however, you will notice something deeper: Pleasure and play have also been responsible for the conception of many of the most important ideas or institutions today.[35] In connection with *The Geography of Genius*, the arts clearly have a prominent place here, as they lead to more play and pleasure. Indeed, one could say, "where play leads, ideas follow." But how often is such a reading debated in knowledge formation and development policy?

Third, as Jared Franz explains, "the economic appeal of learning-by-doing is obvious because it corresponds well with the economic theory of specialization and the division of labor, courtesy of Adam Smith," composer of *The Wealth of Nations*. The idea is that increases in gross investment lead to decreases in unit labor cost. Plus, as Franz goes on to say, "it has intuitive appeal and is easy to model in many economic situations." That said, concerning ideas, Adam Smith was not short of insightful comments.[36] Think about the following quote (aptly cited in *The Economics of Ideas*). Smith employs machinery to present his point. The machines could easily be sticky notes made in Creativeria (see the Overture) or in Nigeria, however:

> All the improvements in machinery, however, have by no means been the inventions of those who had the occasion to use the machines. Many improvements have been made by the ingenuity of the makers of the machines, when to make them became the business of a peculiar trade; and some by that of those who are called philosophers or men of speculation, whose trade is not to do any thing, but to observe every thing; and who, upon that account, are often capable of combining together the powers of the most distant dissimilar objects.[37]

As Franz notes, clearly Smith saw that improvements could also be made by observation, not just through the division of labor, specialization, or learning by doing.[38] And that observation could be observing how the "powers of the most distant dissimilar objects" can work together, as Arthur Fry saw. Whether growth is exogenous or endogenous, is there no need to heed from that insight? Here we can draw lessons from the arts, for they are powerful teachers of observation.

The art of observation might seem just as easy to master. But it requires a clear mind. In this day and age, where we are susceptible to information overload, our minds are easily cluttered. As the neuroscientist Moshe Bar says, we eat food, but we do not taste it; we look at beautiful things, but do not see them.[39] Applying this to development policy, it is remarkable how much gets overlooked, as we clutter our minds with competing interests. We obsess about meeting quotas, for example, regardless of whether problems are solved or not. And we constantly load our thoughts with potential future moves like calculating to get promotions instead of genuinely solving problems.

In the journal *Psychological Science*, Shira Baror and Moshe Bar "demonstrate that the capacity for original and creative thinking is markedly stymied by stray thoughts, obsessive ruminations and other forms of 'mental load.'" They go on to "suggest that innovative thinking, not routine ideation, is our default cognitive mode when our minds are clear."[40] A clear mind is likely to be more observant. And an observant mind is much needed in development policy, because it might allow us to see and tap into what is there – like the cultural wealth of nations – instead of always obsessing on what is not there.

"All knowledge," as Robert and Michèle Root-Bernstein write in *Sparks of Genius*, "begins in observation. We must be able to perceive our world accurately to be able to discern patterns of action, abstract their principles, make analogies between properties of things, create models of behaviors, and innovate fruitfully." That implies observation is hard work and demands a clear mind, and it cannot be simply equated with visual perception.[41]

The fourth point that invokes the sticky-note story is the so-called "analogical transfer." Such a process, according to Gary Magee, occurs when what we know in one situation helps us solve a problem in another distinct situation. "This approach implies that people with different experiences, backgrounds, and specializations may be vital to the firm." This is "because they bring a different set of experiences to the problem."[42] That is true. And to be sure, diversity is a common song today. But just because we know a song, it does not mean we sing it well. In reality, while we know a lot about diversity, we often fall far short of harvesting the benefits of diversified thinking. In development policy, for example – with a few exceptions – many economists and non-economists alike think that economists are the solution to global poverty. Hence despite their promise, areas like the arts are often overlooked in serious development debates in part, because few economists bother to understand what the arts have to offer.

The reason for this might be because, as filmmaker Errol Morris told the experimental social psychologist David Dunning, we are not good at knowing what we do not know.[43] Interestingly, but hardly surprising, the arts can be blunt at reminding us about that blind spot (anyone who gets a memory slip on stage, for example, can attest to this). As they challenge us to become better students of knowing, moreover, the arts lead us to one key insight: curiosity. Another Isaacson biography, the one of the Italian Renaissance polymath and iconic painter Leonardo da Vinci, is yet another testament to that insight: Like Einstein, who once wrote to a friend saying that he "no special talents;" he was "just passionately curious," Leonard, of course, had special talents. But the one trait in which he distinguished himself to become a kernel of inspiration, the one that aided him to know what he did not know, was his "intense curiosity."[44]

If anything, "Curiosity takes ignorance seriously, and is confident enough to know when it does not know," Alain de Botton and John Armstrong write. "It is aware of not knowing, and sets out to do something about it."[45] Such a reminder is especially pertinent because even what we know is also littered with gaps. For example, we have come to cite Adam's Smith invisible hand theorem when it comes to the operations of the free market. But how often do we consider that the forces of creativity may also work as if by invisible thought? Think about the following excerpt from a 1958 essay by the economist Leonard Read on making a pencil. It is often cited to promote free market freedom. In it, nevertheless, there are powerful insights, insights that exhibit the ability to connect distinct items and ideas that, in terms of trade in value added (more on this in Chapter 4), may come from different disciplines and corners of the world:

> I, Pencil, am a complex combination of miracles: a tree, zinc, copper, graphite, and so on. But to these miracles which manifest themselves in Nature an even more extraordinary miracle has been added: the configuration of creative human energies – millions of tiny know-hows configurating naturally and spontaneously in response to human necessity and desire and *in the absence of any human master-minding!*[46]

The tiny know-hows work spontaneously as they come about through linkages of knowledge. They are not masterminded. Nonetheless, like the way genius is interconnected, they are enabled by diverse capabilities. As Smith showed, we can learn these capabilities through observation. Smith never made any mandatory arts education policies – although, again, the arts can teach us immensely about observation. But since education for Smith "is about cultivating the human experience," at a minimum, one could argue that if the arts can enrich knowledge for development, then courting them is a Smithian gesture. That is the American philosopher Jack Russell Weinstein's take in *Adam Smith's Philosophy of Education.*[47] I shall expand on this in the next chapter on arts education. There, via Amartya Sen's capability approach, I will argue that sometimes, by participating in activities like singing in the choir like Fry, we gain capabilities that enrich us in unprecedented ways.

THE CREATIVE ECONOMY

The exchange of cultural goods and services is often encompassed in such terms as the following: "creative economy," "creative sector," "creative industries," and "cultural industries" – the terminology and definitions go on and on (for the full list of definitions, see Annexes 1.1 and 1.2). Moreover, in their work at the Inter-American Development Bank, Iván Duque Márquez and Felipe Buitrago Restrepo suggest that we should just call it the "Orange Economy." (To them, squeezing the orange is an apt metaphor.[48]) I use these terms interchangeably here to imply the same thing.

The term "creative economy" was popularized by John Howkins, a British writer and media manager, in 2001. Howkins applied the "term to fifteen industries extending from the arts to science and technology" – from cultural goods and services to toys, games, and research and development. As a result, he placed the value of the creative economy at the towering figure of "US$2.2 trillion worldwide in 2000 and growing at an annual rate of 5 per cent."[49]

This figure is less than half of Hernando de Soto's estimate of $9 trillion of "dead capital" locked up in land, homes, and businesses belonging to poor people.[50] That said, the $2.2 trillion is probably an annual flow of income, while de Soto's number is a stock. Interpreted that way, this makes the creative economy even bigger, in all likelihood.

The takeaway to bear in mind is that the quantification of assets – whether tangible or intangible – is markedly intricate. In de Soto's analysis, property rights, which are legal instruments, tightly connect law to development.[51] The same is true of Howkins's argument. Intellectual property is a prominent component, as discussed in Chapter 4.

Promoting cultural activities involves externalities for social capital, education, and innovation, as well as direct economic linkages to other businesses. These lead to job creation and tax-generating activities, and much more. This is similar to how academic institutions tend to make major economic and social contributions to the places in which they are located.[52]

But with respect to economic linkages, as much as universities may benefit their respective locales in terms of job creation and commerce, not all graduates are guaranteed good jobs. Similarly, while arts hubs may benefit their locations, this does not put all artists on the path to financial success. There will still be some "starving artists." In any event, since some artists make millions, this raises questions on how the arts industry works, and how it connects to other sectors of the economy.

CASE STUDY: NASHVILLE: THE CITY THAT "MUSIC CALLS HOME"

Take Nashville, Tennessee, a city in the United States that is centered on music. What enabled Nashville to bank on music as the calling card for economic exchange? Was it luck? Unique music? Prudent economic policy? All of the above? What can this city teach us about the creative economy's role in development?

Nashville is "called Music City for a very good reason," the city's Convention & Visitors Bureau says: "In Nashville, music is the heart and soul of the city." No doubt. And one could say, in the beginning there was Nashville, and Nashville was music, and music was Nashville:

> From its very beginnings, Nashville grew from a foundation built on music. Music has been the common thread connecting the life and soul of the city and its people. And visitors have ventured here to experience the music that weaves such a fundamental pattern in its cultural, business and social fabric. Nashville's earliest settlers celebrated in the late 1700s with fiddle tunes and buck dancing after safely disembarking on the shores of the Cumberland River ... Live music can be seen and heard every day and night of the week in Nashville ... And with more than 130 music venues around town ranging from large arenas and concert halls to small clubs and featuring nearly every genre of music, it's easy to see why this is the city that "music calls home."[53]

The similarity with places like Africa is that many communities, rural and urban, live and celebrate their daily activities with music. The difference is that not many of these places have been able to build themselves around their cultural endowments – at least when it comes to direct economic functions. The fact that Nashville grew from an impoverished city to a global music center generating billions of dollars a year[54] provides a repertoire of lessons for arts and development. In the early 2000s, this fact made Nashville the center of discussion at the World Bank's first Africa Music Workshop.

"One of the notable features of the music industry in Nashville is its physical integration," noted David Sanjek, who participated in the workshop. "Recording studios, publishing companies and performance rights agencies are literally within eyeshot and in some cases virtually earshot of one another." These include Broadcast Music Inc. (BMI) and the American Society of Composers, Authors and Publishers (ASCAP). It is "the existence of these other institutions, such as BMI, which are as important as the economic structures that allowed the cultural activity to flourish initially."[55] Here, moreover, music provides employment opportunities not only in the direct music production sector, but also in graphic designing, lighting, sound technicians, marketing specialists, artist services, tourism, and even dry cleaning, to name a few. Even before the Bureau of Economic Analysis revised its methods to record expenditures on creative items in 2013, Nashville had for ages boasted a flourishing arts-based economy.

A study commissioned by the Music City Music Council and developed by the Nashville Area Chamber of Commerce provides the music industry's impact on Nashville's economy: Within the Nashville area alone, the industry is estimated to help create and sustain more than 56,000 jobs paying a total of more than $3.2 billion in wages annually. This suggests that in relation to its population and total employment, Nashville may have more music-related jobs than any other city in the United States, even more than Los Angeles or New York. Moreover, for a total output of $9.7 billion within the Nashville Metropolitan Statistical Area, the local economy is said to gain a whopping $5.5 billion from the music industry.[56]

There are also substantial spillovers from the economy to education – and vice versa. Nashville is also referred to as the "Athens of the South."[57] The city earns this title "not only for [its] appreciation and promotion of fine arts, but also for its renowned devotion to higher education."[58] The Nashville Area Chamber of Commerce reports that today Nashville is home to twenty-one colleges and universities, six community colleges, and eleven vocational and technical schools – all of which are integral to the city's cultural and economic identity.[59]

"There are many programs unique to the area taught in the various schools," Charles Manning, chancellor of the Tennessee Board of Regents, concludes. "For example, Nashville is famous for its music, and there are excellent music industry programs at Middle Tennessee State University and Belmont University."[60]

AN ARTS-BASED CLUSTER MODEL

Nashville's creative economy is powered by a harmonious relationship between music, innovation, and entrepreneurship. It is a relevant model of idea-based innovation in that businesses are not making products like cars, but they are innovating from a musical canvas. "The modern-day empire of Music Row, a collection of recording studios, record labels, entertainment offices and other music-associated businesses," according to Nashville's Convention & Visitors Bureau, "populates the area around 16th and 17th Avenues South."[61] Music clusters can be seen as hubs that stimulate innovation and job creation. Through enterprises such as "Innovation Nashville," the city hosts fora to discuss ideas related to technology, innovation and entertainment entrepreneurship. Held monthly, these conversations "feature thought leaders who understand the past and are creating the next generation of scalable new media companies,"[62] a thought that takes us back to the idea of learning from past as we innovate the future. These exchanges tend to lead to more trade in music and other areas, making Nashville a useful example for arts-based cluster development (see Annex 1.3 for a list of economic linkages within the music industry; arts education, although not highlighted, could be added to this illustration[63]).

The cluster model – as this phenomenon is often called – is common in developing countries. Nonetheless, as Calestous Juma notes, the "presence of a cluster does not automatically lead to positive external effects." There are numerous examples of both failed and successful attempts at establishing clusters in developing countries. "There is therefore a need to look beyond the simple explanation of proximity and cultural factors," as Juma contends, "and to ask why some clusters prosper and what specifically explains their success."[64]

Moreover, since Nashville is in a developed country, there are important questions that cannot be sidestepped. Why has music shaped Nashville, Tennessee? How does Nashville's collaboration and innovation through music add to Tennessee's economy? Would a Nashville replica work in developing countries where regulatory systems are still weak and basics such as electricity are often limited? What kind of public policy framework should governments interested in this idea follow?

WHAT EXACTLY EXPLAINS THE SUCCESS OF CLUSTERS?

It is difficult to tabulate all the reasons why some clusters fail and others flourish. Nonetheless, let us consider some measures that fuel cluster performance. Michael Porter "acknowledges the scope and importance of the state's involvement in the economy..." He is nonetheless "explicit on confining the role of the state in cluster development to that of a facilitator...."[65] In Porter's view, the private sector plays a leading role in the performance of clusters, while states act as facilitators. Yong-Sook Lee and Ying-Chian Tee, however, "contend that Porter's reasoning lacks understanding of the historical legacy of the developmental state, and the complex and embedded interrelationships it has engendered in cluster development."[66] Highlighting examples from Singapore, they argue that a state can play an active role in enabling clusters. For example, to catalyze growth within its biomedical industry, among other things, Singapore provided provision grants and tax incentives, and also introduced regulatory policies to protect intellectual property and risk taking.[67]

As a city-state, Singapore is different from most developing economies. But the examples above show the kinds of policies that developing states could use to engender effective cluster development and innovation systems. While biomedical industries differ from creative industries, there is no doubt that these types of provisions can be key to successful cluster performances, even in the area of the creative sector.

Indeed, in some countries like France, creative clusters benefit from state support. Although creative clusters, particularly in cities, may benefit from local value-added, innovative energy, and other linkages, as Allen J. Scott has argued, their success also depends on their ability to reach national and international markets.[68] And again, even though vibrant local areas tend to reinforce local production, and thereby attract talent,[69] there is no question that, in addition to enabling the private sector, the state can proactively pave the way for markets.

In developing countries, clusters "are usually more dominated by smaller-scale firms, are organized in a more informal manner, have weaker linkages among actors, face more difficulties in achieving a critical mass of firms and have been specialized in lower-value niches," as Eva Gálvez-Nogales points out. That is why "clusters in developing economies require more support."[70] To garner this support, besides engaging the private sector, there is a role for international agencies, national donor agencies, and governments. The action of these agencies should be more than roles between "actors" and "enablers;" they should espouse truly interactive and proactive roles that stimulate mutually inclusive public policy measures. This role is in line with the call for collaboration noted in the Overture to this book. And, as noted earlier, it recapitulates the need to create environments that allow disciplines to interconnect to stimulate creativity and innovation.

MOVEMENT II

BEYOND MONETARY VALUE: THE SOCIAL UTILITY OF THE ARTS

> Interdependency ought to ensure that we will regard one another as the basis of our own well-being, and we will reciprocate, service for service, working out the fine points as circumstance requires. This has been a commonplace since antiquity.
>
> Marilynne Robinson[71]

While the economic impact of the creative economy is huge and growing, the social utility of the arts has also gained attention. Indeed, although economics has yet to fully capture the value of intangibles as noted in Chapter 9, efforts have been made in cultural economics to define and to articulate ways in which cultural value goes beyond monetary measures.

In the process of valuation, however, the distinction between cultural value and economic value can create a dilemma, as David Throsby has argued. Economic valuation of cultural products may certainly appear to occasion "unambiguous estimates" on the one hand. On the other, cultural valuation does not fit neatly into boxes.[72] This is one of those issues that deserve a book of their own.[73] (And in debating whether growth comes first and then culture follows, or vice versa, we may find that the concept of one hand washing the other may come in here.) At any rate, here are some quick points to note:

First, cultural goods and services can be categorized as *mixed goods* – that is, goods that have both private and public aspects. "Private goods and services are those whose benefits accrue entirely to private agents (individuals or firms)," according to Throsby. "Public goods," meanwhile, "are those whose benefits accrue to everyone in a given community."[74]

To properly account for value of culture is to recall that cultural value is multifaceted. It runs from aesthetic to symbolic, and from spiritual to historical. Because valuation can differ from person to person, the way a cultural item is valued can be "reflected in any economic analysis." Nonetheless, there is an unflinching sense in which cultural value can only be realized in collective terms. Consider identity. When we say that culture helps people tell their stories, identify who they are, it is hard to see how identity can be fully assessed in financial terms, as Throsby explains. "Yet identity is something that is valuable to society at large and clearly affects decision-making in the cultural policy arena."[75] Because this issue is beyond the scope of this book, let us turn to just a few aspects of the social utility of culture.

Besides identity, the social utility of the arts can be realized from education and cultural diplomacy to social inclusion and catharsis. In Rwanda, for example, women are using drumming to recover from the trauma of genocide (see Chapter 8). Since wellbeing is not just about accumulating physical assets, it is important to take a closer look at the nonmonetary benefits the arts render. Regarding the World Bank's first Africa Music Workshop, Amartya Sen had this to say:

> Since the language of cost-benefit analysis is more or less obligatory these days, I should translate that transparent thought into justificatory language by noting that the costs incurred in supporting the music industry can produce high returns in terms of quality of life, even if no account whatever is taken of the other benefits that ensue from commercial, political and social contributions that the music industry makes. The contributions to the richness of human lives made by the creative arts – often available free or at little cost – does not figure much in the gross national product (GNP), or for that matter in the Human Development Index (HDI). But that is a problem for the GNP and the HDI, not a reason for the neglect of the creative arts. In the enriching of human lives that development aims at, the augmentation of inexpensive but effective sources of joy and fulfilment has a particularly promising role. Music and the creative arts will never, of course, replace the need for food and medicine, but nor would food and medicine replace the need for the creative arts.[76]

THE ARTS AND INCLUSION

The role of the arts in advancing social inclusion is well known, but not necessarily well quantified.[77] In South Africa, for example, music was a major player in fueling the movement against apartheid. Today, in Venezuela, despite the political and economic challenges in that nation, one program that has often been hailed across the world is El Sistema, a music program that has worked tirelessly to bring disadvantaged kids from a path of risk to a path of promise.[78] One shining graduate of the program, founded by the economist and musician José Antonio Abreu, is conductor Gustavo Dudamel. In Brazil, where, as noted earlier, Temer's axing of the cultural ministry was protested, AfroReggae is helping young people emerge from an existence riddled with drugs and violence in the favelas of Rio (see Chapter 8).

And in many parts of Africa, such creative work as woodcarving has been "an aspect of the creation and maintenance of community identity," as the eminent British historian C. A. Bayly sums it up. "Making images fixed the powerful natural and supernatural forces which bound together human generations, their ancestors, and their descendants" since antiquity.[79]

THE ARTS AND SOCIAL CAPITAL

Social capital was launched as a popular focus for research and policy discussion through the work of Robert D. Putnam, according to the *Encyclopedia of Informal Education*.[80] "Whereas physical capital refers to physical objects and human capital refers to the properties of individuals," according to Putnam,

> social capital refers to connections among individuals – social networks and the norms of reciprocity and trustworthiness that arise from them. In that sense social capital is closely related to what some have called "civic virtue." The difference is that "social capital" calls attention to the fact that civic virtue is most powerful when embedded in a dense network of reciprocal social relations. A society of many virtuous but isolated individuals is not necessarily rich in social capital.[81]

Putnam's work is often associated with *Bowling Alone: The Collapse and Revival of American Community*. In that work, he "shows how [Americans] have become increasingly disconnected from family, friends, neighbors, and [American] democratic structures–and how [they] may reconnect."[82] Even though *Bowling Alone* focuses on the United States, development agencies have picked up Putnam's notion of social capital "as a useful organizing idea." The World Bank, for one, argues that "increasing evidence shows that social cohesion is critical for societies to prosper economically and for development to be sustainable."[83] If development can benefit from trust, moreover, then here is the thing: "Social networks allow trust to become transitive and spread: I trust you, because I trust her and she assures me that she trusts you."[84]

The arts can be useful in building domestic and international social networks.[85] Internationally, they can create social ties (imagined or real) across borders. For example, within local (and international) communities, music "not only helps to strengthen the solidarity that group identities can generate, but can also help to overcome narrowly divisive groupings that tend to split up a culture into battling groups along the lines of artificially sustained 'separations.'"[86] Here is Putnam on the arts and social capital:

> [A] growing body of research suggests that the arts can be a valuable engine of civic renewal. Indeed, more and more arts institutions are directing substantial resources to that cause. The arts can nurture social capital by strengthening friendships, helping communities to understand and celebrate their heritage, and providing a safe way to discuss and solve difficult social problems.[87]

Indeed, to "withstand or forestall shocks – from conflict, violence, vulnerabilities to the impacts of climate change and natural disasters, or economic crisis – countries need strengthened resilience, inclusion, and social cohesion."[88] This may be enabled by the strategic application of the arts, not to force, but to naturally encourage social capital. For "the significance of social capital for civic well-being is more than a theoretical conjecture," as Blair A. Ruble observes in his book *The Muse of Urban Delirium*. "A growing body of evidence drawn from the responses to such recent disasters as Hurricane Katrina and Super-storm Sandy suggests that those communities that have the highest stores of social capital before suffering a communal trauma recover most quickly following both human-made and natural disasters." This capital need not be strong ties any more than "causal sociability" or "weak ties." But whatever the nature of its makeup, this capital allows people to turn to each other in times of pain or joy. And again, the arts' capacity to bring people together to share human moments is invaluable.[89]

Think about choirs. Regardless of whether choral experiences turn out more Arthur Frys, choirs can be good for the community at large: "The harmonies of a choral society illustrate how voluntary collaboration can create value that no individual, no matter how wealthy, no matter how wily, could produce alone. In the civic community associations proliferate, memberships overlap, and participation spills into multiple arenas of community life." That is Putnam's observation in *Making Democracy Work*.[90] Indeed, "Stocks of social capital, such as trust, norms, and networks, tend to be self-reinforcing and cumulative. Virtuous circles result in social equilibria with high levels of cooperation, trust, reciprocity, civic engagement, and collective well-being. These traits define the civic community."[91] And since "social capital" is not simply embedded in the instrumental utilitarian function, we might as well think of it as "social capability" in connection with the capability approach noted in Chapter 2.

That thought notwithstanding, it must be noted that social capital or social networks can also be abused (like any other form of influence or power).[92] And this concern has not escaped scrutiny. Kaushik Basu echoes a longstanding critic: "It is not difficult to see that cooperation promoted by a group, such as a nation, racially homogeneous community, or collectivity of coreligionists, against others can be more ruthless than oppression promoted by individuals."[93] Such positions may fall under "divisive groupings" that efficiently fuel social exclusion.

THE COSTS OF SOCIAL EXCLUSION

Social exclusion is a major deterrent in promoting shared prosperity, citizen voice, and cultural democracy. Yet it is difficult to measure the true costs of exclusion. To complicate matters, when some groups are excluded or marginalized, they often do not figure into official statistics. "For instance," as the World Bank's report *Inclusion Matters* observes, "in many cultures, a disabled member of the household is not reported in the household roster when survey personnel conduct interviews." In other scenarios, common even in the United States and other advanced countries, undocumented immigrants or "refugees who cross borders without documents may actively avoid official contact."[94] These issues interact with any country's economic foundations. And as economic activities become even more globalized, the costs of exclusion may well increase bleeding across borders.

Here is one small example. A World Bank study on the economic costs of excluding the Roma people suggests that the annual productivity and fiscal costs in four Eastern and Central European countries (Bulgaria, Czech Republic, Romania, and Serbia) could be over 2.5 billion euros.[95] Meanwhile, the Roma, also called the Romani, "originally a Hindi people from northern India," have made an immense cultural contribution. "They are often celebrated for their musical heritage, which has influenced jazz, bolero, flamenco music, as well as classical composers including Franz Liszt."[96]

Here is another measure, this time covering an entire region. A series of social experiments conducted by the Inter-American Development Bank found that "there may be a welfare loss of up to 22 percent as a result of lack of trust and cooperation among different groups in selected Latin American countries."[97]

Now, since Latin America is a beacon of ancient and modern arts, one could ask, Why is trust an issue in a place that flourishes with all sorts of artistic manifestations? For we have been told that the arts can help build social networks that in turn fuel trust. There are no easy answers. Maybe if it was not for the arts, things would be worse. Given the historical complexity of social arrangements, it is impossible to dissect the situation and provide a clear-cut answer. What is more, the arts themselves are not immune from boiling divisions.

ON CULTURAL MISUNDERSTANDINGS, CULTURAL ENGAGEMENT, AND ADDING SOCIAL VALUE

Indeed, differences in artistic interpretations can breed tensions. Such statements as "Asians cannot interpret Bach as well as Germans" or "Germans cannot really be good at African drumming" are common. The threads of such thinking may even be why many cultural institutions themselves can be exclusive. This is often oiled by entrenched social norms and identity of both the excluded and the included. On a personal note, as an African who likes Bach and plays the pipe organ – a species of instrument often seen as antediluvian – I can tell you I get my share of bizarre questions. That I also like jazz and African chant does not count. That in such artists as Lionel Richie (who majored in economics) and Lucky Dube (who educated me about apartheid) I find inspiration does not matter. To some, my identity seems to be confined to one corner. Yet that borders on fiction that ignores the innate majesty of the diverse art forms I adore.

On the issue of human identity and its variable manifestations, at the 2013 World Culture Forum, Amartya Sen asked, "Should we allow ourselves to be categorized – and partitioned – in terms of exactly one of our many identities and affiliations?" Undoubtedly, he said, "our inherited traditions are important, given by our race, religion, language, nationality, or ethnicity, but there is a plurality of identifications even here. And we can acquire new identities in terms of location, education, profession, politics, and social commitment." To "overlook the inescapable plurality in our identities and to place us into a singular box of one identity – be it race, or religion, or community, or whatever – is a remarkably efficient way of *misunderstanding* nearly everyone in the world."[98]

Consider the recent conflict in the West African nation of Mali, one of the cradles of African music. As the fighting intensified there in 2012 – its population was estimated at 14.85 million with a GDP of $10.39 billion in that year – Mali's GDP contracted by 0.4 percent and inflation shot up to 5.4 percent.[99] But, as is true in any war, the cost of human lives lost and dreams shattered will perhaps never be known. Moreover, as is always the case in such conflicts, women and children are especially vulnerable. Indeed, in addition to "pillaging of hospitals, schools, aid agencies, warehouses, banks, and government buildings," as Human Rights Watch reports, Mali did not escape the use of child soldiers and the raping of women.[100]

Although Mali's conflict can be linked to various aspects, including economics and politics, cultural confusion and intolerance exacerbated the situation. Whereas "music anchors every ceremony, from births and circumcisions to weddings and prayers for rains" in Mali, a top Islamist commander declared it necessary to target musicians:[101] "Music is against Islam," said Oumar Ould Hamaha, the military leader of the Movement for Oneness and Jihad in West Africa, one of the three extremist groups controlling the north. "Instead of singing, why don't they read the Koran? Why don't they subject themselves to God and pray? We are not only against the musicians in Mali. We are in a struggle against all the musicians of the world."[102]

Such extreme positions fueled by historical and cultural misunderstandings cannot be avoided by economics alone. Such troubling cases could crop up anywhere, reversing the progress made.

Therefore, we need to ask how we should recalibrate and sharpen our tools of engagement. We need to take the time to understand cultural activities and how they can play a meaningful role in building a more secure and peaceful world amidst modern globalization. There is a pressing need "to save globalization from being exploited for the cultivation of divisiveness and inter-group hostility, with hugely flammable consequences, and instead draw on global cultural interactions to advance our future, even as we admire the past."[103]

In advancing our future, as we admire our past, the arts have the ability to build positive relations. Along those lines, they surely not only help us to draw on the past as we innovate for the future as *The Geography of Genius* shows, they also help us build trust, a high "input" crucial in strengthening "resilience, inclusion, and social cohesion."[104]

Moreover, in a process that could be called "where trust leads, development follows," "New research in economics shows that one important trait that helps a nation or a community prosper economically is trust."[105] Such a reading, of course, deserves a careful look. But as we saw earlier, for example, the conclusion by the Inter-American Development Bank study that "there may be a welfare loss of up to 22 percent as a result of lack of trust and cooperation among different groups in selected Latin American countries"[106] is difficult to dismiss. And as economists Algan Yann and Pierre Cahuc note, citing Kenneth Arrow, "'Virtually every commercial transaction has within itself an element of trust, certainly any transaction conducted over a period of time. It can be plausibly argued that much of the economic backwardness in the world can be explained by the lack of mutual confidence.'"[107]

Certainly, from economics to politics, and from public diplomacy to cultural cartography, it can be argued that trust drives all sorts of progress; this issue will get more treatment with respect to nation branding in Chapter 4. The following coda presents, meanwhile, one idea for building trust by strengthening the commerce of the arts.

CODA: ON CULTIVATING TRADE IN THE ARTS

Given all the benefits of the arts – tangible and intangible, measurable and unmeasured – they need to be supported. As this book will argue in the chapters that follow, we need creative solutions for the creative sector. The policy option highlighted in Box 1.1 presents one such idea. The idea has Africa in mind, because as we shall see in Chapters 4, 5, and 6, African trade still far lags behind more than in other regions. But the thoughts here apply elsewhere. After all, "[a]s

BOX 1.1 **Regional and Global Partnerships for Cultural Trade**

The New Partnership for Africa's Development (NEPAD), the African Union's vision and policy framework for encouraging socioeconomic development, acknowledges that African countries need to "find ways to diversify their economies, namely by boosting non-traditional sectors; expanding their range of products and exports; and engaging with new economic and development partners."[111]

African countries should go further and implement a cooperative New Partnership for Africa's Cultural Trade (NEPACT) to promote small-scale creative enterprise. This policy could work under special trade arrangements where, for example, member African nations could come together to negotiate their cultural export provisions with the European Union, the Americas, and elsewhere.

To look beyond Africa, other countries could go ahead and consider New Partnerships for Cultural Trade to promote regional cultural trade provisions for development. Governments will indeed need to find better ways of protecting intellectual property with copyright and related measures; many artists in are deprived of their rightful earnings by piracy (see Chapter 5). But it can be done. Creative solutions can help grow the creative sector.

Source: Kabanda 2014a.

a result of the growth of disposable consumer income and the expansion of discretionary time in modern society, the consumption of cultural products of all kinds is evidently expanding at an accelerating pace, and the sectors engaged in making them constitute some of the most dynamic economic frontiers" today, as Allen Scott points out.[110]

2 Arts in Education

Cultivating Creative Minds for Development

Education is the most powerful tool you can use to change the world.

Nelson Mandela

In the beginning there was knowledge, and knowledge was art, and art was knowledge. But somehow, somewhere in the course of history, the arts were left behind. There are many reasons for this.[1] But one key element is that we began to believe that math and science were the only causes of wealth. Hence education systems across the world would focus on these subjects – even though, ironically, many still do not measure up – to augment their "human capital." These attempts are not entirely futile. Nonetheless, since the arts embody creativity and innovation they have a major role to play in fostering knowledge for development. Also, their contribution to making learning more enjoyable and transformational cannot be discounted. This chapter seeks to distinguish between the concepts of "human capital" and "human capability" to show that arts education does more than augment production possibilities. It also helps students develop curiosity, make connections with other subjects, embrace collaboration, realize that winning is not always gaining, deal with ambiguity, and so on. Such knowledge also helps students become more civic-minded and imaginative individuals. Such attributes cannot but make arts education relevant in realizing the full dimensions of development.

***

THE AFGHANISTAN NATIONAL INSTITUTE OF MUSIC

There is a music school in Afghanistan that has cropped up against all odds. All odds, because this is perhaps a place where a bassoon could easily be confused for a bazooka.

A typical development framework, which pivots on the idea that the poor do not have the luxury to enjoy poetry, might say: Provide security before even thinking about music. Security is certainly important. In fact, the music school itself probably needs sustained security.[2] But if we acknowledge that development does not translate readily into some simple formula,[3] and that security is not just military might, then we can take a different path. We are less likely to overinvest our energies and resources (including media coverage) on things that have traditionally and conventionally been deemed important. We are challenged to open our eyes, to see spots that need attention but do not get it because they are considered "soft," irrelevant, not a priority.

The World Bank might not be known to be in the business of building music schools. But whether it was a stroke of luck or not, the Bank was one of the earliest donors to the Afghanistan National Institute of Music (ANIM).[4] Located in Kabul, the Institute is a place that, among other things, seeks to foster social inclusion in a country that has had its share of long-running wars – including culture wars. Afghanistan was subject to extreme music censorship under Taliban rule. While the British ethnomusicologist John Baily notes that it is incorrect to say that the Taliban have banned music[5] – some religious songs and the so-called Taliban chants were allowed[6] – the extreme music censorship could be seen as "competition between different kinds of music."[7]

Today, students come to the Institute from diverse ethnic, religious, and economic backgrounds. They include orphans (from such provinces as Bamiyan, Farah, Jalalabad, Kunar, and Nuristan) and a number of female students. ANIM aspires to show a new face of Afghanistan: a place tolerant of freedom of expression, intercultural dialogue, and social progress.[8] Through partnerships, concerts, and an annual Winter Music Academy, ANIM has built local and international bridges. The curriculum includes both Afghan and Western music. The school's global presence, meanwhile, is augmented through such things as tours and music festivals.

In 2013, ANIM made a historic tour of the United States. The sixty-member group performed at such venues as Carnegie Hall, the Kennedy Center, and the World Bank. The group also visited a few schools. Beyond arts education, such people-to-people interactions provide meaning beyond measure in the form of cultural diplomacy. This tour aided this exchange. And its long-term strategy is to counter negative stereotypes that hobble Afghanistan – to teach us something unique about Afghan society. In addition to the students' human development, ANIM has become a place that embodies learning and collective action in a region almost written off by the rest of the world.[9]

With the way world crises unfold, it is difficult to understand how supporting music education in Afghanistan could rapidly diminish the problems there. Moreover, for outsiders, including me, there is a lot we do not know. Is the school's leadership sound? Does the program live up to its ideals? Such questions linger. But still, what can we learn here?

BEYOND THE MOZART EFFECT

What the example of the Institute teaches is that there is more to arts education than its direct, instrumental value (although that value is itself great, as we will see in a moment). Yet many children, especially the underprivileged, generally do not get a fair chance to engage in the arts, or even in general education. The reasons for this are various. For example, whereas I cannot picture Adam Smith in, say, the Uganda 1700s – even in Afghanistan I am not sure – what this Scottish philosopher noted centuries ago persists even today, despite the progress made in promoting education: From remote villages in the developing countries to inner cities in the United States, it is likely that many children from low income families,

> have little time to spare for education. Their parents can scarce afford to maintain them even in infancy. As soon as they are able to work, they must apply to some trade by which they can earn their

> subsistence. That trade too is generally so simple and uniform as to give little exercise to the understanding; while, at the same time, their labour is both so constant and so severe, that it leaves them little leisure and less inclination to apply to, or even to think of any thing else.[10]

To center on arts education is to restate that such severe constraints leave underprivileged children fewer chances to engage in "ornamental knowledge." Meanwhile, because of such theories as the "Mozart Effect" (as we shall see shortly), parents with means are more likely to court arts education for their children – even if for unrealistic motives. This wedge adds to the hypothesis that arts education is for the privileged, the elite, or the intellectuals.

On the macro level, it is easy to see why some claim that arts subjects are a luxury compared to more "useful" subjects like math and science.

This was a common refrain when I was growing up in Uganda. I grew up bearing the burden of hearing that music was connected with stupidity. And I have met a few prominent Ugandans who told me that they were forced to abandon music growing up because they were told it would compromise their brains. In fact, at Makerere University, Uganda's major institution, once considered the Harvard of Africa, music, dance, and drama students have heard their share of crude invectives. Time and again, they were called *Musiru Dala Dala*, which means very, very stupid.

But then in my adult life, I kept hearing a counterargument. It is not unusual for many parents in the United States and elsewhere to push their children to practice long hours of piano, violin, or other instruments on this premise: Music makes kids smarter. In fact, the "disciples of the 1993 'Mozart Effect' study made impressive claims: Listening to music, they said, could boost Junior's math scores and maybe even get him into Harvard. The idea sparked a cottage industry of CDs, classes and books for babies and toddlers."[11] In policy spheres, Governor Zell Miller of the US state of Georgia took this to heart: Out of his $12.5 billion budget proposal for the fiscal year 1999, he requested $105,000 to provide classical music CDs to every child born in the state of Georgia.[12]

A recent Harvard study puts a damper on these claims. The "effects of early music education on children's cognitive development are unknown,"[13] it found. The "report provides no consistent evidence for cognitive transfer from music training: preschool music classes did not cause detectable skill increases in the cognitive domains of spatial, linguistic, or numerical reasoning."[14]

This observation is critical. In the argument for the developmental role of the arts in education, the arts do not have to make children smart to be valuable. If they do, I am all for that. But this should not be the principal yardstick for assessment. And to borrow Howard Gardner's theory of multiple intelligences: What exactly do we mean by "smartness" here?

HUMAN CAPITAL VERSUS HUMAN CAPABILITY: THE ROLE OF ARTS EDUCATION

Those who advocate that arts education must be "useful" or "make us smart" in the instrumental sense are falling into a trap of seeing education merely as capital to augment production possibilities.

Education is more than instrumental. As the Namibians put it, learning expands great souls. Indeed, from Namibia to Norway, education is generally considered a trajectory to both social and economic advancement. As Theodore W. Schultz reminds us in "Adam Smith and Human Capital," "[a]dvances in knowledge are a decisive factor in economic progress. The increases in the quality of both physical and human capital originate primarily out of the advances in knowledge."[15]

No doubt. But let us explore the dimensions of "human capital" – a notion that has sparked critical debates. First, as Schultz stresses, people "are first and foremost the end to be served by the economy; they are not property, nor are they marketable assets." With respect to arts education, a person should not be trained in the arts only to be seen as a mere form of property. "The mere thought of treating human beings as investment objects is offensive."[16]

Second, as Serbian-American economist Branko Milanović points out, the term human capital "obfuscates the crucial difference between labor and capital by terminologically conflating the two. Labor now seems to be just a subspecies of capital."[17]

Third, as Amartya Sen notes, "At the risk of some oversimplification, it can be said that the literature on human capital tends to concentrate on the agency of human beings in augmenting production possibilities." Given Sen's attention to "human capabilities," his critique opens the way to consider the closely related but distinct perspectives of "capital" and "capability."[18] I turn to that aspect now.

A person's value of education (gains in human capital) can enable that person to contribute to the economy and also make more money. "But even with the same level of income, a person may benefit from education – in reading, communicating, arguing, in being able to choose in a more informed way, in being taken more seriously by others and so on. The benefits of education, thus, exceed its role as human capital in commodity production."[19]

This perspective hinges on human capability. It looks at "human beings in a broader perspective," as Sen has argued in *Development as Freedom*.[20] Yet among the reasons marshaled against spending money on areas like arts education is the view that there is generally no money in arts vocations. But this is a problem with society; it is not a problem with the arts. In fact, this view, which more or less borders on capital and commodity production, ignores the noninstrumental values the arts contribute to human progress and enriching people's lives.

In realizing the enrichment of people's lives in a broader perspectives, "[t]he capability perspective involves, to some extent, a return to an integrated approach to economic and social development championed particularly by Adam Smith (both in the *Wealth of Nations* and in *The Theory of Moral Sentiments*). In analyzing the determination of production possibilities, Smith emphasized the role of education as well as division of labor, learning by doing and skill formation," as Sen goes on to say. "But the development of human capability in leading a worthwhile life (as well as being more productive) is quite central to Smith's analysis of 'the wealth of nations.'"[21] With that in mind, if the arts can even reach orphans in Afghan schools in ways we will never know, why should not they get sustained attention?

If you think about it, education is full of complementarities. For instance, to strike a pitch on the piano or on the sitar is to set into motion a complex chain of math and physics. That is the case for even for the vibrations of the pitches. Math did not come easily to me in school, but the math I did understand was aided by music. For example, I quickly realized that 2+2 could be 5 if you combined a duple unit (2 beats) and a compound unit (3 beats) in the same measure at the same duration. The rhythm in music helped me appreciate math, and the math in rhythm helped understand the music. I also gained knowledge about the arts and human civilization, cross-cultural understanding, and what happened to African arts at the dawn of colonization. And, if I may add, school was much more fun with music. When music activities were going on, I showed up; when they were absent, I disappeared. Though my arts education was informal, I gained a number of skills. I learned the discipline, the urgency of working with others – even keeping up with jerks – and many other transferable skills.

But the tunnel vision affecting education, as many have noted, is creating a narrow class of specialized learning. This is especially a loss in an era of rapid technological advance, cross-border influences, massive information flows, and shorter and shorter attention spans. Think about the work of Su Tungpo, who lived in ancient China. A "much-beloved governor" of Hangzhou, Su was a poet, a painter, and a skilled engineer. "His best known project was a causeway that traversed West Lake and still does today," according to Eric Weiner. "Su was a Renaissance man three hundred years before the Renaissance." Why are there few people like Su today? Weiner has asked. He answers his own question by "imagining what would happen if a polymath like Su walked onto a modern college campus."[22]

> "Is it literature that you're interested in, Mr. Su? Then please see the School of Humanities. Oh, you're a painter? Please drop by the Department of Fine Arts. What's that? It's engineering that piques your interest? We have an excellent school for that, too."
>
> "But I want to do it all."
>
> "I'm sorry, Mr. Su. We can't help you there. Please return when you've clarified your career objectives. Meanwhile, if you like, I can direct you to Mental Health Services."[23]

The rationale for specialization is taken as a given. Weiner's friend deduced that there was less specialization in Su's time, because "the world was less complicated." There is some truth to that. But Weiner argues the opposite: less specialization is what made the world less complicated. One could argue that specialization is not the problem per se, but rather, the way we have come to interpret, or to overstretch it.

I personally relished the hours I spent trying to learn Frédéric Chopin's waltzes on the piano, for example. Yet when I realized that Chopin was a pianist who also took dance lessons, interpreting his waltzes became much clearer. One could argue that music and dance are close enough. Even so, to consider the sciences, for instance, is to note that "many of our great scientists had formal art training"[24] Yet today the following scenario is commonplace: "The specialist is encouraged, rewarded, for parsing his chosen field into smaller and smaller morsels, then building high walls around those tiny bits. A narrow outlook naturally follows."[25] And this has terrible consequences.

As Weiner notes, for the death of the Renaissance person we mourn, oblivious to the fact that we killed this person "and continue to do so every day on college campuses and in corporate offices across the land."[26] All the while in *Out of Our Minds: Learning to be Creative*, Sir Ken Robinson has this to say: "Creativity often comes about by making unusual connections, seeing analogies, identifying relationships between ideas and processes that were previously not related. This is precisely why some of the most effective creative teams are interdisciplinary."[27]

The need for interdisciplinary or multidisciplinary ways of thinking and learning is greater than ever. And here, many non-Western societies have an advantage, as subjects tend to be part of daily life in their cultures.[28] Yet they often neglect this blessing, as they look West. The Western model of education has its merits, no doubt. There is a need to curb its tendency to put subjects into boxes nevertheless. This is especially necessary because what Robert and Michèle Root-Bernstein note in *Sparks of Genius* is not fiction:

> Despite the current lip service paid to "integrating the curriculum," truly inter-disciplinary courses are rare, and transdisciplinary curricula that span the breadth of human knowledge are almost unknown. Moreover, at the level of creative process, where it really counts, the intuitive tools of thinking that tie one discipline to another are entirely ignored. Mathematicians are supposed to think only in "mathematics," writers only "in words," musicians only "in notes," and so forth ... By half-understanding the nature of thinking, teachers only half-understand how to teach, and students only half-understand how to learn.

This kind of education leaves out "huge chunks of creative processes."[29] And this needs to be reversed.

In fact, if ancient wisdom matters today more than ever, we can learn greatly from such places as Polynesia, which Wade Davis describes in his book, *The Wayfinders: Why Ancient Wisdom Matters in the Modern World*, as "the largest culture sphere ever brought into being by the human imagination." Of course, just as a master pianist may isolate note by note, chord, by chord or phrase by phrase before putting a piece together as a whole, so we can draw lessons from deconstructing what allowed Polynesians to achieve their extraordinary brilliance in the field of navigation, for example. "But as we isolate, deconstruct, even celebrate these specific intellectual and observational gifts, we run the risk of missing the entire point, for the genius of Polynesian navigation lies not in the particular but in the whole, the manner in which all of these points of information come together in the mind of the wayfinder."[30]

Since we are all wayfinders in the quest for learning, let me stress what legendary artists like cellist Yo-Yo Ma have said: For goodness' sake, we need to turn STEM education (science, technology, engineering, and mathematics) to STEAM education (science, technology, engineering, arts, and mathematics).[31] This call is generally concerned with the situation of arts education in the United States. But, as I noted earlier, there is need to bank on the complementarity of these subjects across the board, around the world. They cannot remain seen as hostile competitors. The silo-minded education formats could use some steam.

One could in fact argue that music education should connect to STEM more directly rather than loosely, as Brian Ruble told me. For, in many ways, music has math properties.[32] This connection takes us back to the days of Ionian Greek philosopher and mathematician Pythagoras of Samos. An average teenager today may surely know Pythagoras for his right triangles concerning the Pythagorean theorem. But his mathematical ratios "are the corner stone of every pop song on Spotify." To explore this linkage, we can again turn to ancient wisdom: "The study of musical ratios marked one of the very first moments in the history of knowledge where mathematical descriptions productively explained natural phenomena," as Steven Johnson explains. "In fact, the success of these mathematical explanations of music triggered a two-thousand-year pursuit of similar cosmological rations in the movements of the sun and planets in the sky – the famous 'music of the spheres' that would inspire [the German mathematician, astronomer, and astrologer Johannes] Kepler and so many others."[33] If we consider all, is advocating for arts in education a huge ask?

THE WIDE-RANGING VALUE OF ARTS EDUCATION

The value of arts education is wide ranging. In the instrumental dimension, there are direct and indirect benefits we take for granted,

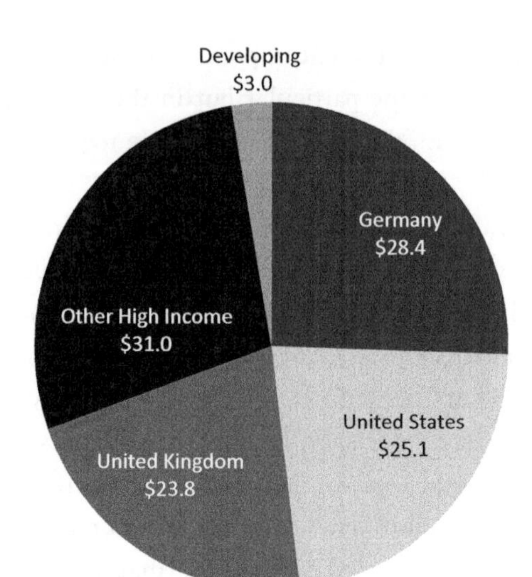

FIGURE 2.1 Printed Music World Exports in 2012 – Trade Value in 1000 USD (Millions of Dollars)
Source: WITS Trade Data (UN Comtrade). Kabanda 2014b.
Nomenclature: H4 | HS 2012 (Selected classification) | Code 4904 – Music, printed or in manuscript, whether or not bound or illustrated. World exports, nominal US dollars, millions. Sample size (Reporters) – Developing countries: 22; High-income countries: 29; Total = 51

or we simply do not see – see Chapter 9. For example, one unlikely micro sector that deserves scrutiny is the area of music notation. Musicians in a number of developing countries tend to play by ear. These skills have been passed on this way from generation to generation. In places like Africa, however, if musicians can notate their music, they can enjoy added benefits. They can sell their music scores both in hard and soft copies, they can collaborate with other artists more efficiently, and their music could easily be taught, as Makhtar Diop, vice president for the Africa Region at the World Bank said.[34]

Revenues from global musical scores rarely make headlines. Nevertheless, who knew that trade in this area is in the millions of dollars? See Figure 2.1 on the breadth of this trade among select countries.

The system of Western music notation cannot capture all the global music traditions. Therefore, artists in their respective countries could develop their own methods of notation and teach them to the rest of the world. This could be done via such channels as YouTube or other mediums. Besides enabling the trade of music scores, however, arts education could also extend to providing instruction in areas like sound engineering – in a number of developing countries such combinations of arts and technology are rare. These innovations are not new. But they have yet to catch on. As Nashville discussed earlier and the Banū Mūsā brothers discussed later show, artistic activities can induce a culture of learning, innovation, and entrepreneurship. Indeed, on the features of social dynamics, human capability, one is tempted to connect such ingenuity to Adam Smith; it is a key pillar to the teeming wealth of nations.

And here is another example: In December 2013, the National Endowment for the Arts in partnership with Bureau of Economic Analysis published preliminary estimates from America's first Arts and Cultural Production Satellite Account. The account seeks to help us answer this question: What is relationship of arts and cultural industries, goods, and services to America's GDP?[35]

"The numbers are still a work in progress," as Sunil Iyengar and Ayanna Hudson wrote in their article, "Who Knew? Arts Education Fuels the Economy." Published in the *Chronicle of Higher Education*, "arts education" in this article "refers only to postsecondary fine-arts schools, departments of fine arts and performing arts, and academic performing-arts centers. Yet even for this limited cohort, the findings are impressive:" Arts education contributed more than $7.5 billion to America's GDP in 2011.[36] For an economy whose GDP is measured in trillions of dollars that may not be much. Seen another way, however, that was more than 40 percent of Afghanistan's GDP, which was less than $18 billion in 2011 (World Bank).

But even in the United States, a place where the conversation on jobs and employment is gaining heated attention and skewing political priorities, the jobs arts education contributes to the nation do not count for little: In 2011 alone, the industry (and to be sure, this just a sliver of it) "employed 17,900 workers whose salaries and wages totaled $5.9 billion." Moreover, an additional 56 cents is generated elsewhere in the American economy for every dollar consumers spend on arts education.[37]

And again, as Sunil and Hudson note, "the figures do not include design schools, media arts departments within schools of communications, or creative writing programs – to name just a few notable omissions from the world of higher education. And yet the results are in line with a series of claims that have fueled arts advocates in recent years. While not grounded in economic theory, those arguments have portrayed arts education as a conduit to greater creativity and innovation in the work force."[38] It must be remembered, though, that even arguments grounded in economic theory often miss important insights. Whatever the case, if many American policy makers understood the diverse contribution of arts education, threats to cut the already miniscule budgets of the National Endowment for the Arts and the National Endowment for National Endowment for the Humanities would perhaps not come up.

Indeed, when you listen to policy makers who get it, the idea of nurturing the arts is not fluff. Consider the work of the sixty-first New Orleans Mayor Mitchell Landrieu. Speaking at the Wilson Center in December 2016 at the celebration of the fiftieth anniversary of the National Endowment for the Arts, Landrieu insisted that since the arts allow a sense of freedom of expression, "art is the oxygen of democracy." It is not an add-on, Landrieu said, building on remarks by the Wilson Center's director, president, and CEO, Jane Harman; rather, it is a "critical part of national security and policy infrastructure." Landrieu encouraged the audience not to approach "the table of the powerful" as though they are supplicants, but to understand that they are a critical part of what makes America strong.[39]

Louisiana has surely demonstrated how the arts can make America strong. In this cultural haven, when natural disasters like Hurricane Katrina strike as winds from hell, the arts can help bring recovery. This may be attributed to the arts' capacity to galvanize social capital as we saw in Chapter 1. Also, in terms of putting

Americans back to work, the arts are not just "an add-on to what corporations should be thinking about."[40]

Landrieu said that when the city conceptualized the creative economy and went to the appropriation table, sitting next to the oil and gas industry, the port, etcetera, they were able to identify the return on investment in the arts. In Louisiana more than 140,000 people make a living around culture. Once people in these sectors found each other, they realized that they had common interests: education, health care, transport, and so on. In order for the arts economy to grow, like any other industry, it needs nurture. Yet when it comes to nurturing the arts in America, the otherwise commonplace notion of public-private partnership leans more toward "private-a-little-bit-public." But the government has a stake in this nurturing, Landrieu concluded. It can support arts education through schools like the arts-based Lusher Charter School in New Orleans, for example, not to mention through providing a favorable tax policy and other incentives.[41]

As we have seen, the instrumental contributions are important, but they are just one side of the coin. Again, there are many other compelling noninstrumental benefits of arts education that are extremely important, as Sen's capability approach shows.

Arts education engenders many traits, including curiosity, creative thinking or imagination, discipline, empathy, dealing with ambiguity, learning by doing, learning from mistakes, social engagement, and observation – traits that are hard to quantify, but nonetheless essential to innovation, overall wellbeing, and even success (in whatever way this may be interpreted).[42]

What is more, if acquiring observational skills is critical – observation is more than visual, as it includes aural, touch, and even smell and taste – then, as noted in Chapter 1, we can turn to arts education for help.[43] But since we have preconceived notions, our observations are not bias-free, even if our minds are uncluttered. "Thus the mind must be trained to observe just as much as we train the eyes, the ears, the nose, or the hands," according to the

Root-Bernsteins: "Clues as to how to do this come from one of the greatest observers of all time: Sherlock Homes, the violin-playing detective who, like a perfect artist, could size up a situation or an individual with a moment's glance."[44] Other compelling clues may come from lessons in dance and poetry, and from painting and drawing. Still others may come from reading and writing: "Writing and reading literature can be valuable for those who deal with people, whether in the social, legal, or medical professions."[45]

Gardner adds other benefits from arts education: "Among them are the likelihood that skill and craft gained in the arts help students to understand that they can improve in other consequential activities and that their heightened skill can give pleasure to themselves and to others."[46] These qualities are often neglected in education policy, as curriculums follow the template of standardized tests.

Moreover, if innovation and creativity are as important as we are told, I am not sure we are doing the right thing to cultivate innovative and creative minds. Innovation and creativity are being preached to death. Yet they are becoming tired words. It seems highly unlikely that corporate retreats to "cultivate creativity" produce sustainable outcomes, for instance. If we want to be life-long students of creativity and innovation, Steven Johnson has argued, we may do better to observe one area in which the arts grant us delight: play.

"Because play is often about breaking rules and experimenting with new conventions, it turns out to be the seedbed for many innovations that ultimately develop into much sturdier and more significant forms," Johnson says. To demonstrate that music, the "most abstract and ethereal of entertainments . . . has a longer history of technological innovation than any other form of art," as Johnson put it, is to consider a historic example: The three gifted toy designers from the Islamic golden age called the Banū Mūsā brothers, who introduced something called "The Instrument Which Plays Itself" to do nothing but satisfy the human desire for play and delight.[47]

I was delighted to learn that this self-playing instrument was a water-powered organ (the precursor of the synthesizer). Although this hydraulic organ was similar in design to Greek and Roman instruments built centuries before, it employed a new feature: The organ notes were triggered not by human fingers on a keyboard, but by a pinned cylinder – "a barrel with small 'teeth,' as the brothers called them, irregularly distributed across its surface. As the barrel rotated, those teeth activated a series of levers that opened and closed the pipes of the organ. Different patterns of 'teeth' produced different melodies as the air was allowed to flow through the pipes in unique sequences."[48]

Moreover, the cylinder could be swapped out and encoded with new information to play different sounds when placed back in the organ. This Banū Mūsā innovation – the brothers were associated with the "House of Wisdom," a kind of think tank for engineers and tinkers in 800AD when Baghdad was the center of global wisdom – was the genesis for programmability and the difference between software and hardware.[49] As Johnson explains, it introduced "important concepts of the digital age more than a thousand years before the first computers were built."[50] So if we talk about "programming," "cutting melody," and "coding," we have these brothers to thank.[51] What if these brothers had attended a school where play had no place, because they needed to cram for standardized tests, where they were told that tinkering with musical instruments was futile, because music had no market, where they were pushed to dump programming melody, because music would make them stupid?

"The entrepreneurs and industrialists may have turned the idea of programmability into big business," as Johnson concludes, "but it was the artists and the illusionists who brought the idea into the world in the first place."[52] Indeed, if we broaden the concepts of "culture" and "trade," this is another reminder that "where culture leads, trade follows" is not just a theoretical conjecture. And so, although this is not to say that art is just play and never serious work, one could argue that "where play leads, ideas follow."

Another important point to note is that when the arts induce play, they are also likely to induce engagement that leads to trust. And this is especially crucial in students' formative years. According to the *World Development Report 2015: Mind, Society, and Behavior*, "Primary school is a formative experience for children. The experience can shape the mental models that the individuals possess as adults."[53] Clearly, children do not interact with one another only through the arts. Sports and debates, for instance, also engender these interactions. But if the arts increase these interactions, then there is an added advantage. "There is some evidence that 'horizontal teaching systems,' in which children interact with one another and engage in class discussions, are an important learning tool and increase their level of trust. This body of evidence suggests new policy options."[54] Without doubt, a "shift in teaching strategies – incorporating more group work projects, especially in education systems that have traditionally relied heavily on rote learning and memorization – may be a promising avenue for improving social capital."[55]

But even if the arts simply keep children engaged in school – as I vividly recall in my own Ugandan experience – then that is justification enough. Student disengagement is rampant, and school dropout rates are unacceptable, in many schools around the world.

It is especially important to emphasize this in development policy, because the traditional models of education are not sufficient to address challenges like youth unemployment and other aspects of human development. This is true from rural places across the world to American inner cities like Newark, New Jersey, discussed in Chapter 8. Arts education is not all about making children first-rate artists to get jobs in the arts world – although that may not hurt. It is about giving them social behavioral, innovation, knowledge formulation, risk-taking, and observation skills, and much more. These capabilities are indispensable. As widely cited, they are not only important in job creation, they also equip people to lead a better life aided by development in full dimensions.

Policy debates ought to extend beyond the narrow confines of enrollment and attendance, if children are disengaged and not learning while at school. We must wake up. We cannot fail our children.

Mike Huckabee, an American presidential candidate more than once, as governor of Arkansas in 2005 pushed through a law "requiring elementary schools to offer 40 minutes per week of music and art and requiring high school students to take at least a half-year of art, music or dance to graduate,"[56] as Alec MacGillis writes. Huckabee, a conservative politician, wielded "a plank that would warm the hearts of many a liberal mom in Cambridge," Massachusetts and arts advocates elsewhere:

Indeed, on the economy of the future, in which we are told creativity will be front and center, Huckabee's observations are music to the ears of those who have long argued that science, technology, engineering, and mathematics should go hand in hand with the arts: Echoing Steve Jobs, he said, Even scientists and engineers will be better served if they are inventive (and here the idea is to put imaginative processes into practice). For just knowing the periodic table of elements will not be enough.[57] A "passionate advocate" who calls the arts "weapons of mass instruction,"[58] Huckabee says it is a mistake for schools to cut arts programs in favor of standardized tests:

> The biggest single mistake we've made in the last generation is that we've created a left-brain education system. And when you do that, it's like having a computer that has a wonderful database and no operating system. We have 6,000 kids that drop out of school every day in this country—6,000. There are millions more kids that lay their heads on the desk and take the most expensive nap in [America] – at the expense of the taxpayers – and its not because these kids are dumb. These kids are bored.[59]

Huckabee is certainly not talking about the kind of boredom in which delight in tedium, as Jude Stewart writes, can spur creativity.[60] But inasmuch as he is of the thought that eliminating the arts means not stimulating both sides of the brain, not generating its full capacity, Huckabee recapitulates the broader capabilities the arts can teach: "Ask a CEO what they are looking for in an employee and they say they need people who understand teamwork, people who are disciplined, people who understand the big picture. You know what they need? They need [artists]."[61] No wonder he concludes: "This whole idea that music and art are great programs if you can afford them and have room for them – that's utter *nonsense*. It's the stupidest thing we've done to education in the last two generations.'[62]

THE ROLE OF THE ARTS IN TEACHING NEW MODES OF BEHAVIOR

Although Huckabee was speaking with America in mind, the notion that arts education is a luxury looms large across the world with extraordinary unthinking. But as Huckabee said, it is *utter nonsense*. This is because even beyond stimulating creativity and keeping children engaged, the arts can "affect" human behavior. Indeed, in changing minds and mindsets, are the arts not an effective communication tool?

Theater for Development

The arts can be teachers and conduits of pedagogy, whether consciously or subconsciously. The use of the arts in positive information delivery has never been more important, since attention spans are getting shorter.[63] Moreover, as Gardner concludes, "the arts allow us to express what is important but cannot be captured in words – at least not in poetic words."[64]

Consider the global practice of Theater for Development. *Jana Sanskriti*, a participatory theater group in India, addresses contemporary social problems by requesting viewers to participate in skits on stage. "Through its interventions Jana Sanskriti seeks to stop the oppressed people from thinking that they are inferior, weak and incapable of analytical thought. They must become aware of their ability to plan constructive action and provide dynamic leadership in the process of development."[65]

Around the world, entertainment education has been shaping behavior in socially beneficial ways. "In Brazil, access to the TV Globo network – which was dominated by soap operas with independent female characters with few, or even no children – has been linked to the country's rapid drop in fertility. Viewing the soap operas had an effect equal to 1.6 years of additional education. In India, access to cable television reduced fertility and son preference and increased women's autonomy."[66] The arts can even help where imposing penalties and fines hit gridlock.

Former mayor of Bogotá Antanas Mockus, a professor of philosophy, said he "had little patience with conventional wisdom," in a *New York Times* article "The Art of Changing a City." Nonetheless, he knew that "people respond to humor and playfulness from politicians." And he recognized that new methods were needed to deal with the many problems his city faced.[67]

These included traffic that was not only chaotic, but also dangerous. He devised radical strategies that helped drop Bogotá's traffic fatalities to an average of about 600 per year from 1,300 within a decade. "Contributing to this success was the mayor's inspired decision to paint stars on the spots where pedestrians (1,500 of them) had been killed in traffic accidents."[68] And in one area, he replaced "corrupt traffic police officers with mime artists. The idea was that instead of cops handing out tickets and pocketing fines, these performers would 'police' drivers' behavior by communicating with mime – for instance, pretending to be hurt or offended when a vehicle ignored the pedestrian right-of-way in a crosswalk." Skeptics scoffed, "but change is possible. People began to obey traffic signals and, for the first time, they respected crosswalks."[69]

The test is how to sustain this change, as Mockus observed. But we should never forget that surprisingly small steps can lead to huge changes.[70] Hopefully, these steps, however tiny, will one day help people in Bogota and elsewhere cross a road safely.[71]

ON THE NEED TO LEARN ABOUT THE VALUE OF ARTS EDUCATION

As economists Edwin Mansfield and Gary Yohe highlight, "one of the benefits of education is that it allows individuals to appreciate and enjoy various forms of experience more keenly than they otherwise would."[72]

Beyond the creative benefits of arts education, there is a practical reason for extending it. As proponents of arts education have long preached, exposure to it helps create demand for more culture. And while philanthropists continue to support opera and ballet, for example, cuts in arts education continue and overall funding is meager. This is shortsighted. Broadly speaking, if expenditure on arts education on global cultures is minimal, then demand for such products is likely to be constrained. So another role of arts education in development is to increase demand for more trade in the arts.

But there is need to think beyond such rationales. For policy makers to comprehend the value of the arts in people's lives – for them to pass the test on the value of arts education – they badly need to do some learning. Too often, artists have been asked to demonstrate or find some quantitative way to prove what the arts can do for education.[73] This request is not entirely hopeless. In fact, earlier, we spent time explaining how that may be achieved. But some scholars like Jessica Hoffmann Davis, founding director of the Arts in Education Program at the Harvard Graduate School of Education, have come out and said: Enough of this. It is time to stop asking what the arts can do for education, and instead ask what education can to for the arts.

This observation is critical because, as I have tried to demonstrate, the arts enrich us even in ways that are difficult to measure or to describe. Moreover, according to Patricia Goldblatt, "every person," as the philosopher John Dewey believed, "is capable of being an artist, living an artful life of social interaction that benefits and thereby beautifies the world." Art conveys "messages that stimulate reflection on purposeful lives. It "[changes] perceptions, [increases] interest, and moral sensitivity." And it engenders "thoughts and actions in regard to societal roles and responsibilities."[74] Reflecting on such thoughts, no wonder "[m]any of us have questioned, albeit facetiously, why math teachers aren't asked to demonstrate how their teaching of math enhances students' ability to express themselves in any arts media," as Davis observes. "A frequent reason for dismissing the arts in education has been because so few students will grow up to be artists. We do not dismiss other subjects because so few students will grow to be mathematicians or scientists or historians or writers."[75] (Recall our previous discussion on production possibilities versus human capabilities.) What is more, as Davis notes, "Let's not worry about how what students learn in the arts 'transfers' to other subjects; let's consider how the arts 'transform' the learning and living of students who pursue them!"[76] On the macro level, we cannot but challenge ourselves to consider how arts education can *transform* our communities. That is the topic of Chapter 3. In the meantime, consider the following policy options.

CODA

Increase the Use of the Arts to Educate People about Social Issues

The arts can influence minds and address social issues, through such areas as theater for development or mimes for road safety, as we saw moments ago, or through music to promote HIV/AIDS awareness. This message extends to environmental stewardship (discussed in Chapter 3). And it can also be used to tackle superstitions. One such example is occurring in Asia, whose economic growth today is contributing to the extinction of African elephants and rhinos thousands of miles away.

In Vietnam, for instance, the superstition is that the rhino horn has medicinal properties (there are none). Furthermore, rhino horn is a status symbol. It is ground up, mixed with tea, or simply snorted to induce an experience dearer than cocaine.[77] In China, ivory is a longstanding symbol of wealth and status.

Tackling this crisis requires increasing such measures as combating militias and illegal cartels involved in this tragedy and enacting full-fledged game protection. Changing the myths and mindsets that fuel this demand is also key, though. The arts can help. More development organizations could engage the arts to help do this. Specifically, there is a need to build upon the example set by the United Nations Environment Program (UNEP). To bring the issue of poaching to public attention, UNEP has worked with its goodwill ambassador, actress Li Bingbing, and the city of Shanghai.[78] If such initiatives (or their variants) help curb such deadly demand, then there is no reason why they should not be replicated and scaled up.

Fund and Scale Up Arts in Education Initiatives

There is great need to generously fund and scale up arts in education initiatives in development. As seen in Afghanistan, besides providing physical infrastructure and the like, building a nation is about building its people. In this war-torn country, the contribution of the World Bank and other organizations to the Afghanistan National Institute of Music has touched on many mutually beneficial angles, including social inclusion (such as gender equity and ethnic equity), employment, infrastructural development, intercultural dialogue, and human development.

Yet such investments often receive meager funding, even if their impact can be grand. For example, the Afghanistan National Institute of Music's tour to the United States in February 2013, which brought together the World Bank, the United States Embassy, Carnegie Corporation, and the American Asian Cultural Council, cost about $600,000. Yet it was the largest and most successful exchange in the history of cultural relations between Afghanistan and the United States. In addition, the tour, which included some sixty Afghan students and teachers, not only allowed students to hone their skills; it also expanded their horizons. They saw another side of America, and America saw another side of Afghanistan. We could all learn from this. The World Bank's Multilateral Investment Guarantee Agency and the International Development Association, for instance, could do more to support such soft and smart development initiatives in select countries.[79]

3 The Arts and Environmental Stewardship

The world sends us garbage, we send back music.

Favio Chávez

Since the God versus Science debate comes up in environmental discussions, consider the following story a priest named Edward T. Kelaher told organists at a dinner in January 2017 at All Saints Church in Chevy Chase, Maryland: At one church gathering, a notable scientist told his audience that he had searched all planets in the universe, but could not find God. The church was dead silent. You could hear a pin drop from heaven. Everyone, including distinguished scientists, scratched their heads for counter arguments. It was the organist who raised his voice and said, Sir, your argument is limited. It is like saying if I take this organ apart and search all its bits and pieces, I would find no music.[1] This chapter is not about the God versus Science debate. Rather, it attempts to illustrate how artists and their art can often explain difficult subjects, including climate change, even better than scientists. This is badly needed because climate action requires changing mindsets. And sometimes the lesson is just about how art can inspire us to make use of the little we have to live more sustainable lives. To invoke that relationship, this chapter begins in Paraguay where, in an attempt to make their lives a little better, the world sent the people garbage, and the people sent back music.

***

There is a small town called Cateura in Paraguay, located about six miles from Asunción, and home to a trash dump that has become famous. To mention Paraguay is to invite comment on one of the major issues of our time: inequality. "Paraguay is one of South America's most unequal countries. A third of its people are poor and 18 percent extremely so, while 6 percent of farms occupy 85 percent of farmland."[2] Perhaps the residents of Cateura see the landfill as their own farm. Amidst biting poverty, they pick scrap to try to eke out a living. As you can imagine, opportunities for children in this place are few. More than 40 percent of children do not finish school because their parents need them to work.

One day, an environmental engineer, Favio Chávez, who also happens to be a musician, decided to try something to keep the children from playing in the landfill: He offered them music lessons. "At first it was very difficult because we had no place to rehearse and we had to teach in the same place where the parents were working in the trash," said Chávez. "The children knew nothing about music and it was very difficult to contact parents because many of them do not live with their children." But the lessons caught on, with children and parents alike. Soon they became so popular that the supply for instruments could not keep up with demand among the children. So, like a scavenger, Chávez looked left and right, until he and "Cola," one of the garbage-pickers, stumbled upon an idea: They experimented with making instruments from the trash. They used cans, forks, bottles, wires – whatever would work.

Over time, they and the children made improvements that made some of these "recycled" instruments sound even better than the wooded instruments "Made in China," Chávez said. The recycled instruments had another advantage: The young musicians could carry them around safely. "For many children," Chávez added, "it was impossible to give them a violin to take home because they had nowhere to keep it and their parents were afraid they would be robbed or the instrument would be sold to buy drugs."

In this way, the Recycled Orchestra of Cateura was born. In summing up what this is all about, Chávez is poetic: "The world sends us garbage, we send back music."[3] I heard that music in person when I met Chávez in September 2016 at the Avalon Theater in Chevy

Chase. He had come to Washington for a performance by the orchestra after a showing of a documentary film about it, called – wait for it – "Landfill Harmonic."

Although we cannot predict the future of these children, their story could teach us a thing or two about recycling and environmental sustainability. This lesson is vital, especially if we consider the situation in the United States: "Despite decades of exhortations and mandates," the American journalist and author John Tierney said, "it's still typically more expensive for municipalities to recycle household waste than to send it to a landfill."[4] That observation deserves a hearing, especially in the short run. But how about in the long run? Should we not prioritize better – how we spend, use, share, repurpose, and create?[5] After all, we are in the age of climate concern and environmental stress, which demand resourcefulness and imagination to tackle.

At any rate, who knows which direction this recycled orchestra will take as it becomes famous.[6] The donations coming in now include instruments from well-wishers. This well-intended kindness may in fact diminish the invention that was propelled by necessity in the first place (this catch-22 is not new in development aid). All in all, however, this example shows how the arts can inspire a better existence.

In Louisiana, where Hurricane Katrina left the city of New Orleans "fighting for its life,"[7] the New Orleans Jazz & Heritage Foundation is also finding inspiration in recycling. In 2013, the Foundation created a program called Second-Life Recycling, whose main goals are to provide employment opportunities for low-income youth and to advance environmental awareness. I am not sure if this event uses jazz as a metaphor for recycling. But in charting its goals, the Foundation seeks to make its "events 'greener' by disposing of recyclable waste properly."[8]

The mission of the Foundation, created in 1970, is to "promote, preserve, perpetuate and encourage the music, arts, culture and heritage of communities in Louisiana through festivals, programs and other cultural, educational, civic and economic activities." The group's annual Jazz Fest did not instantly become world-famous, but today, the Foundation says, it "attracts hundreds of thousands of visitors to New Orleans and pumps $300 million a year into the local economy."[9] The way the tentacles of the so-called creative economies stretch, who knows how many of these millions promote "green" jobs? The organization's Second-Life Recycling program, however, could be seen as a vector from which jazz and climate policy can be inferred.

CLIMATE CONFUSION + ART = CLIMATE ACTION?

Even though we have facts about climate change, the climate debate – or perhaps climate confusion – is far from over. Climate action therefore requires changing mindsets and pursuing systematic, multidimensional approaches to policy. This is important because there is a lot of skepticism about the whole idea of climate change.

Physicist Robert Davies, it is fair to say, was not particularly interested in climate change a decade ago. But while working at Oxford, he decided to visit the university's Environmental Change Institute. After seeing some of the evidence with his own eyes, he was struck by the gap between what the "science understands" and what the "public understands." This, he assumed, might be a science communication problem. So, he decided to start giving public lectures ... only to be further surprised by what he found: People would connect intellectually, but they would not act. "It was as if he were informing people about the dangers of smoking, and then watching them go out afterward and light up cigarettes."[10]

As he thought of what to do next, he decided to try music. So when he took a job at the Utah State University Climate Center, he partnered with the Fry Street Quartet, which is resident at the Caine College of the Arts there. That collaboration led to the establishment of something called the Crossroads Project,[11] which has so far enlisted the composer Laura Kaminsky, the painter Rebecca Allan, the sculptor Lyman Whitaker, and the photographer Garth Lenz. Its mission is to bring "the power of performance art to bear one of the great conversations of our time – human civilization's growing unsustainability and the quest for [a] truly meaningful response."[12] As Davies explains, "The project isn't meant to convert skeptics." It is about getting the converted to act.[13]

NATURE AND ART: BOTH TAKEN FOR GRANTED

Nature inspires creative work, but this inspiration often escapes our attention. In my case, I grew up being surrounded by sounds of nature. I vividly recall Uganda's frog choruses, birdsong, and much more. Yet it was not until I seriously studied music theory that I realized that these sounds were music – a cultural center, a treasure-trove for artists. There are a great many examples across the world of how nature inspires creative work. Consider birdsong. Bird music has inspired scores of compositions. Yet many birds have not escaped the destruction that too often claims their habits and their livelihoods.

This destruction often comes in the name of progress. In her remarkable 1962 book, *Silent Spring*, Rachel Carson notes that our modern, chemical-drenched insecticide practices also ended up killing many birds. Sometimes this spraying is meant to save trees. But one woman from Milwaukee, Wisconsin, questioned this premise, Carson wrote: "'Taking a long look, can you save trees without also saving birds? Do they not, in the economy of nature, save each other? Isn't it possible to help the balance of nature without destroying it?'"[14] I cannot help but ask: What would composers like the French organist and ornithologist Olivier Messiaen say about climate change and its toll on nature, including the jubilant birds? How often does it cross our minds to protect Mother Nature because she is a spiritual haven? If the arts enrich our lives, does it ever occur to us to debate protecting the environment because it inspires creative work?

Even if that is a huge ask, I am inclined to say that the arts and the environment seem to share a common conundrum: they both enrich humanity, yet they are relentlessly taken for granted. This alarming situation requires that all disciplines aggressively join hands to tackle the problem. But even if all disciplines join hands, this does not necessarily translate into meaningful action. Why? We have been locked into our ways. And human behavior can be hard to change. It is in this premise of behavioral change that the arts could help lead the way. As we concluded in Chapter 2, they can transform us.

THE ARTS AND ENVIRONMENTAL STEWARDSHIP

The arts have long had a sense of stewardship toward protecting the environment and mitigating climate change. Photographers, painters, and others use their work to portray the reality of our increasingly deteriorating environment. After all, wonders of nature inspire artists. Targeting the biggest polluters is critical, because, as widely noted, their actions indirectly affect the poor, especially those in remote coastal villages. Some work has been done in this area, most of which can be found on the Web. Consider the following examples.

In China, the world's largest carbon emitter today, an art exhibition titled "Unfold" was staged in Beijing in 2013 by a nonprofit called Cape Farewell. The aim of this exhibition, which also traveled to Vienna, London, New York, and Chicago, was to prompt a "cultural response to climate change." Showcasing more than twenty artists, it merged culture and science to provoke a debate on climate change in China. The art, in a nonconfrontational way, asked people to reflect on actions connected with their daily living and what this means for climate change.[15] Meanwhile, in the United States, the second largest carbon emitter colleges have increased courses on the arts and climate change.[16]

In Europe, the Imagine 2020 – Art and Climate Change network, funded by Creative Europe (a cultural framework under the aegis of the European Commission), has brought together a number of European arts organizations with the mandate of increasing climate change awareness within the arts community and the public at large. Ultimately, the network says, art "should provide a physical and imaginary space where people can take a step back, away from the corporate, the commercial and the educational, to exchange and engage with each other."[17]

Similarly, artists like Bono can use their stardom to sensitize the public about climate change. "An Inconvenient Truth," a documentary about former US Vice President Al Gore's efforts to promote awareness on global warming, garnered international acclaim. These artistic endeavors communicate in ways policy speeches may fail to deliver.

THE GREEN BELT MOVEMENT: ON TAKING ROOT AND BECOMING A HUMMINGBIRD

In Kenya, Wangari Maathai founded the Green Belt Movement in 1977 "to respond to the needs of rural Kenyan women who reported that their streams were drying up, their food supply was less secure, and they had to walk [farther and farther] to get firewood for fuel and fencing."[18] It has since spread across Africa "and contributed to the planting of over thirty million trees."[19] In the words of the citation that made her the first African woman to be awarded the Nobel Peace Prize, in 2004, Maathai was recognized not only for her contribution to sustainable development, but also to democracy and peace.[20] Operating under the auspices of the National Council of Women of Kenya, the Green Belt Movement has "encouraged the women to work together to grow seedlings and plant trees to bind the soil, store rainwater, provide food and firewood, and receive a small monetary token for their work."[21]

More about Maathai's work can be found in her books *The Green Belt Movement, Unbowed: A Memoir, The Challenge for Africa*, and *Replenishing the Earth*. Her work is documented in the award-winning documentary "Taking Root: The Vision of Wangari Maathai." The film, by Lisa Merton and Alan Dater, tells a compelling story about Maathai and her movement. "Through cinema verité footage of the tree nurseries and the women and children who tend them, 'Taking Root' brings to life the confidence and joy of people working to improve their own lives while also ensuring the future and vitality of their land."[22]

Another scene in another movie "animates a story from [Maathai], about a brave hummingbird who struggles to do good while others just look on."[23] The story is concerned with a situation in which a fierce fire engulfs a huge forest that a number of animals call home. Instead of doing something to stop the blaze, however, other animals – including big elephants that could use their big trunks to collect water from the nearby stream to extinguish the fire – do nothing. It is the tiny hummingbird that makes an effort, fetching water, drop by drop, back and forth, to fight the fire. When other animals question the tiny bird of its seemingly tiny actions that could even get its little wings burned, the bird says it is doing the best it can. The moral of the story, according to Maathai, is this: All of us need to become humming birds. To do the best we can, however little, to fight the climate crisis.[24]

If this story sounds familiar, it is because the movie where the scene is found, "Dirt! The Movie," is inspired by William Bryant Logan's groundbreaking book *Dirt: The Ecstatic Skin of the Earth.* In a fascinating account (narrated by Jaimie Lee Curtis), we are reminded that "four billion years of evolution have created the dirt that recycles our water, gives us food, and provides us with shelter." Yet "humanity has endangered this vital living resource with destructive methods of agriculture, mining practices, and urban development, with catastrophic results: mass starvation, drought, and global warming."[25]

In an effort to showcase hummingbirds among us, people who are doing their best to avert the climate crisis, the filmmakers of "Dirt! The Movie" continue their global mission: They "travel around the world to capture the stories of global visionaries who are discovering new ways to repair humanity's relationship with soil," engaging Vandana Shiva "to discuss her fight to prevent world hunger by preserving biodiversity in India, and documenting the tree planting work of renowned photographer Sebastião Salgado and his wife Lélia in Brazil."[26]

SIREN SONGS IN SILENT SPRING

Another story that captures new ways to repair our relationship with nature cannot but take us back to *Silent Spring,* which arguably altered "the course of history."[27] This landmark book, which inspired the creation of the Environmental Protection Agency in the United States, raised questions about the irresponsible use of toxic chemicals to kill off unwanted pests. The modes of action that Carson suggested to replace pesticides are varied. Still, who knew that sound could be one sustainable way of containing pests?[28]

In charting a more chemical-free future, Carson listed experiments on siren songs and other ultrasonic sounds to attract and repel insects. Although the research here is not about linkages of creative work and climate action per se, the idea of influencing insect behavior with sound is not far fetched. It "only awaits discovery of the proper key to unlock and apply the vast existing knowledge of insect sound production and reception." Although I have heard about how listening to Mozart can make kids smarter (see Chapter 2), I have yet to hear about how Mozart can contain mosquitoes. But in some experiments, airborne ultrasonic sonic sounds have killed yellow fever mosquitos, mealworms, and blowflies "in a matter of seconds." "All such experiments," Carson argued, were "first steps toward wholly new concepts of insect control which the miracles of electronics may some day make a reality."[29] It is not difficult to find ultrasonic sounds as insect repellents on the market today. And, as more research is carried out, such electronic miracles would certainly benefit from the dance between environmental science and music technology.

DANCE FOR CLIMATE ACTION

> Dance, like every other artistic expression, presupposes a heightened, increased life response.
>
> Mary Wigman[30]

In March 2015, the American Museum of Natural History in New York put on an unlikely event. The museum, whose history goes back to 1869, showcased choreographer Karole Armitage's dance about climate change in our contemporary cultural context. The dance, titled "On the Nature of Things," was tailored for the Museum's Milstein Hall of Ocean Life. The Hall, we are told, "highlights the drama of the undersea world and its diverse and complex web of life in a fully immersive marine environment."[31] It is in this immersive spirit that dance and science came together, not to compete but to collaborate.

Armitage, the daughter of a biologist, is concerned about the divide between climate data and human behavior: Scientists are frustrated, she said. They have been presenting facts for over twenty-five years, yet this has done little to change people's behavior.[32] So it perhaps should not be a surprise that Armitage, whose love with nature is deep, would team up with the biologist Paul Ehrlich of Stanford University.

Ehrlich, author of the controversial best-seller *The Population Bomb*, is deeply concerned with the so-called "culture gap." In "The Culture Gap and Its Needed Closures," an essay he wrote with his wife, Anne H. Ehrlich, they argue that for people to detect the overall environmental deterioration, they need to do such things as the following: "interpret a graph of CO_2 concentrations in the atmosphere ... understand how the scientific enterprise works, and become accustomed to thinking about such things as risk analysis, fat-tailed probability distributions, population externalities, resilience, synergisms, tipping points, and complex adaptive systems."[33] The list goes on and on. But here is the couple's point:

> That few people think about or do many of those things is a result of a vast "cultural gap." In modern societies, knowledge has become deliberately and excessively divided into even smaller units – "siloed" – and isolated from the related information. Knowledge and information are so compartmentalized that even the most

> brilliant leaders do not see (or choose for political reasons not to point out) obvious crucial connections. Because of the cultural gap and a public education system that fails to make important connections and draw important inferences, few people in our society are able to describe how the climate works.[34]

Their observations echo the *World Development Report 2015*, which notes that "people interpret scientific information in light of their cultural worldviews, obtain information through social networks and favored media channels, and rely on trusted messengers to make sense of complex information."[35] Speaking about the combination of science and dance, Armitage concurs with this point: we badly "need a new method of presenting climate change as an issue we can't ignore." By putting on three one-hour performances over three days, the troupe of over thirty dancers played its part in spreading the word about climate change.[36]

The dance was designed to bring "visceral emotion to the topic of climate change," Armitage explains. "The arc of the production started in peace and harmony, gradually became disturbed and then more and more perilous, violent, and unpredictable. Once the dancers (standing in for people) opened their eyes and looked at the state of things, they changed course and harmony returned. The ballet showed how a change in consciousness can make a change in the world."[37] The dance was accompanied by Ehrlich's narration (adapted from his culture gap essay) and the music was written by such figures as John Luther Adams, Philip Glass, Michael Gordon, Henryk Górecki, and Arvo Pärt.[38]

The movements "'are meant to evoke the perils and harmony and chaos of our world, which comes through in the music and body language,'" Armitage said. "'Our job was about balancing a very non-judgmental, objective text with the dance and the music.'"[39]

The central mission here is to see how projects like dance and science can work together on promoting effective climate action. The old adage comes to mind: You can take a donkey to the river, but you cannot make it drink. Similarly, science can take people to the well of facts, but it cannot necessarily make them act.

On that premise, Ehrlich cofounded MAHB, the Millennium Assessment of Human Behavior (pronounced "mob"). The cofounders "emphasise that it is *human behavior*, toward the planet that sustains us all and toward one another, that requires rapid modification." MAHB's founders acknowledge that their organization cannot do it all[40] – in fact, the organization has since been renamed the Millennium Alliance for Humanity and the Biosphere.[41] They nonetheless pose important questions: "How can critical parts of the culture gap be closed? What can be done to make the needed changes on a time scale of years, not decades?"[42]

Reflecting on those questions, Armitage says: "'Art is often a portrait of being alive in your time . . . Climate change is part of our time.'"[43] As this iconic choreographer noted, for those who showed up, "On the Nature of Things" was probably preaching to the choir. These people probably believe what they saw. Not everyone does, though. Here are just two lines from a critical comment on the dance: "This is like a parody. Something normal people would joke about liberals doing."[44]

That opinion is loud and clear. But here is the thing: "Evidence of early dance, such as artifacts and cave paintings, indicates that among ancient peoples dance was one of the first arts, existing long before written language."[45] As we have seen, scientists have presented data. Yet despite the urgency of the matter, these facts are having a hard time changing people's attitudes. So perhaps it is not a parody for dance and science to merge. That this merger can promote behavioral changes would be a welcome step. And if action is as individual as it is global, it is also as cross-cultural as it is intergenerational. It therefore remains to be seen if people like Armitage and Ehrlich will one day enlist such groups as the Paraguay's recycled orchestra. For dance, an ancient ritual, heightens our sense of purpose.

PART II Trade in Services: A Three-Part Suite

4 International Trade in Cultural Services

Services represent the fastest-growing sector of the global economy and account for two-thirds of global output, one-third of global employment and nearly 20 percent of global trade.

World Trade Organization

This chapter begins a series of discussions on the role of trade in cultural services that will be carried through Chapters 5 and 6. Trade has become a dirty word these days,[1] but we should never forget that people have been engaging in trade for millennia – long before modern globalization or objections to it. International trade is not like playing a competitive sport, with just winners and losers; it is about mutual benefit.[2] What is imperative is to make sure trade liberates the poor from poverty, and here the exchange of cultural goods and services can play an important role. Nonetheless, while it is easy to see the exchange of goods, the exchange of services is hard to visualize. Yet services are very much part of the modern economy. The reason why a country like Nigeria now has a larger economy than previously thought, as noted in Chapter 1, is in part because of the explosive growth of its movie industry, "Nollywood." This chapter introduces the World Trade Organization's modes of supplying services and it touches on the concept of trade in value added. With a focus on Africa, it carries Nollywood along as it examines how areas, including nation branding and intellectual property, can contribute to development.

***

Imagine you are seated on your sofa one Sunday afternoon somewhere in the Republic of Creativeria. As you flip your TV channels, you land on a teaser for a film from Nigeria's movie industry, Nollywood. You pause. But the teaser grabs your attention. It tells the tale of Osuofia, a poor hunter from rural Nigeria who inherits the fortune of his brother, who has died in London. Osuafia quickly travels to London to claim his share. Once there, British culture confuses and alarms him, as "various run-ins with fast-food cashiers and convenience store clerks" make clear. He meets his brother's fiancée and travels back to Nigeria with her. It soon becomes clear that she is just pretending to be interested in him; she is really after his money.[3] You stay put, glued to the screen. The movie is great; hooked, you decide to buy a subscription to Nollywood movies. Do you know what you have just done? You are now participating in a form of international trade in services.

Technically speaking, services are those intangibles that range from architecture to space transport, according to the World Trade Organization (WTO).[4] In colloquial terms, imagine "'everything you cannot drop on your foot.'"[5] In the diverse structure of creative work, intangible trade in the arts is trade in services. And trade in the arts can induce investment in other areas.

If this all sounds abstract, it is. But its importance is undeniable. Services, the WTO notes, "represent the fastest growing sector of the global economy and account for two-thirds of global output, one-third of global employment and nearly 20 percent of global trade."[6] Why does this matter for development? Services "are the largest and most dynamic component of both developed and developing country economies. Important in their own right, they also serve as crucial inputs into the production of most goods."[7]

TRADE IN CREATIVE SERVICES: A CREATIVE BOON FOR DEVELOPING NATIONS

Recognizing the potential and the diversity of trade in services from tourism to education, from insurance to banking, the WTO came up with not one, but four modes of supply (Box 4.1). The important point, for the purposes of trade in the arts, is that one mode can lead to another, in a self-reinforcing cycle that can create jobs, spur

BOX 4.1 The Four Modes of Supply

These modes appear in the General Agreement of Trade in Services (GATS), which entered into force in 1995. "The GATS distinguishes between four modes of supplying services: cross-border trade, consumption abroad, commercial presence, and presence of natural persons":

I. "Cross-border supply is defined to cover services flows from the territory of one Member into the territory of another Member (e.g. banking or architectural services transmitted via telecommunications or mail)";
II. "Consumption abroad refers to situations where a service consumer (e.g. tourist or patient) moves into another Member's territory to obtain a service";
III. "Commercial presence implies that a service supplier of one Member establishes a territorial presence, including through ownership or lease of premises, in another Member's territory to provide a service (e.g. domestic subsidiaries of foreign insurance companies or hotel chains)"; and
IV. "Presence of natural persons consists of persons of one Member entering the territory of another Member to supply a service (e.g. accountants, doctors or teachers). The Annex on Movement of Natural Persons specifies, however, that Members remain free to operate measures regarding citizenship, residence or access to the employment market on a permanent basis."

Source: WTO n.d. "The General Agreement on Trade in Services (GATS)." www.wto.org/english/tratop_e/serv_e/gatsqa_e.htm#4.

investment, boost growth, strengthen the bonds among people and cultures, and promote the arts. Those links are traced in this chapter and the two that follow.

These four modes, operating separately and together, could unleash a creative boon for developing countries. Why? Well, as this book insists, every nation, big and small, has immense cultural wealth. But if creativity is ripe even in the poorest of nations, why are services not well harvested? There are plenty of political and policy issues at play. Nevertheless, one common challenge is their intangibility. To understand the problems and the potential of trade in creative services, let us return to Nigeria and Nollywood. In the WTO's GATS-speak, if you have streamed a movie like *Osuofia in London* outside Nigeria, you have participated in the "cross-border supply" (Mode I). If you saw this movie in Nigeria, you participated in what we may call "in-border supply." Either way, you have now participated in the second largest movie industry in the world in terms of production.[8]

Nollywood: Learning How to Climb Walls[9]

Nigerian film producer Bond Emeruwa once quipped, "In Nollywood we don't count the walls. We learn how to climb them."[10] Production crews function on shoestring budgets. One source put the average cost of a movie between $15,000 and $30,000;[11] another, more recent source, estimated it to be between $25,000 and $ 70,000.[12] Besides tight budgets, there are many problems that can arise, as one account summarized: "Electricity goes out. Street thugs demand extortion money. The lead actor doesn't show. During one crucial scene, prayers blast from loudspeakers atop a nearby mosque."[13] Such obstacles, however, have not deterred entrepreneurs from investing in an industry that now generates about 2,500 movies a year.[14]

Nollywood today is considered the second largest employer in Nigeria[15] – behind agriculture – and in 2013 contributed around 1.4 percent to Nigeria's GDP of more than $500 billion dollars.[16] That 1.4 may not sound like much, but hang on. The potential is huge.

Nollywood movies, which were simply called Nigeria's home videos back in 2002, became popular at first through videotapes traded across Africa. But now – and this is especially important with respect to our discussion on trade in creative services – "Nollywood is available on satellite and cable television channels, as well as on streaming services like iRokoTV." Norimitsu Onishi, a Japanese Canadian journalist who helped coin the term "Nollywood," has this to add: "In 2012, in response to swelling popularity in Francophone Africa, a satellite channel called Nollywood TV began offering round-the-clock movies dubbed into French. Most Nollywood movies are in English, though some are in one of Nigeria's main ethnic languages."[17]

Across Africa, Nollywood is not only becoming more popular in terms of content. It is also becoming a movie production model. For example, in Kitwe, Zambia, "local filmmakers were recently making their latest movie in true Nollywood style: a family melodrama shot over 10 days, in a private home, on a $7,000 budget. Burned on DVD, the movie will be sold in Zambia and neighboring countries."[18] We should not be surprised if more and more of these movies will be distributed via streaming, satellite, and the like.

On the Nature and Method of Trade in Value Added: A Brief Inquiry

If distributing movies via streaming or satellite to other countries is one thing, accounting for the inputs that make up products is another. So consider the idea of trade in value added (TiVA).

And what is that? Think about a pencil you might use to write *Osuofia in London* on a sticky note.

As we saw in Chapter 1, the bits and pieces that make up a pencil include graphite, rubber to name a few etc. The pencil may be made in the Republic of Pencilaria, but its graphite may come from Sri Lanka, the rubber from the Congo, and the wood from America, not to mention the know-how of consulting services from the creative natives of Creativeria.[19] So TiVA is simply a "statistical method used to estimate the sources of value added when producing goods and services for export and import." TiVa "traces the value added by each industry and country in the production chain to the final export, and allocates the value added to these source industries and countries. TiVA recognizes that exports in today's globalized economy rely on global value chains." These chains "use intermediate items imported from various industries in a number of countries."[20] Therefore, the pencil example also applies to cars, iPhones, movies, and so on.

Although trade in value added does not fully capture how an economy benefits from trade, it gets us somewhere:[21] It casts light on the "double counting" or "multiple counting" problem,[22] and it reveals a picture that can be a vector for trade policy debates. For example, not long ago, "the iPhone contributed $1.9 billion to the US trade deficit with China, using the traditional country of origin concept," as former WTO Director-General Pascal Lamy has pointed out. "But if China's iPhone exports to the US were measured in value added – meaning the value added by China to the components – those exports would come to only $73.5m."[23]

It is easy to see how this works for goods such as iPhones. But what about movies like those made in Nollywood style, which you can watch on your iPhone assembled in China, accompanied by a sound track of Zambian rhythms played on a keyboard from Japan? I cannot help but borrow an idea from "I, Pencil":

> *I, Movie, am a complex combination of miracles: stories, music, scenery, and so on. But to these miracles, which manifest themselves also in Nollywood-style movies, an even more extraordinary miracle has been added: the configuration of creative human energies, often called intellectual property.*
> *My director may come from Nigeria, but my script may come from Zambia; my soundtrack may employ African rhythms, but it may be played on a Japanese keyboard; and my animation may be drafted in Lagos, but it may be produced in London.*[24]

Such a setting is of course imaginary, but it challenges us to imagine how movie making might work in the complex web of value added. Doing so, the following points come to mind: First, the direct services of making a movie may be based in Nigeria or in Zambia, but when it comes to, say, designing software for a Nollywood movie app, that function could be outsourced to Kenya or to Korea. And a movie animation or video game may be conceived at home. Yet its production could be realized elsewhere and then returned home for completion.[25]

Second, DVDs, jackets, booklets, and the like could be produced elsewhere. A DVD burned in Zambia may come from Japan. All the while, the inputs the make that DVD may comprise of plastic from other countries; the same could be said of booklets and jackets. (If any of these inputs come from Zambia, then you can see the problem of "multiple counting.") To complicate matters, the booklet may include a French translation automated by software from Korea or done by a French speaker in Senegal, for example.

The third point is related to intellectual property. A movie may be based on a novel written by a Nigerian author, say, the Nobel laureate Wole Soyinka, employ a soundtrack by a South African composer, and use photographs by a Ugandan photographer. While the movie may be produced in the United States, it clearly carries intellectual roots from Africa. The trade in value added approach might aim to index the breakdown of such roots, and again, thereby inform trade policy debates. There is, however, a longstanding critique that when African music or movies are produced elsewhere, for instance, this creates jobs not in Africa but elsewhere. Although infrastructure and facilities may be the determining factors (regarding final production) – and, of course, there are other nontradable goods and services that add value – branding and marketing also wield immense power. And that brings up another issue: Africa's image. That issue has implications on how Africa might attract investments related to outsourcing and local business development. We may not know much about Africa's trade in value added, but when it comes to nation branding, Africa surely has a huge wall to climb. Can the arts help? Let us see.

THE ARTS, INVESTMENTS, AND NATION BRANDING

The Happy Meeting: How Cross-Border Services Can Induce Domestic Subsidiaries

Any smart investor today may have reason to consider Africa. Whilst the Chinese have been savvy about this, the reality is that many still view Africa as a dark continent. From AIDS to Ebola, political instability to corruption, the portrait is largely dark. The time has come to do away with this view. And we can start by positively branding African countries, with the arts and culture leading the way.

Branding is not advertising, although the two are interrelated. A country's brand is closely tied to the full spectrum of its political, cultural, and commercial history. Why does this matter for development? "Country branding is a vital element in both domestic and international affairs," as the global company FutureBrand explains. "The difference between a successful, defined and understood brand and a weaker, less differentiated one can have a significant impact on a nation's attractiveness for investment as well as tourism, and can compromise domestic confidence and social unity."[26]

Through the power of branding, a good movie (or other positive developments) can paint a positive image. Hollywood probably wins America more hearts and minds around the world than nearly anything else. And this likability attracts talent to American schools, induces sales of American iPads, American jeans – you name it. All this fuels America's GDP, which amounts to trillions of dollars. And it buys America great influence across the world, regardless of what you may think of American values.

Conversely, a bad country brand can diminish a country's attractiveness. Nigeria's image has been tarnished by a succession of fraudulent e-mails, oil scandals, and kidnappings, including the tragic case of abducted schoolgirls.

Many countries could use a better brand. On a global comparison, many African countries, in particular, have abysmal scores in the annual FutureBrand Country Brand Index (CBI). That should not surprise us. But even though Africa has much to do for Africa, lighting its own candle of destiny, consider what America's foremost novelist and Nobel Laureate Toni Morrison captures in her book *The Origin of Others*: "As the original locus of the human race, Africa is ancient, yet, being under colonial control, it is also infantile. A kind of old fetus always waiting to be born but confounding all midwives. In novel after novel, short story after short story, Africa is simultaneously innocent and corrupt, savage and pure, irrational and wise." From one example to another, it is inevitable that Africa would be portrayed this way: "A huge needy homeland to which we were said to belong but which none of us had seen or cared to see, inhabited by people with whom we maintained a delicate relationship of mutual ignorance and disdain, and with whom we shared a mythology of passive, traumatized Otherness cultivated by text books, film, cartoons, and the hostile name-calling children learn to love."[27]

Africa's negative perception, often fed by issues ranging from disease to wars, translates into poor nation brands. This is what William Easterly might call the "tyranny of negative bias." And negative brands stick. We know from behavioral economics that people tend to hold onto negative images and stereotypes longer than positive ones. Indeed, as Daniel Kahneman cites the paper "Bad Is Stronger Than Good" by Roy F. Baumeister and others in his book *Thinking, Fast and Slow*, "'Bad impressions and bad stereotypes are quicker to form and more resistant to disconfirmation than good ones.'"[28]

Besides compromising domestic confidence and social unity,[29] such negativity can diminish a nation's attractiveness for investment and tourism.[30] Investors can become more risk averse. As my Nigerian friend Abdul-Rahman B. Akande at the International Finance Corporation told me, this makes business investments in places like Africa more expensive, as investors pile up more and more safeguards to avoid losses. The "asymmetric intensity of the motives to avoid losses and to achieve gains," as Kahneman observes, "shows up almost everywhere."[31] It is not surprising, therefore, that "the strategic development of country brands and their marketing has become big business and will undoubtedly continue to fuel economic growth in the years to come."[32] Moreover, investments often spur increases in trade, as Simon Lester and others explain:

> [I]nvestment and trade are the two ways to sell in foreign markets. With goods [as well as services], a company can either export its products to a foreign country or open a factory in that country to

> produce and sell there. Thus, the goals of trade and investment overlap to some extent. In addition, foreign investment often spurs increase in trade. As multinational corporations seek the ideal location for their production, they often plan for that production to service regional or even global demand. As a result, foreign investment often leads to increased exports from the host country.[33]

Since a country's image does indeed matter in such considerations, the strategy to promote country branding via creative trade in services for developing countries is timely: particularly so, since target 8.a of the Sustainable Development Goals is to increase Aid for Trade, including technical assistance to the so-called least developed countries.[34] This aid for trade could pay a closer look at how countries with poor brands do in the complex world of global commerce. Here, in the parlance of WTO's four modes, expanding trade in services as the arts could serve as "crucial inputs" or "infrastructure" for trade in other areas. These "crucial inputs" and infrastructure are more than cement and steel. They could be architectural renditions that inspire a bridge – or, in moments of human interaction, they could be bridges that build trust: creating an environment that enables people to learn more about one another. What is more, as an aspect of "soft power,"[35] the arts have "the ability to entice and attract," as Joseph Nye has argued.[36] (See the coda of Chapter 6 for other suggestions on building a national brand.)

But this process of enticing and attracting not only concerns branding; it also induces investments in other areas, leading to direct, hardcore economic growth. Consider this example from the United States, where movies and music have sparked billions in investment.

When cable companies first began to provide an internet service that eliminated the need for telephone lines, few customers signed up. "One issue was, and continues to be, cost," as economists Edwin Mansfield and Gary Yohe explain. But more to our point, "few consumers saw a fundamental need for more speed for the services that they were then demanding." Then things changed:

> Major companies have become convinced that movies on demand, instant music downloads, and the next generation of broadband software and interactive television will begin to increase consumer demand for nanosecond communication. Indeed, Comcast, Inc., of Pennsylvania used backing from Microsoft to win a bidding war with AOL Time Warner for AT&T Broadband in December 2001. The combined bid of $72 billion speaks volumes about what these companies see as the future – a future that must be driven by consumer demand.[37]

As this example demonstrates, consumer demand for cultural products can help drive major investments in other areas.[38] This evokes that idea of "where culture leads, trade follows."[39] To return to the WTO's GATS treaty, the flow of services from country A to country B (cross-border supply, Mode I) can induce a service supplier in country A to establish a "territorial presence" in country B to provide a service (commercial presence, Mode III). Let us consider another example – and, on a practical bearing, this touches on the subject of outsourcing that can be mirrored in trade in value added: if an American cable company decides to establish a subsidiary in Nigeria to tap into the flourishing creative sector there, it could be said that Mode I is inducing Mode III. This movement, moreover, can occur in the other direction: Nigerian firms could start investing in the United States. It could even induce domestic direct investment. Indeed, if Nigerian movies continue to crescendo, this might induce investments in Nigerian telecommunications and broadband connectivity. As we saw in the discussion about Nashville (Chapter 1), creative hubs or clusters or regions tend to compose a harmonious symphony that inspires and accelerates innovation. This contributes to progress, be it economic or social.

For example, in many parts of Africa where a cellphone is "a digital Swiss Army knife: flashlight, calculator, camera and, yes, audio player," consider what Lydia Polygreen saw "on the sun-blasted streets of Bamako, Mali's capital." A "new kind of merchant has sprung up along Fankélé Diarra Street":

> Seated practically thigh to thigh, vendors crouch over laptops, scrolling through screen after screen of downloaded music. They are known as *téléchargeurs*, or downloaders, and they operate as an offline version of iTunes, Spotify and Pandora all rolled into one. They know what their regulars might like, from the latest Jay Z album to the obscurest songs of Malian music pioneers like Ali Farka Touré. Savvy musicians take their new material to Fankélé Diarra Street and press the *téléchargeurs* to give it a listen and recommend it to their customers. For a small fee – less than a dime a song – the *téléchargeurs* transfer playlists to memory cards or USB sticks, or directly onto cellphones. Customers share songs with their friends via short-range Bluetooth signals.[40]

Regardless of the viability of this business model or concerns about intellectual property rights, there is innovation at work under the sun of Mali. Indeed, this example seems to also support Steven Johnson's theory that where play leads, ideas follow. And while we often hear how Islamic fundamentalists lob a combustible cocktail of hostility toward the tradition and practice of music in Mali, the people of this West African nation have kept music close to their heart.

Technology is accelerating connections like the ones on Mali's streets (see Chapter 5). As creative economies become more and more intertwined, including in the area of services, we might continue to see the process that Nobel-economist Paul Krugman identifies: "Regions that for historical reasons have a head start as centers of production will even attract more production."[41] In a way, that was the case in Nashville, and it could be the case in the Nollywoods and Bollywoods of the world. Whatever the case, what is happening on Mali's Fankélé Diarra Street somehow exhibits how culture can be the taproot from which rootlets of ingenuity spring. *The Geography of Genius* (introduced in Chapter 1) makes that point clear.[42] And if nurturing creativity "is not a private act, but a public commitment,"[43] then: We need a development commitment to unleash culture's role in emancipating homegrown ideas to attack the tyranny of poverty.

But to recapitulate the concepts of value added and nation branding, there is a need to see how culture here can help guide new approaches to development. Here is why. There is "the tendency to think of value-added as pertaining only to components: the memory function, touch screen and applications processor in an iPhone, rather than the logistics, R&D, marketing and branding," as Lyndon Thompson has written.[44] Now, if marketing and branding are part and parcel of the value chain phenomenon, is nation branding not too important to ignore?

On Promoting Nation Branding

Nation branding rarely shows up in development policy. Therefore, it is no surprise that country image is not considered in many development frameworks. To address this issue, there is a need to apply such ideas as the "evidence-based and selective country engagement model" noted in the World Bank Group Strategy. The idea is to assess the relationship between weak country brands and trade, tourism, and investment. This could occur under, say, the auspices of the World Bank's Systematic Country Diagnostic.[45] For countries where it is clear that a weak image is likely to constrain their competitiveness and economic growth (see the discussion on Haiti in Chapter 6), the following steps could be considered.

First, there is a need to explore the promise of cultural diplomacy and nation branding.[46] Details for this require careful articulation that goes beyond the scope of this book. This could nonetheless be done in partnership with embassies, as well as cultural and educational institutions and the private sector, including airlines, cruise ship operators, and hotels. Embassies and hotels are particularly "crucial for national identity because they are the places where outsiders encounter a society."[47] The second step may entail building closer linkages between cultural institutions, ministries of culture, the private sector, and development agencies. The main focus here would be to close the gap between poor country brands and private sector investment. Moreover, this may also touch on the issue of geographical indications, trademarks, and other aspects of intellectual property in tandem with linkages to trade in value added.

At any rate, the following points should be kept in mind: First, investments made in image building are not easy to measure and may take a long time to pay off. That said, the costs incurred in engaging the arts to build a positive image could be offset by major returns even beyond pure economic gain. Second, since every nation has its own unique culture and heritage, each nation has an opportunity to excel in promoting its own image, fully and positively. Third, for countries with a poor image, the major challenge is to turn their cultural assets into "perceived strengths through clear and consistent" communication.[48] Of course, it will take more than clear and consistent communication to turn around the problems that underlie a bad image. Such an intervention is nonetheless better than nothing. Finally, in conflict-affected countries and in countries with other extreme governance challenges, on the other hand, one could argue that solving directly these constraints to investment is a priority.

THE DELICATE DANCE BETWEEN CREATIVE WORK AND INTELLECTUAL PROPERTY[49]

Trade in creative services needs to solve the problem of how to protect intellectual property to really take off. Since a large portion of trade in services interacts with intellectual property, it is an area of law "too important to be left to lawyers."[50]

Broadly speaking, intellectual property "means the legal rights which result from intellectual activity in the industrial, scientific, literary and artistic fields."[51] (For more on definitions, see Annex 4.1.) Legal scholar Robert P. Merges argues that intellectual property today is like the character of the "chaotic, sprawling mega cities in the developing world" such as Mexico City or Shanghai[52] or Lagos. Merges's illustration depicts the tension between the excitement and the chaos and confusion that accompanies growth – and illustrates the complex nature of intellectual property, particularly in the global economy.

In the arts, intellectual rights normally interact with copyright, but also extend to patents, trademarks, and even industrial designs and geographical indications. To see why it is so important, let us return to Nollywood.

Service Flows and Intellectual Rights

Though Nollywood is standing strong, piracy is hitting it hard. "Nollywood insiders estimate that up to 50 percent of the industry's profits are currently being lost to Nigeria's endemic piracy and corruption problems."[53] Indeed, if you maintain your Nollywood licit subscription, you might be in the good half. Emmanuel Isikaku, whose résumé includes such titles as president of Nigeria's Film and Video Producers and Marketers Association, told CNN that "[p]iracy has dealt a big blow to the industry." His 2007 film, "Plane Crash," was popular, but it is as if it crashed his wallet: he says that he lost so much money that he failed to break even. "A lot of people watched the film," Isikaku said, "but unfortunately they watched pirated copies."[54]

Piracy problems are common worldwide. For example, we are told that in 2008, piracy cost India's Bollywood industry $959 million and about 571,000 jobs.[55] In the United States, where in 2014, the economic activity of arts and culture accounted for over 4 percent of GDP, or more than $726 billion,[56] Hollywood claims that its piracy-related losses amount to billions – it is difficult to provide a specific figure, as these numbers are often disputed.[57] Whatever the case, they are further demonstration that creative intangibles are simply hard to harvest effectively.

When the United States created a category called "intellectual property products,"[58] its economy suddenly grew by $400 billion. Such growth can be attributed to factors such as strong legal systems and infrastructure. Nonetheless, even developed countries are not immune from piracy and unfair shares of income from creative work.

As my Belgian friend Alain Ruche, who has advised the Office of the Secretary General at the European External Service told me, rights arrangements even in "developed" countries should be looked at more critically. For example, he said, his wife, who runs Garage Culturel, "a dynamic and original place," faces "permanent problems" in collecting intellectual property rights fees. In some cases, a *private* collection firm takes half of what the artist gets. Indeed, as Scott Timberg makes clear in his book *Cultural Crash*, too often big tech corporations are the ones enjoying the pots of gold induced by creative work. Meanwhile, the pots of many nonmogul artists and people who labor around creative work only rattle with pennies.[59]

Of course, as I will explain in Chapter 5, technology can provide creative opportunities, and even promote little-known artists and art forms. All the same, Ruche told me, "as nicely said by Susan Jones: 'The artist feeds our soul, but who feeds the artists?' The artist is at the end of the food chain, and is [often] exploited."[60] Yet from Belgium to the United States, something digital pioneer Jaron Lanier said also corroborates the concern here: "I actually helped make the argument that music should be free and would ultimately benefit culture and musicians," Lanier said. "But the way we are doing it means everybody becomes a servant of a tiny handful of large tech companies, and that's really pretty stupid."[61]

That reading should remind us that rich countries are not always the model for everything. We have to be careful though not to just blame technology for enabling inequality. As Amartya Sen said, if you hire an engineer to build a bridge and the bridge breaks down due to bad engineering, blaming science does not help. The blame should go to the bad engineer.[62] Likewise, if the way the West has engineered its aspects of intellectual rights ends up benefitting a few large tech companies, that does not make technology bad altogether. The reasons for this are many. One of them could be that the laws are not keeping up with the relentless technological changes of our time. So one endeavor might entail continually updating policies to make sure they work for people who labor in and around creative work in the digital age.

Here developing countries have an opportunity to avoid mistakes made by the West. But though developing countries have

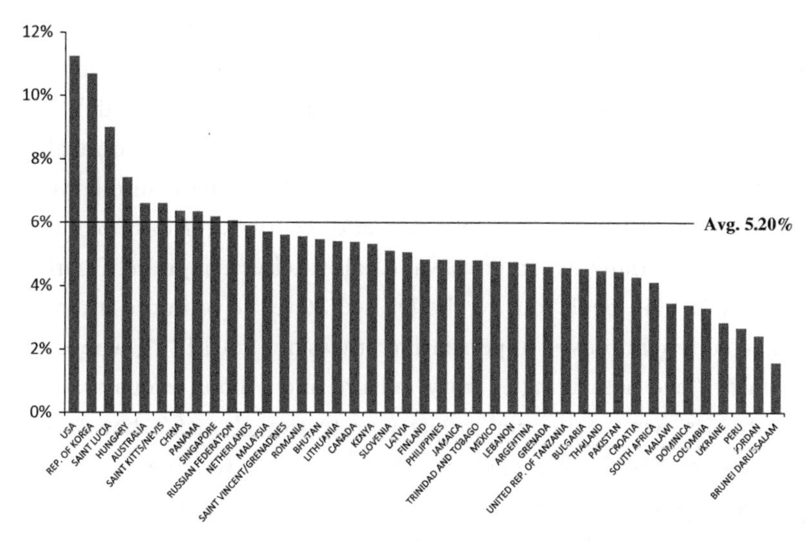

FIGURE 4.1 Contribution of Copyright Industries to GDP (select countries)
Source: WIPO 2014. Note: UN 2013, 164.

immense cultural resources, their intellectual property protection remains notoriously weak. Thus, artistic creations – from music and literature, to dance, film, and the visual arts – are by and large untapped. Copyright "has underpinned an extraordinary modern economic success story, accounting for tens of millions of jobs worldwide," as the African Regional Intellectual Property Organization observes.[63] Nevertheless, many developing countries have yet to maximize this phenomenon.[64]

Just consider Figure 4.1 on the contribution of copyright to the GDP of select countries (for definitions related to copyright industries see annex 4.1 B). The Republic of Korea is an interesting success story. Korean Pop ("K-pop") "has become a fixture of pop charts not only in Korea but throughout Asia," as cited in Chapter 1.[65]

But as Figure 4.1 also shows, many developing economies have yet to catch on. Indeed "there is a continuing drive" – or rather need – "to obtain maximum economic benefits for developing countries from their enormous resources in indigenous creation, arising from traditional knowledge and indigenous arts, creative crafts and folklore."[66] And that drive might expand to harvesting the benefits of geographical indications, patents, branding, and value added.

Service industries like Nollywood could do better economically with stronger intellectual property laws. Nonetheless, intellectual rights are controversial. In the nineteenth century, for example, the rapidly industrializing America was a bold intellectual pirate. Charles Dickens's 1842 book tour to the United States to promote international copyright proved unpersuasive. It was not until 1891, when the country "had a thriving literary culture and a book industry that wanted its own intellectual property protection abroad," that action was sought. "So Congress passed a copyright act extending protection to foreign works in return for similar treatment for American authors overseas."[67] Steve Lohr amplifies the point:

> Indeed, the economies that were shining success stories of development, from the United States in the 19th century to Japan and its East Asian neighbors like Taiwan and South Korea in the 20th, took off under systems of weak intellectual property protection. Technology transfer came easily and inexpensively until domestic skills and local industries were advanced enough that stronger intellectual property protections became a matter of self-interest.[68]

In a related path, creative industries like Nollywood and Bollywood in developing countries are likely to go through a process similar to Hollywood's earliest days. Hollywood's beginnings were linked to escaping intellectual legal troubles elsewhere. "In the early 1900s, filmmakers began moving to the Los Angeles area to get away from the strict rules imposed by Thomas Edison's Motion Picture Patents Company in New Jersey. Since most of the moviemaking patents were owned by Edison, independent filmmakers were often sued by Edison to stop their productions," according to the "History of Hollywood." "To escape his control, and because of the ideal weather conditions and varied terrain, moviemakers began to arrive in Los

Angeles to make their films. If agents from Edison's company came out west to find and stop these filmmakers, adequate notice allowed for a quick escape to Mexico."[69]

Unlike the United States, many developing countries do not enjoy the option for a quick escape anywhere. They have to encounter a whole body of intellectual property law and international agreements that do not, as of now, reflect their interests. Complicating the picture is the fact that there are diverse interests and widely differing viewpoints about just what – if anything – constitutes proper intellectual property protection in developing countries. This diversity of viewpoints and interests was clear in my trips to South Africa and East Africa.

Policy Lessons from What I Saw in Southern Africa

On a trip to southern Africa to research music as social action in 2005, I found two opposing views of intellectual property – communal sharing and respecting property rights. Lindokuhle Mpungose, who has lectured at the University of KwaZulu-Natal, told me that to boost creativity, enthusiasm, and a sense of pride, some traditional music teachers encourage students to make their own instruments.[70] Unlike countries in West Africa, Southern Africa is not known for a diverse drumming culture, Mpungose observed. So instead of constantly purchasing imported drums, the students started to make their own, based on West African designs. In my presence at Fields of Rhythm, a music shop in Durban, Mpungose, with a drum on his lap and a pocketknife in his hand, was concentrated, completing a drum that he modeled from a "Nigerian design." What if it was impossible for Mpungose and others like him to copy ideas from a particular Nigerian drum under patent protection? His activities to disseminate knowledge would be diminished, and in the end students would be hurt the most.[71]

On the other hand, some musicians in Cape Town, Durban, and Gabarone were reluctant to talk to me when I asked to interview them. They were tired of people from the West taking their knowledge and writing books or papers about their work, or reproducing their music and profiting from it. They were angry that they never hear from these people again. They said that they needed to be compensated fairly; in one instance, I had to absorb a significant charge in order to interview a traditional music virtuoso.[72]

That virtuoso was a South African woman known for her expertise playing the Uhadi, a single-string gourd bow. As a major African economy, her country has many systems that many other African nations have yet to obtain. One of them is the Southern African Music Rights Organization (SAMRO), a copyright administration business that was created in 1961.[73] At SAMRO's headquarters in Johannesburg, I met Mzilikazi Khumalu, a celebrated South African composer. Khumalu told me how SAMRO benefits South Africa's traditional music:[74]

The "traditional music sung by Ladysmith Black Mambazo is making lots of money; they sing beautifully, and their music is accepted all over the world," he said. "I have visited many parts of the world, and have been to America many times," added the professor, whose opera "Princess Magogo" has been presented at Chicago's Ravinia Festival, the oldest outdoor music festival in North America. "I have been particularly happy about the wider acceptance of our music."[75] The key issue here is to see how that acceptance can be fully harvested for development in economic diversification strategies that can even be linked to value added and branding.

And speaking of economic diversification, if "developing countries wish to overcome the problems caused by the fluctuating and low levels of export earnings, they must do everything they can to diversify their economies and their markets. By diversifying their economies, they would put an end to the present, only too frequent situation where concentration on a very restricted range of export commodities means that the entire economy is dependent on world market conditions [for] those exports," as Julio A. Larcarte said. "The geographical diversification of their markets would make them less dependent on trade with one or two countries and considerably improve marketing possibilities for their products. Steps cannot be taken in either direction alone; they must be co-ordinated and integrated. The domestic economy must be diversified so as to produce exports that can be sold on many different markets."[76]

In terms of diversifying the economy and exporting music to different countries, SAMRO's impact on abating piracy in southern Africa is unclear. But this organization, which so far has been collecting most of its foreign income from Europe, is affiliated with a number of international collection agencies. And this collective action is as important to organizations as it is important for individuals. It is difficult for African artists – and indeed artists elsewhere – to fight piracy and to negotiate fair pay without organizing themselves. I do not know how well SAMRO lives up to its standards – its mandate is to "protect the intellectual property of composers and authors and to ensure that their creative output is adequately accredited and compensated both locally and internationally."[77] SAMRO demonstrates the need for a collective force nonetheless. And it might provide lessons emanating from where it fails and where it succeeds. While it is true that intellectual property rights could discourage the sharing of ideas, there is strong evidence to consider where protection is needed. Africa has some rights organizations such as the Uganda Performing Rights Society, but few have strong muscles and the reach they need. Strong advocacy organizations such as SAMRO could be useful elsewhere. An effective intellectual property regime needs to be created to support artists and the broader communities and nations within which they work.[78]

On the Ground in East Africa

When I was growing up in Uganda, I lived in two worlds. My first world was immersed in music. But access to music scores, whether classical, jazz, or pop, was difficult. My peers and I ended up copying not one or two pages, but complete music books and CDs. That was the easiest way to access materials that extended our music horizons. When we were touring neighboring Tanzania and Kenya, people who attended our performances, including European diplomats, wondered how we got our music education. Some of us later received scholarships to study in the United States and in Europe. We competed with some of the most talented musicians from around the world, whose beginnings in music education were far different from ours.[79]

Meanwhile, back home, many more talented Ugandan musicians who had no access to music books and records, whether illegal or otherwise, were less well positioned to improve their talents. Many of them were stuck – simply because they had little or no access to educational resources, a legacy of the untoward nature of my second world. In cases like these, multiplied thousands of times across the developing world, intellectual property rights could hamstring the very people they could help if they are not calibrated with great care. It is clear that those who seek to *learn* from copied works, as opposed to profiting from them, should have the opportunity to do so – especially if they cannot afford to pay for access to knowledge. Intellectual property frameworks should allow that.[80]

Years later, as we started performing, composing, and collaborating with other artists professionally, something else became clear: we did not and do not want our works to be copied illegally. Moreover, the goal in performing and composing music was not only for our emotional satisfaction; it was also to support ourselves, as professional artists. We realized that our income possibility would disappear if our creations are widely pirated.[81]

Even state-owned radio and television stations abuse copyright laws. The Uganda Performing Rights Society has asked the Ugandan government to help enforce copyrights. Licensing all users, the Society argues, will expose infringers, increasing the revenue of the artists. James Walusa, in his capacity as secretary-general of the Society, described the benefits of government involvement: "If the government can work with us to enforce copyright and other relevant laws, music will be among the top 20 taxpayers in the country."[82]

The Society collected sixteen million Uganda shillings in fees in 2009 (about $7,804, back then). Nearly 300 copyright owners shared that sum. Yet only eleven radio stations out of the 200 broadcasters paid copyright fees. That figure could dramatically multiply if all broadcasters complied with the copyright law. Moses Matovu, the Society's chairman and the leader of Afrigo Band concluded: "If the government supports us, we can collect over Ush3 billion ($1.4 million) annually."[83]

More generally, copyright infringement in Africa is stunting cultural creativity, Ghanaian representative Betty Mould-Iddrissu reported at the 1999 World Intellectual Property Organization Roundtable on Intellectual Property and Traditional Knowledge. She had Ghana in mind. Nonetheless, it is likely that for any "developing country whose national identity and cultural roots are inextricably linked with its national economic development," cultural piracy "may have far-reaching consequences."[84]

The Knowledge Gap versus the Knowledge Bridge

These examples show that intellectual property rights are too important to be ignored, let alone left to lawyers. But where to draw the line?

Some say that intellectual property rights make it harder for people, especially the poor, to access knowledge. With the immense challenges in development, the last thing any policy should do is to inhibit easy access to knowledge.

As legal scholar Irwin A. Olian, Jr., noted in 1974, in a comment that still rings true today: "Of the many problems facing developing countries, none is more urgent than the need for wider dissemination of knowledge, for ultimately this will act to further the educational, cultural, and technical development of their people."[85]

Similarly, Joseph E. Stiglitz, former World Bank senior vice president and chief economist, comments: "It was increasingly clear that what separated developing countries from developed countries was not just a gap in resources but a gap in knowledge ... It was imperative that this gap be closed."[86]

Indeed, some argue that intellectual property protections widen the knowledge gap: They are designed to keep knowledge in the developed world, and make people in developed countries pay for it. In response to Stephan Faris's article, "Can a Tribe Sue for Copyright? The Maasai Want Royalties for Use of Their Name,"[87] one commenter barked: "Finally! Africa is working the same system used to exploit them and their land. Prediction – this will be kept under wraps. Do you think businessmen would want Africans to know about rights!!"[88]

There are lots of practices widening the knowledge gap, instead of shrinking it. But knowledge in developing countries, despite its richness and diversity, is often neglected in development practice.[89] Even worse, as Wade Davis shows in *The Wayfinders*, it is often looked down upon,[90] if not outright pirated by some parties in rich countries.[91]

For example, one day in 2009, when the legendary African saxophonist Manu Dibango, known as "the Lion of Cameroon," was listening to the radio, he heard music familiar to his own. Dibango was at his apartment in Paris, and soon, he started receiving one phone call after another. The calls were like those Nigerian phishing emails; they seemed too good to be true. But Dibango, who has "played almost every style of music you care to mention: soul, reggae, jazz, spirituals, blues,"[92] and whose 1972 single "Soul Makossaa" was an international hit, was not being phished. "Friends and relatives were calling to offer their congratulations: Michael Jackson was singing his song! But Dibango's pride turned to puzzlement when he bought the album, only to find that the song was credited to Michael Jackson and no one else," Kelefa Sanneh wrote in the *New Yorker*. His song was the first one in Jackson's "Thriller" album, but his "value added" was not credited. Dibango, who was not thrilled at all, "eventually worked out a financial agreement with Jackson," Sanneh wrote, "and he made his peace with 'Thriller,' which might be (depending on how you keep score) the most popular album of all time."[93]

But it turns out things did not end there. "In 2007, the pop singer Rihanna had a hit with "Don't Stop the Music," which was based on "Wanna Be Startin' Something" – that Jackson song with motifs from Dibango. "Once again, Dibango heard his chant on the radio, and, once again, he noticed that he wasn't given credit," Sanneh reports. "And so the process started anew. When Jackson died, Dibango was still waiting for a French court to decide whether he was owed damages for Rihanna's use of Jackson's version of Dibango's chant."[94]

That example illustrates the urgent need to support policies that can effectively render *all* artists their rightful royalties. Moreover, giving credit to Dibango may help brand his native Cameroon as a beacon for thrilling African rhythms, rhythms worth acknowledging even in the indices of cultural trade in value added.

Yes, intellectual property is controversial, but what do you make of that almost broken dance between Dibango and the King of Pop? One problem is this: The concept is seen as a Western tool. But you might be the surprised to note this: Intellectual property traces its roots in a country where River Nile terminates its journey after criss-crossing several African nations.

ON THE ROOTS OF INTELLECTUAL RIGHTS

Intellectual rights apparently existed in ancient Egypt, Michael A. Gollin writes: "The ancient Egyptians' respect for trade secrets is clear from Stele C-14 of Irtisen, a hieroglyphic tablet from 2000 BCE on display in the Louvre museum" in Paris.[95] Along with trade secrets, trademarks also existed in antiquity. "Egyptians branded cattle, Chinese marked their porcelain, and Romans used logos and brand names for stores, lamps, and other products."[96] Marking items was perhaps the first practice of separating goods, Christopher May and Susan K. Sell argue: "Marks could indicate reliability and the reputation of the craftsman [or] maker as well as origin. Marking to establish ownership long precedes formalized laws to adjudicate disputes regarding ownership."[97] Here is May and Sell on "Greek Ideas about Owning Ideas":

> Intellectual property did not emerge (in any form) in Greek society of Simonides and other poets, but they seem to be the first "creatives" to become intellectual entrepreneurs in a sense that we

> might now recognize. Prior to the Greeks of sixth century B.C., patrons "kept" artists, poets, or singers, as well as intellectuals, who were expected to perform on demand. In the Greek city-states, direct support by patronage began to be supplemented by prizes for recitations in public as well as paid performances (similar to recitals).[98]

Trips or Tripped Up?

Today, at the international level, intellectual property coordination is centered on the controversial TRIPS (Trade-Related Aspects of Intellectual Property Rights), an international agreement administered by the WTO that sets down minimum standards for many forms of intellectual property regulation as applied to nationals of other WTO members.[99] But as many voices insist, this Agreement does not effectively address the needs of developing countries.

Stiglitz, who won a Nobel Prize in economics "for his analyses on markets with asymmetric information,"[100] opposed TRIPS when he served on President Bill Clinton's Council of Economic Advisers. "I had no illusions: it was special-interest legislation," he said. That lemon-like legislation was shaped by American "pharmaceutical and entrainment industries."[101]

A colleague, J. Michael Finger, former lead economist and chief of the World Bank's Trade Policy Research Group, echoes Stiglitz. He asserts that TRIPS "is about the knowledge that exists in *developed* countries, about developing countries' access to that knowledge, and particularly about developing countries paying for that access."[102] He goes on to add, "TRIPS is about collecting across borders." But "if you are a Senegalese musician" or a Nigerian movie maker, for instance, "and your problem is piracy within the local economy, then the TRIPS Agreement has no relevance."[103] Indeed, Nigeria might have its own domestic needs to protect Nollywood. And it might have other Nigerian "creations of the mind" to protect. But the TRIPS Agreement is more about cross-border supply of services

(Mode I). It is not really about collecting copyright fees or other related creative measures within Nigerian borders.

There is a strong argument that piracy is good for artists, their respective industries, and the public at large. For one, movies or songs that promote positive social messages may be a public good that should be widely circulated. As Nollywood producers argue, their work helps to educate Africans about social issues. The documentary film "This Is Nollywood" directed by my friend Franco Sacchi, sums up that philosophy: "Many of the films deal with AIDS, corruption, women's rights, and other topics of concern to ordinary Africans. The impetus behind Nollywood is not purely commercial; the traditional role of storytelling is still alive and well – just different."[104] In the doctrine of "knowledge for development," if Nollywood is seen as a public good, one could argue that fighting Nollywood piracy may not be the best development strategy.[105]

Moreover, artists themselves may benefit from piracy via marketing and name recognition. That said, it is difficult to accept that artists should not have a say on matters of piracy and marketing. At the end of the day, in terms of freedom and choices, artists may have reason to reject piracy, even if this comes at the cost of exposing their work.[106] Investors, moreover, invest in creative projects as they do in any other sector: They want a return on their investments.

On the Cost of Fighting Piracy

Another important aspect to consider is this: Fighting piracy is not cheap. This added cost puts further strain on the already scarce resources. In the United States, it is common for the Federal Bureau of Investigation (FBI) to conduct piracy investigations at, say, high school and college campuses. Can this approach take root in developing countries? A report commissioned by the United Kingdom's Department for International Development has this to say:

> Establishing the infrastructure of an IPR [intellectual property rights] regime, and mechanisms for the enforcement of IP rights, is costly both to governments and private stakeholders. In developing countries, where human and financial resources are scarce, and legal systems not well developed, the opportunity costs of operating the system effectively are high. Those costs include the costs of scrutinising the validity of claims to patent rights (both at the application stage and in the courts) and adjudicating upon actions for infringement. Considerable costs are generated by the inherent uncertainties of litigation. These costs too need to be weighed against the benefits arising from the IP system.[107]

I cannot see the FBIs of the world following around intellectual pirates from year to year. Indeed, when I sat down with former World Bank President James D. Wolfensohn, his concern was apparent. "I'm all in favor of protecting the creative artists and ensuring that they can have some return on what they do," Wolfensohn, a cellist who has performed at Carnegie Hall, told me. "But it is not without difficulty within a lot of the poor developing countries. I mean if their song comes out on the radio in a village 500 miles from the capital, and the kids start playing it, and enjoying it, and you come along and say – 'Well, I really need to get my share of the amount of money that's due to me on this,' – it is pretty unlikely that you will get it."[108]

It will take time and creativity to solve the problem. After all, intellectual property protections evolved over decades and even centuries in developed countries. Along the way, a diversity of ideas and approaches will be needed, including meaningful collaboration.[109]

In striking a balance between where the laws should allow copying, especially for educational purposes, and penalizing those who abuse the system, strong legal and public policy mechanisms are needed. Amartya Sen argues that:

> a prominent place must be given to the economic returns from well-designed programmes of distribution at home and abroad, with adequate protection of rights and entitlements. . . . This can not only

> be a significant revenue earner (especially for some of the economically marginalized people), but also the support that this will provide to musicians can be expected to play a constructive role in making the industry and the practitioner's more secure and resourceful.[110]

Sen's reading extends to other creative areas. But given the broad nature of intellectual property – from computer software to pharmaceuticals and movies – major misunderstandings are common. One of them is this: to some, protecting intellectual property generally means "no cheap drugs to HIV/AIDS patients in the developing world." This has truth to it. Nevertheless, protecting a Nigerian movie from piracy, for example, is not the same thing as protecting patents for drugs. This begs clarity regarding the debate on intellectual rights and the role of culture in development. In this complex area, one of the best policy interventions is education.[111]

EDUCATION FOR INTELLECTUAL PROPERTY IN DEVELOPMENT

There is a pressing need to teach policy makers and the public alike about the costs, benefits, and even limitations of intellectual property. Nonetheless, intellectual property, because of its intricate and extensive nature, can be difficult to teach.[112] There are many reasons for this. For one, the way intellectual property law interacts with economic realities is often changing, especially due to relentless technological transformations (see Chapter 5). For another, from Nigeria to Uganda, China to Mexico, intellectual property regimes vary by country; they are often on different levels of application (or "maturity"). Hence cut-and-paste policies are notoriously difficult to orchestrate.

That noted, there is a need to strengthen the understanding of intellectual property in development. This could be done under the framework of augmenting practical skills, training the judiciary and businesses, as well as general public awareness. The next subsection outlines what could be achieved via education.[113]

The Judicial System and Intellectual Property Training

In many countries, justice systems are weak. Training the judiciary about the benefits and limits of intellectual property could be a viable policy intervention. How can this strategy work in countries that wish to reform or understand how matters of intellectual property interact with the creative sector, indigenous knowledge, international trade, job creation, youth employment, and the like?

The Taiwan Intellectual Property Training Academy (TIPA) presents a practical example. TIPA offered professional intellectual property training courses "for over 300 judges and prosecutors in order to develop necessary IP-related expertise among judicial officials in Taiwan."[114] It is difficult to evaluate the performance of such initiatives. Nonetheless, the idea is to draw lessons, learning from what works and what does not. If Nigeria adapts such a program, for example, the idea is to see how this works for Nigeria in a Nigerian framework.

In order to increase internal research and development (R&D) capacity, TIPA held intellectual property training courses for "over 600 people, including teachers of secondary and elementary schools, staff of state-owned enterprises, university technology licensing and R&D personnel."[115] Artists could also be trained directly in intellectual property protection.

In the early 2000s, the World Bank spent some $321,700 to help develop the music industry in Africa. The project planning and feasibility studies were conducted in five African countries: Ghana, Kenya, Mali, Senegal, and South Africa.[116] Musicians in Senegal, for example, engaged in workshops to learn the basics of copyright. As part of that program, the Ford Foundation sponsored a training program for musicians on the basics of intellectual property protection. The program drafted contract templates and taught musicians negotiation skills and how to write a basic contract. These were simple skills. But this knowledge made a difference. The musicians became better equipped to effectively negotiate with private entities, the collection agency, and the Ministry of Culture. As Finger points out, many foundations want to work on "big news" items and tend to neglect such nuts and bolts projects.[117] The Ford Foundation's involvement in Senegal, however, shows that NGOs can play a significant role in training and promoting intellectual property.[118]

Such workshops can also be done or complemented by distance learning. In any case, countries and development agencies could work with NGOs and other partners here.

A Study on Intellectual Property and Culture in Development

Studies can easily end up in cabinets and never read – yet it is crucial to deepen our understanding of intellectual property in specific contexts across the world. The concern about trade treaties like TRIPS, Lohr notes, "is that it is too much of a one-size-fits-all approach that works to the detriment of developing nations."[119] Economist Jeffrey D. Sachs agrees: "'It would be fine if we lived in a world of all rich people … The danger with TRIPS is that it will mostly hurt the developing countries' access to ideas.'"[120]

These statements suggest that more learning is needed here. And this means funding cutting-edge research on the relationship between intellectual rights and culture in development. An example is the commission that was "set up by the British government to look at how intellectual property rights might work better for poor people and developing countries."[121] Recall that while the Nollywoods of the world are up and coming, the knowledge bridge from the developing countries to the developed is weak or nonexistent. The knowledge gap from the developed world to the developing world is well known. But how often do we hear about the knowledge gap from the developing world to the developed world? And how often do we ask how this matters for development? Answering such questions could also be useful in helping artists in the developing world net income from digital technologies, a topic discussed in Chapter 5. Meanwhile, the following coda provides other immediate considerations.

CODA

The music initiative mentioned moments ago was the first time the World Bank engaged in such a project. But this area is largely dormant among development agencies and governments, despite the great need to fund artistic initiatives. In the medium of film, besides augmenting global reach via services trade, one opportunity is to develop local cinemas. For example, in India, where the population is over 1 billion, Indian films should effectively reach the country's middle class of about 300 million people. Instead, they reach only 45 million. One constraint is this: India does not have "many cinemas for people to go to – less than 13,000, versus almost 40,000 in the United States (a country which has only one-fourth of India's population)."[122] Yet over 70 percent of Bollywood's revenues are from domestic sources.[123] It is likely that a similar situation exists in Nigeria and elsewhere.[124]

Along those lines, many countries have cultural industries that need capital – for example, the Kitwes of the world that seek to expand their reach across the globe. And here, we must bring in the issue of licit and illicit tax evasion – consider Gabriel Zucman's book *The Hidden Wealth of Nations*. This evasion especially hurts developing countries, in unimaginable ways. Even before the Panama Papers were leaked and captured the attention of people all over the world, Kofi Annan was arguing that Africa was losing twice as much in illicit financial flight as it gets in international aid.[125]

And this problem may be larger than previously thought. Consider the Paradise Papers, documents that were leaked even before the dust on the Panama Papers settled. As they reveal the iniquitous dealings of some politicians and world leaders, celebrities, multinationals and universities, the papers expose such activities as tax-engineering methods, tax haven shopping sprees, and dubious negation deals. As they spill the beans, they cast light on a classic case: The "secretive deals and hidden companies connected to Glencore," one of the world's largest natural resource companies.[126]

Apparently, "one of the companies Glencore currently controls got a $440 million discount on the price it paid for access to some of the Democratic Republic of Congo's best mines." To the bewilderment of those concerned, including Resource Matters an organization that has looked into this matter, Glencore said, "the price was 'essentially correct.'" [127] The "correctness" of that price notwithstanding, in a nation "where more than a third of adults are illiterate," consider what the investigative Journalist Will Fitzgibbon reports: The $440 million "was almost as large as [the Congo's] total expenditures on education at the time."[128]

This is not the moment to invoke the call-and-response of naming and shaming. Still, if we are really talking about domestic resource mobilization to finance initiatives that run from education to health, culture to energy, then such tasks as taking on dubious mining deals and attacking the tyranny of tax evasion cannot remain sidestepped.[129] For some of these funds could help finance many programs mentioned in this book.

Now, one could argue that many rich people and corporations support cultural activities via such mediums as corporate social responsibility. That is fine where it works. This practice, however, does not guarantee the much-needed equal distribution of resources to programs that may not fall under the radar (or the interests) of corporations and the economic elite. And if such a model is sustainable in a development policy, these "gifts" tend to focus on nonentrepreneural activities. This issue is beyond the scope of this discussion, but we must note that corporate social responsibility should also mean paying a fair share of taxes in countries where companies operate. If taxes are paid, then governments can be held accountable for using these recourses for collective good. But anticipated government errors should not always be the supreme excuse for not paying taxes and then turning around and saying that foreign aid programs should bear the burden. At any rate, besides funding, advisory services are key, as many countries take the creative sector for granted. Working with such agencies as the International Finance Corporation (IFC) and other partners, countries could convene monetary and advisory services to develop concrete arrangements that benefit local arts-related businesses, and the like.

And that echoes the need to cultivate partnerships. Partnerships to promote culture in development are needed between agencies like the IFC, the WTO, UNCTAD, UNDP, UNESCO, development banks, and NGOs and the public and private sectors. Whether we are talking about accounting for trade in value added, promoting nation branding or intellectual property, that is the case. This is particularly important because each partner could bring their "value added." And that value could be funds or knowledge.

Moreover, although many cultural agencies are custodians of knowledge, they are often scraping by for funding. And worse, instead of winning benediction, sometimes they are just closed due to shifting political and policy priorities. That was the case for Kultur og Udvikling (CKU), or the Danish Center for Culture and Development, whose programs stretched from trade to education. Although we may not fully know what led to CKU's demise, from 1998–2016, CKU implemented programs in thirteen countries in Africa, Asia, and the Middle East, cooperating not only with Danish embassies and representations, but also with local organizations and institutions. For that we know. It also held cultural exchanges in Denmark.[130]

As an autonomous organization under the Danish Ministry of Foreign Affairs, CKU believed what this book is all about: That "art, culture and creativity are central parameters for sustainable human and social development ... that art, culture and creativity are determining factors for democratization, respect for human rights and enhancement of economic growth."[131] But that did not deter its closing at the end of 2016.

What happens to CKU's activities remains to be seen. Nonetheless, one could insist that partnering with such agencies could help fuel the diverse promise of culture in development. And this may include how the WTO's modes of supply could benefit low-income countries as they seek to promote their cultural trade.

Partnerships, however, should not be formed for the sake of partnerships. That would be like arranging marriages of convenience that will remain feckless, as another hilarious scene of "Osofia in London" may show.

5 Artists without Borders in the Digital Age

> Connectivity is vital, but not enough to realize the full development benefits. Digital investments need the support of "analog complements": regulations, so that firms can leverage the internet to compete and innovate; improved skills, so that people can take full advantage of digital opportunities; and accountable institutions, so that governments respond to citizens' needs and demands.
>
> World Bank, *World Development Report 2016*

Digital technology has the potential to contribute to development, and its ability to carry creative output from tiny villages to the global stage cannot be underestimated. After all, as we saw in Chapter 4, the transmission of movies and music via the internet is part and parcel of international trade in services. But focusing on connectivity is not enough. For having potential is one thing, and realizing that potential is another. "Analog components" are much needed for digital creative trade to be able to make meaningful contributions to development.[1] This chapter considers the need to invest in media startups, internet access within and between countries, and the like. And it touches on how services trade can induce companies to open offices in places where they want to expand their reach. Since piracy is not ending anytime soon, the chapter goes on to propose an artists' visa to encourage live performances. The visa could be given to artists who may not be the Michael Jacksons of the world, but are nonetheless virtuosos in their own right. Such an arrangement is also part of international trade (Mode IV, presence of natural persons; see Box 4.1), as the "mighty throat" singers of Tuva exemplify.

***

More than two billion people interact with the internet today, notably via social media. Actors large and small on the world stage have brought this about. In technology and policy affairs, Estonia and Finland have played leading roles. Estonia unveiled extraordinary e-services, and Finland in 2010 became the first country in the world to make broadband a legal right for every citizen.[2]

The internet and the ever-emerging technologies invite piracy. At the same time, however, they also make it easier to share knowledge, conduct research, and fuel commerce. In the cultural dimension, they can even help promote obscure artists and art forms. As Edna dos Santos-Duisenberg, former chief of the Creative Economy Program of the United Nations Conference on Trade and Development, put it, "New technologies and the internet give developing countries a feasible option to promote their creativity and entrepreneurship in the global market."[3]

To return to Chapter 4, again, if you subscribed to see movies like *Osuofia in London*, you are shaking the digital hand of service delivery. Certainly, the four service modes of the World Trade Organization are all the more robust today because of technology. (This is especially true with respect to Mode I, cross-border supply.)

The lion's share of revenues in creative goods and services is realized in developed countries, however. Still, the UN *Creative Economy Report 2010* provides figures that, while dated and incomplete, give a glimpse of what has been happening: "South-South trade of creative goods reached nearly $60 billion in 2008, tripling in six years." This "represents an astonishing rate of 20 percent annually, while South exports to the North has been growing at an impressive, but relatively slower, annual rate of 10.5 percent."[4] A considerable share of this growth can be traced to the internet. An excursion to the world of digital music shows the possibilities.

MUSIC SERVICES IN THE DIGITAL AGE

In 2015, digital music revenues surpassed those from physical formats, according to the International Federation of the Phonographic Industry (IFPI). For the first time in nearly two decades, the industry's total revenues grew over the previous year's, by 3.2 percent, to

$15 billion. Music subscription services have a lot to do with this. "An estimated 68 million people worldwide" as of 2016, paid for "a music subscription service, up from 41 million in 2014 and eight million when data was first compiled in 2010."[5]

A study by the International Trade Centre examines the "long tail" "of niche product distribution over the Internet and on cellular networks."[6] These avenues offer tremendous possibilities: they enable "musicians, producers and record companies around the world to cater to small groups of consumers at much lower costs than in the physical world," the study says, (again connecting with the web of trade in value added). Unlike many such studies, this one involved a survey of Brazil, India, Mali, Senegal, Serbia, and Tajikistan, all of which, in one way or another, fit the bracket of developing countries. The study reports that "newly digitized recordings of traditional music from Tajikistan could be made available to world music amateurs and ethnomusicologists."[7]

Similar technology could be applied to export ethnic music from developing countries to music amateurs and ethnomusicologists worldwide, promoting education and cultural democracy. The economic interactions do not end with uploading and downloading music moreover. As the Nashville example in Chapter 1 shows, there are other businesses from printing to hotels that also crop up. And since the "music market is extremely fragmented with thousands of independent artists and bands that function as small companies,"[8] the potential for small-scale businesses that are directly or indirectly induced by creative activities is huge, not to mention the linkages with outsourcing and value added.

Whereas digital revenues from the music industry have enjoyed steady growth, it would nevertheless be premature to see this as slam-dunk evidence that the music industry is on its way to reclaiming its past revenue glory. Many people like enjoying music for free, and the internet enables this behavior on an unprecedented scale. In addition, as just noted, sizable commercial interactions remain limited mostly to the developed world.

How can music industries from developing countries effectively tap into this global music market via new technologies? These countries have a unique product that could attract global audiences. But it needs to be marketed strategically and it needs seed funding.

Since the arts are not as capital-intensive as extractive industries, provisions such as tax credits for innovative and eco-friendly jobs should be considered. These could also be linked to broader frameworks of economic diversification and rural development. Agencies such as the International Finance Corporation (IFC) could play a leading role in financing and providing advisory services for media startups in developing countries. Since many of these ventures may not have the guarantees that the IFC might require to fund them, there is a need to find innovative ways of financing. Meanwhile, for firms with guarantees (such as those likely to be in middle-income countries), the question is to see how they could employ the IFC's resources. Some of them may not even know that such financing and advisory services exist.[9]

The reality, however, is that international trade in music has been dominated by an oligopoly of four major labels: Sony/BMG, Universal Music, EMI, and Warner Music. Based in developed countries, these labels have subsidiaries across the world.[10] Where independent labels are making strides (at least in the United States),[11] the system seems to be working in favor of enabling providers or media enterprises in developed countries to effectively capture markets in developing countries (even if piracy cuts into their profits). It generally does not work the other way around. Indeed, what the UN Creative Economy Report noted in 2010 may have not changed much today: "Developing economies and economies in transition are both net importers of recorded music, primarily because the music is created, recorded and commercialized by transnational companies. As a result, developing countries import not only foreign music but also their own music."[12] This pattern echoes the concerns about the TRIPS framework and it recapitulates the issue of double or multiple counting trade in value added is trying to solve.

Moreover, technological platforms[13] that offer an option for developing countries to trade cultural products via the internet are also dominated by service providers in developed countries. In a letter to the *Economist*, Wolf Kramer makes a salient point: "Today, music is being used to sell smartphones, tablets, computers, recurring subscription fees, operating systems and to generate market share. There is no reason or incentive to build an artist's career or sell the music." He goes on to lament: "Many of the board members and management of these new companies are not from the music industry; they are from the world of technology, banks, software, hedge funds, private equity or technology firms. The interests of the artists and the music services are no longer aligned."[14]

These charges echo findings from a 2015 report by the International Federation of the Phonographic Industry:

> Many pirate websites are funded by advertisers from well-known brands. Despite initiatives either underway or being discussed in a number of countries including the US, UK, Spain, France and others, the advertising industry [has] yet to take effective action. Research for the Digital Citizens Alliance, published in February 2014, and conducted by MediaLink, for example, found that 596 infringing sites generated $227 million a year in advertising revenue, with adverts appearing from blue chip firms . . . Driven by the demand for music, this advertising generates exposure for the brand, and revenues for the pirate site and the advertising industry companies involved in placing the advertising, yet the songwriters, artists and labels whose music is involved receive nothing.[15]

CROSS-BORDER SUPPLY MEETS COMMERCIAL PRESENCE

Returning to Nigeria, let us consider iROKO, "one of Nigeria's largest internet and entertainment companies."[16] It presents a typical case of demand often inducing supply, and it also shows how innovation can move things regardless of geographical limitations. With offices in "Lagos, London, New York, Johannesburg, and Kigali and a team of over 100" as of 2015, iROKO is another example of how Mode I (supplying services) can induce Mode III (territorial presence) (see Box 4.1). The company is the parent of iROKOtv, a platform that delivers Nollywood movies (you may have watched *Osuofia in London* on this platform). Its music-distributing arm is called iROKING. Not long ago, the company launched "a global content distribution and licensing division, iROKO Global."[17] The company's business model states: "What iROKO Partners does is brutally simple: we buy the online licenses of movies and music directly from producers and recording artists and stream them online to a global Diaspora audience. In doing this, iROKO Partners has assembled the world's largest online library of awesome African content and has made us West Africa's fastest growing Internet company."[18]

The company has enticed investors, including $10 million in funding from American and Swedish investors in 2012.[19] The global reach, not to mention the spin-off of other entrepreneurial and employment opportunities, is significant. "But is all the excitement warranted?"[20] The following extract from the *Economist* shows the limitations of this approach:

> Femi Longe, co-founder of the Lagos-based Co-Creation Hub which seeks to harness technology to tackle social problems, says it may be premature. It is dangerous when entrepreneurs see funding as "an end-game, as opposed to an enabler," he says, adding that Nigerian entrepreneurs will have to choose between creating businesses that "make money from customers" and those designed primarily to attract funding from investors. Doing business in Nigeria is notoriously challenging: the country ranks 131st out of 185 in the World Bank's [2013] Doing Business Report. Its infrastructure is poor: Co-Creation Hub spends $3,000 a month on fuelling its own power generators.[21]

The situation described above is not that different in many developing countries, where poor infrastructure and corruption tend to be acute and are not easy to escape. And the current modes of investment are generally not helping to address those problems. As Longe notes, many investors, social entrepreneurs, and nonprofits tend to focus on designing initiatives that primarily attract funding from investors; these happen to be mostly foreigners. By relying on such sources, they fail to "make money from customers" or build models that can be sustained by customers.

But this is a larger problem not unique to companies like iROKO. Governments have for too long ignored the role of enablement in many growing countries. When they request funding from agencies like the World Bank, it is rare that they seek to support cultural ventures.

At any rate, as we have insisted earlier, one of the universal challenges around online content distribution is piracy. Notwithstanding other challenges, iROKO "tirelessly battles online piracy, investing tens of thousands of dollars each year in shutting down illegal sites, ensuring that movie producers' intellectual property is protected."[22]

But this is a perennial battle worldwide; people like to get services like music and movies for free. Online services make this all too easy. Recall Napster. This American online music-sharing service began shaking the music stage in 1999 in Shawn Fanning's dorm room at Northeastern University. Fanning's invention was nothing like the infamous phishing emails. All it did was "let users trade songs for free." But "it triggered a financial tsunami in the music industry."[23] And indeed, the "amount of content available over the Internet took a quantum leap in late 1999 with the introduction of Napster's peer-to-peer network technology." Some suggest that it was the first of its kind, and that it started the digital music revolution.[24]

Another site, called The Pirate Bay, elevated copying to an art form. The site, founded in Sweden in 2003, facilitated peer-to-peer file sharing, and Swedish authorities charged it with assisting copyright infringement. In the so-called Pirate Bay Trial, the defendants (four of them) were found guilty. In addition to jail time, they were to pay back millions in damages.[25] But no sooner did its cofounder Peter

Sunde come out of jail than he built an "ultimate piracy machine," following his belief in "people's inherent drive to copy things."[26]

It is estimated "that 20 percent of fixed-line internet users worldwide regularly access services offering copyright infringing music," based on data from comScore and Nielsen.[27] And this estimate "does not include the emerging, but as yet unquantified, threat of smartphone and tablet-based mobile piracy as consumers migrate to those devices."[28] It is important to note, however, that the true cost of piracy is hard to pin down. Further, "just because the movie and record industries lose a certain amount of money from online piracy in the United States," for example, that "doesn't mean the economy as a whole suffers by that exact same amount – particularly if the money that would have been spent on those pirated movies and albums just ends up getting spent elsewhere."[29] The counterargument here might be this: while the economy as a whole might not lose, it is not hard to see how piracy may contribute to the "starving artist" problem, and even diminish jobs related to the copyright industries.[30]

But piracy aside, there are many other aspects needed for indigenous creative businesses in the developing world to flourish, including broadband connectivity, net neutrality, financing mechanisms, and regulatory frameworks.

Even more important, there is a need to make sure that new models of economic and social participation (such as the ever-mushrooming technologies) do not simply widen the gender gap rather than diminish it (see Chapter 7). I say this because women are less likely to be connected than men in the developing world. So the digital divide could leave some women behind, as activities increasingly become driven by digital technologies.[31] Indeed, women who might be artistically inclined to explore the digital space in creative work may be left behind in this new and evolving area.

It is reasonable to ask what could be done to help them. But generally speaking, for all artists in growing countries, there is need to expand their reach into both domestic and international markets. And the answer to the policy question here is clear: enablement.

General measures, such as tax incentives and access to finance, are needed. So are specific measures tied to the arts and trade in such areas as marketing (including at embassies and international organizations), supporting youth cultural entrepreneurs, implementing effective cultural trade provisions for developing countries, forming oversees employment agencies, considering the pros and cons of intellectual rights, and so on. The list is long, and some of it is familiar. But this is another area where complementarities come into play, because many of the same measures that could enable the arts could also promote trade in services and growth and equality in general. Here are some policy options:

Augment Internet Access within, and between Countries. Internet access and broadband services are still limited in many developing countries, especially in rural areas. Yet e-services "now have the potential to deliver rapid economic growth," as Paul Collier notes. For landlocked countries this provides more trade options because e-services make distance irrelevant.[32] Nonetheless, while the internet and other digital technologies offer potential gains, most of these gains often remain unrealized.[33]

The way things stand, it is difficult to see how digital media industries from the developing world could monetize their functions effectively (at home and abroad) without adequate technological infrastructure. Moreover, adequate services are not only about promoting the arts industry; they are also necessary for other sectors. Therefore, there is a need to consider such technical infrastructure as fiber optic networks within and across countries. This is a promising engine for economic diversification and innovation in the digital age. Connecting small towns and rural areas is particularly critical, as private service providers normally bypass them in favor of profitable intercity routes.[34]

Yet increased access to technology is not enough, as World Bank President Jim Kim said; online networks must reach and benefit the intended parties.[35] The most important element may not be connectivity per se, but rather the assurance that this activity fundamentally bears fruit for the unconnected poor, in tiny remote villages and elsewhere. This connects to all sorts of issues – ranging from levels of education to customary behavioral shifts and efficient monetary to distribution mechanisms and branding – that are beyond the scope of this book, but nonetheless need careful scrutiny.

The *World Development Report 2016* makes a fundamental point about how to reap "digital dividends": "Connectivity is vital, but not enough to realize the full development benefits. Digital investments need the support of 'analog complements': regulations, so that firms can leverage the internet to compete and innovate; improved skills, so that people can take full advantage of digital opportunities; and accountable institutions, so that governments respond to citizens' needs and demands. Digital technologies can, in turn, augment and strengthen these complements – accelerating the pace of development."[36]

Develop a Website of World Music for Development. A number of platforms, including iROKING, Apple Music, Beats 1 radio, iTunes, Pandora, and Spotify, are presenting music using digital technologies. While some of this music can be accessed for free, membership fees are a big feature. In development policy, a similar arrangement could be adapted to benefit indigenous musicians, including traditional artists in remote places. It could be structured as follows.

A platform would be created for people to subscribe to plans allowing them to listen to indigenous, local, or traditional music from developing countries. (The site could be called dTunes or "Tunes for Development.") In turn, the membership fees would then be remitted to artists or to community development projects (perhaps after deducting operational costs). Specific arrangements need to be carefully crafted so that this innovation does indeed benefit the intended recipients. But the idea is to have people subscribe to this platform not because they cannot get this service elsewhere, but because they want to support artists and community development via this channel. Putumayo World Music has a similar arrangement in a CD format.[37]

This platform, which could operate as a social business, could function as a place for digital music for development. This innovation could also contribute to the positive branding of nations via the cultural front (see Chapter 4). Since partnerships are crucial, enlisting artists like Bono, Manu Dibango, Angélique Kidjo, Yo-Yo Ma, and Paul McCartney could help bring stakeholders to the table. These partners could include Apple Music, Spotify, and other such businesses in the private sector.[38]

Development organizations could play a leading role as connectors and conveners of resources and partnerships, and hence help foster the actualization of the site. The glitches in America's website for the Affordable Health Act rollout give ample evidence how such sites can be difficult to pull off. This project may require major feasibility studies, providing another reason why multistakeholder involvement is relevant. This again could be under the strategy for rural development, even if development organizations opt to lead such a venture from behind, letting other actors with a comparative advantage in technical and artistic matters administer the site.[39]

Artists without Borders

Over the years, Nigeria and Russia have become well known for their oil exports. In fact, historically speaking, among the reasons the "Soviet Union progressively took greater interest in Nigerian affairs" around the mid-1960s, Achebe writes, was because of Nigeria's emergency "as an important oil exporter."[40] That noted, a protectorate of Russia, the Tuvan People's Republic (also called Tannu Tuva, or simply Tuva), has a unique creative product that it is exporting. It is a technique inspired by nature, *khoomei,* whereby a singer can sing several notes at once. For skilled musicians, singing *khoomei* around the world has become a career path. In our context, when these "mighty throat singers"[41] perform on the global stage, they engage in the WTO's Mode IV, presence of natural persons.

Whether or not you have heard of these mighty singers, Tuva "is easy to miss." It is located along Mongolia's northern border. You cannot fly there directly from Moscow. "The only ways in," according to the *Economist*, "are turbo-prop planes from nearby Siberian cities or a long drive through the surrounding mountains." For sure, "as Oksana Tyulyush, artistic director of the Tuvan National Orchestra, quips, 'God is a long way up and Moscow is a long way away.'"[42]

Tuva is the childhood home of Sergei Shoigu, Russia's defense minister since 2012 and the longest-serving cabinet member. Dubbed "master of emergencies," the man could be Russia's next president. Nevertheless, the *Economist* notes that even "Russians typically know little of the region, which lived under Mongol or Chinese rule for most of its history." But Tuva has a rich cultural history that supports the hypothesis of this book: that every nation, big and small, bears unique creative wealth. At an imaginative level, one could argue that Tuva's culture could drive dynamic cultural tourism under strategic creative economy planning. The place, after all, has "delighted philatelists by issuing a series of oddly shaped stamps."[43]

Tuva: Pumping the Economy with Throat Singing

In Tuva, "most of the region's 308,000 people are native Tuvans, a Turkic people some of whom still practice a traditional nomadic lifestyle."[44] On the idea of the arts for development, and how Mode IV can be feasible for even the most depressed of regions, consider what the *Economist* has to say: "Khoomei is inspired by nature, as performers seek to channel the waters, winds and beasts of their surroundings. In Tuva harking back to tradition has helped fill the void left after the Soviet collapse. Throat singing has also become a career path in one of Russia's most depressed regions. The most skilled musicians perform around the world – though some feel the music only works in its native habitat."[45]

Singing *khoomei* would probably make more sense when you "have to live in a yurt and see the stars," a stark contrast from living in an apartment and dealing with the hustle and bustle of international travel. Yet when we hear that "*Khoomei* is inspired by nature, as performers seek to channel the waters, winds and beasts of their surroundings" there is a motif – a motif that transports us back to Chapter 3 on climate change, where we saw that nature itself is a beacon of creative work.

One complication in traveling from Tuva, and back again, are local surnames. ("When Soviet officials came to distribute passports, they found that everyone in the home village of Sergei Shoigu's family had the same surname, Kuzhuget. They solved the problem by reversing some inhabitants' first and last names."[46]) These days, changing names presents lots of problems. For one, there is the scrutiny of visas. The next discussion ventures into the technical aspects of the visa issue. In the journey of creative commerce across borders, this issue cannot be sidestepped. It is important for understanding the dimensions of Mode IV services (presence of natural persons) for the many artists who may not be the Michael Jacksons of the world, but who have a spectacular talent to offer abroad.

Artists, Visas, and Headaches

Services, as we have seen from Nigeria to Tuva, are increasingly becoming a major part of global trade. Yet evidence suggests that piracy is not going to abate any time soon and that battles to fight it may be futile. Therefore, a model that espouses live performances can be one way around this problem. These performances normally help artists capture their income directly, while also selling CDs and other related articles. In another example of trade following where culture leads, provision of items like t-shirts and other memorabilia can fetch extra revenue.[47]

But since live performances involve the movement of people, this provision is loaded with challenges – visas, for example. In areas where arrangements like bookings, advertisements, and ticket sales are time sensitive, visa delays or denials can have far-reaching consequences. With respect to the United States, since 9/11, artists have had their share of visa headaches[48] – headaches that entail social and economic costs. Even famous artists with common names are not spared. As Larry Rohter reported in the *New York Times* in 2012, the rising Spanish flamenco singer Pitingo got in trouble because of his name, but things did not end there:

Even though his producers had prepared his American début as best as they could, booking the Grand Ballroom at Manhattan Center, preparing tickets and the program, and even purchasing nonrefundable air tickets, when Pitingo went to the American Embassy in Madrid to pick up his visa, he instead picked up something else: The rising star learned that he had somehow become a falling star, a persona non grata, on the "no fly" list.[49]

Pitingo, who probably would have preferred to see his name flying across shiny billboards in Manhattan, had "fallen victim [to] the complex visa laws." For his real birth name, Antonio Manuel Alvarez Velez, is similar to that of a terrorist suspect. But, as the UK-based American Visa Bureau reported, although embassy officials realized that "Pitingo was not the target they were looking for," the singer "was still subject to immigration checks, and by the time they were complete, he had missed his show at the Grand Ballroom at the Manhattan Center, costing his producers almost $25,000 (£16,000)."[50]

That episode is not an isolated one.[51] The Halle Orchestra from Great Britain "no longer bothers to book shows in the United States due to the unlikelihood of being able to receive visas in time." Whether that decision changed, or will change anytime soon, who knows. But the British theatre director Tim Supple has had his own headaches. When he attempted to stage *One Thousand and One Nights* at the Chicago Shakespeare Festival, of the 40 participants in this Arabic show about the Arab Spring, nine faced their own Pitingo-visa moments: "[they] were denied visas, and the show had to be cancelled."[52]

In 2009, the Skirball Cultural Center in Los Angeles found itself entangled in other versions of Pitingo-visa cadences: It ended up cancelling scheduled performances of an Argentine music group. The reason? Immigration officials in California were not convinced that the group's fusion of tango and Jewish Klezmer music met the distinguished criteria of "culturally unique." In other cases, according to Teresa Watanabe writing in the *Los Angeles Times*, "California officials also challenged visa petitions ... that aimed to bring in an Indian group to perform at a California festival honoring the Hindu goddess Durga, a Chicago opera company seeking to bring in a Spanish singer and an African musical group."[53]

Every nation has a right to protect its security, and that point, made by *One Thousand and One Nights'* producer Roy Luxford, deserves respect. Nonetheless, engaging cultural exchanges in the United States has surely become an onerous undertaking. "If all the rhetoric about open societies and cultural exchange is to be believed," as Luxford concluded, "then the agencies involved in that process need to own up to that."[54]

It would be naïve to assume that the ever-fluctuating political climate would have no influence on what "agencies involved" can do. But what would one make of these data from the Department of Homeland Security, cited in Rohter's article?

Overall "requests for the standard foreign performer's visa declined by almost 25 percent between 2006 and 2010, the most recent fiscal year for which statistics are available. During the same period the number of these visa petitions rejected, though small in absolute numbers, rose by more than two-thirds."[55]

Although the visa difficulties described above pertain to the United States, many other developed countries have difficult processes for visas, especially for applicants who are not multimillion-dollar investors, whose names may be questionable, or who may simply not hold the right passport. Consider Sylvester Okwunodu Ogbechie.[56] Ogbechie, a Nigerian, organized and coordinated the First International Nollywood Convention and Symposium, in Los Angeles, in June 2005. The convention "evaluated new media in contemporary African Visual Culture from the perspective of the internationally acclaimed Nigerian Video Film Industry. He subsequently founded the Nollywood Foundation in 2006 to formalize study and research of this phenomenon and produced annual international Nollywood conventions from 2005 to 2009."[57] But when it comes to travelling, this artist and scholar has his own headaches. He is sometimes treated as if he will be the next Nigerian underwear bomber.

An entrepreneur and professor of Art History and Architecture at the University of California, Santa Barbara, Ogbechie wrote about the difficulty he experienced when securing a ten-day German visa.[58] This was when he was preparing to travel to Kassel to view "Documenta XI," one of the world's most celebrated exhibitions of contemporary art: "At the German [Consulate] in Los Angeles, it took me three days to explain to the officials there why I, an art historian and professor in a major department of art history at a major American university, should be interested in attending the most important contemporary art exhibition on the planet." On the issue of the movement of African artists, he asks: "what kind of exchange occurs when African artists and scholars are actively denied a chance to engage their counterparts in the West by being subjected to stringent applications requirements for a visa? What does this do to the production of knowledge about their spaces of practice?"[59]

There are visas such as the United States' O-1B for "individuals with an extraordinary ability in the arts or extraordinary achievement in motion picture or television industry."[60] Nevertheless, such visa categories are not enough. There is a need to explore more possibilities for artists from developing countries who may not be big names, but who nonetheless play an important role in commerce and cultural exchanges, especially in the area of traditional arts.

Creating a Temporary Artist Visa

One idea is to create an artist visa provision akin to, say, the temporary program for agricultural workers in the United States (H-2A or H-2B visas). This provision "establishes a means for agricultural employers who anticipate a shortage of domestic workers to bring nonimmigrant foreign workers to the United States to perform agricultural labor or services of a temporary or seasonal nature." There would be major structural differences, however. Employers seeking H-2A visas "must file an application with the [US Department of Labor] stating that there are not sufficient workers who are able, willing, qualified, and available, and that the employment of aliens will not adversely affect the wages and working conditions of similarly employed US workers."[61]

But artist visas would be aligned with cultural exchanges, including trade in cultural services. The goal is to make it easier to fuel cultural exchanges and generate income from live performances for artists from developing countries. Like the seasonal agricultural visas, artist visas could be provided, say, during the summer, with artists getting a three-month visa to perform in host countries.[62] The requirements of this visa depart from those of the O-1B, as compared in Annex 5.1.

Artists and the Freedom of Economic Migration

People migrate for a number of reasons, economics being one of them. Indeed, the whole idea of international trade is about movement of goods and services. Although people are not commodities,[63] international commerce today involves a number of services provided by people.

"It is estimated that a modest increase in industrial countries' quotas on incoming temporary workers, equal to an aggregate of 3 percent of the current workforces, would result in increased world welfare of more than $356 billion a year by 2025," according to a 2006 study by the World Bank Independent Research Group.[64] How much of this commerce would be related to trade in cultural services is unknown. But at the same time, cancellation of live performances involving major losses due to visa delays or denials is not sustainable commerce. Imagine if it took a year to arrange for the Tuva's "mighty throat singers" to appear at Carnegie Hall, and that they would later tour the rest of the United States for three months. If they were denied visas at the last minute, think of the business and diplomacy losses.

With respect to the benefits of temporary worker arrangements, under which provisional artist visas may fall, consider what the Walmsey-Winters model suggests, as Joel P. Trachtman observes in his book *The International Law of Economic Migration*: "[A]lthough 'developing countries are the main beneficiaries of [an increase in quotas for temporary migration], the initial residents of most of the industrial countries also experience increases in welfare from the higher returns to capital and increased taxes collected.'"[65] Indeed, "Preference of temporary migration over permanent migration may arise from a concern to ensure that arrangements benefit developing countries."[66]

At this juncture, another idea worthy mentioning is Edward Pearlman's proposed Cultural Exchange Free Trade Agreement (CEFTA). Pearlman, a performer and teacher particularly specializing in the fiddle music of Scotland and Cape Breton, is, at the time of this writing, seeking signatures to submit a petition to the United States Administration and Members of Congress to create CEFTA. Here is the gist of his proposal: CEFTA "would permit temporary visits for the purposes of cultural exchange by acknowledged experts in traditional arts among countries participating in this agreement. It would seek to separate cultural exchange visits from commercial visits, by setting criteria to distinguish the two."[67]

Whilst Perlman acknowledges that CEFTA participants would need to be compensated for their time and expenses, his take on the noninstrumental value of culture particularly noted in Chapter 1 is apparent. It is also apparent if we acknowledge that the learning in cultural exchanges can also give us language on "how to recover the animating spirit of humanism." On the point, ponder what Marilynne Robinson, one of the leading American novelists as well as "a rigorous thinker and incisive essayist,"[68] has to say: "For one thing, it would help if we reclaimed, or simply borrowed, conceptual language that would allow us to acknowledge that some things are so brilliant they can only be understood as virtuosic acts of mind, thought in the pure enjoyment of itself, whether in making a poem or a scientific discovery, or just learning something it feels unaccountably good to know."[69]

In their contribution to that line of thought, in celebrating the humanities of the world, CEFTA's virtuosos would be dedicated to the augmentation of their cultural heritage's appreciation. Their focus will not be primarily commercial. They will concentrate on the propagation of cultural traditions, an idea that will no doubt involve of a great deal of cultural learning and teaching without borders.[70] It may also be linked to the Cultural Exchange Index noted in Chapter 9.

It is important to note, however, that even CEFTA and provisional artist visas are not abuse-proof. Stories of "fake artists," or people disappearing when they come from low- and middle-income countries to perform in North America or in Europe, are not new.[71] Even more, contracts need to be carefully crafted to ensure that artists are not exploited. "Although singers and musicians from the Philippines can be found performing in many hotel lounges around Asia," Floyd Whaley reported in the *New York Times*, for example, "the field is actually quite specialized and highly competitive. 'A hotel might need many waiters, cooks and housekeepers,' Mr. Celso J. Hernandez of the Philippine Overseas Employment Administration said. 'But they only need one or two musicians.'"[72]

This makes the field unstable. With so much competition in a strange land, the problem of exploitation can get right down to the piano keys: Josetoni Tonnette Acaylar, who has been singing and playing the piano throughout Asia for more than three decades, was told in one job in Japan "to take off his tuxedo and work in the kitchen, washing dishes and scrubbing floors. 'Sometimes,' he recalls, 'they would pull me out of the kitchen, give me a jacket and yell, 'Play the piano!'"[73]

What is more, as Kevin Erickson of the Future of Music Coalition and others point out, tours also come with their own set of direct and indirect costs. For example, some artists may not be able to travel because of health issues, the financial cost of tours themselves, age, family obligations like taking care of children, and so on. Such transactional and opportunity costs (or whatever they may be called) need to be taken into account; they cannot be ignored.[74] But our point of analysis here is to seek a fair and equitable way to get artists from developing countries to perform around the world on a temporary basis without the labyrinthine or arbitrary procedures clogging the system today.[75]

This is an opportunity for the governments (in both developed and developing countries) and other parties involved to work out provisions that are mutually beneficial and responsive to the reality of our increasingly globalizing world. Here, there is need to augment analytical efforts on how temporary workers (like artists) from the developing world could contribute to development gains via Mode IV of supplying creative services. This may sound like high-minded theory. But as an example, let us reflect on the Philippines, a country that has built remittances into its national economic planning.

About 1.6 million Filipinos worked overseas in 2011 as nurses, waiters, welders, plumbers, caregivers, and so forth. Workers from rural areas with a basic education can earn about $400 a month, plus room and board. "Musicians, meanwhile, can earn as much as $2,000 a month working in five-star hotels, or $800 to $1,500 a month working on a cruise ship, according to performers and government officials," reports Floyd Whaley. But, as we have noted, "[T]hey are also vulnerable to exploitation," cautions Yolanda E. Paragua, a senior official with the Philippine Overseas Employment Administration; some "earn $400 per month."[76]

On Neighbors and Trade

The movement of artists abroad is not only about exporting cultural services. It also reminds us that neighbors, geopolitics, and regional economic activities are important. To illustrate this, let us turn to Paul Collier's conjecture that neighbors matter. Collier was not talking about Nigeria or Tuva, but comparing two landlocked nations – my own country of Uganda, and Switzerland:

> Maybe landlocked countries depended upon their neighbors not just as transport corridors to overseas markets but also directly as markets. Maybe Germany and Italy were not *in the way* of Switzerland's market, they *were* Switzerland's market. Switzerland was not cut off from its market, it was surrounded by it. Well, why not Uganda? All landlocked countries are by definition surrounded by neighbors. Unfortunately, some neighbors are better as markets than others. Switzerland has Germany, Italy, France, and Austria. Uganda has Kenya, which has been stagnant for nearly three decades; Sudan, which has been embroiled in a civil war; Rwanda, which had a genocide; Somalia, which collapsed; the Democratic Republic of the Congo, the history of which was sufficiently catastrophic for it to change its name from Zaire; and finally Tanzania, which invaded it.[77]

It may be lucrative for Filipino musicians to emigrate to Japan, Malaysia, Korea, and China for work. The story is different when Ugandan musicians, for example, emigrate to Kenya, Sudan, Tanzania, and Ethiopia for work. This is not to say that some Ugandan musicians have not had any success working in a place like Kenya – and things may have changed for the better since Collier's take in *The Bottom Billion* in 2007. It might nonetheless make more sense for Ugandan musicians to work in places like Europe or the United States. Yet that too is not an easy way out.

Working under the cross-cutting themes of global concern, there is a need to strengthen the links with the International Labor Organization, the WTO, and the wider international community. One area of intervention could be capacity building. This "building of capacity" sounds like fluff. But its foundation could be laid by building rigorous research and support to set up such schemes as Overseas Employment Agencies (like the one in the Philippines). Such agencies could be the means where negotiations, information, and assistance for overseas workers can be administered. This provision could be attractive for countries where trade in services – including the movement of performing artists (under Mode IV) – provides a clear advantage. The private sector could also be engaged.

The Presence of Natural Persons and Future Prospects

In *Global Economic Prospects 2004*, Pierre Sauvé notes that of the six proposals tabled for the WTO's Mode IV (presence of natural persons), only two were submitted by developing countries: Colombia and India.[78] The rest were from Canada, the European Union, Japan, and the United States. The Nigerias and the Tuvas of the world were absent. The reason for this may include the fact that some developing countries tend to pursue bilateral trade agreements over multilateral agreements.[79] Nonetheless, "this also may reflect the difficulties many developing countries have faced in identifying their export interests in services trade, an area of high demand in trade-related capacity building."[80]

The last point provides ample reason why meaningful capacity building is crucial. It could be the concrete policy instrument to ease the difficulties workers face in moving across borders – movement that could carry artists (from developing countries to the global stage) in seasonal employment arrangements. In Chapter 6, the final part in our examination of the WTO's mighty modes, we turn to the inverse of Mode IV, which is Mode II. This is where a service consumer moves from country A to country B to receive a service. Let us take a trip through the world of cultural tourism.

6 On Cultural Tourism

By 2030, devise and implement policies to promote sustainable tourism that creates jobs and promotes local culture and products.

Target 8.9, UN Sustainable Development Goals[1]

The travel and tourism industry has enjoyed unprecedented growth in recent years. In 2014, it accounted for more than $7 trillion and for 1 in 11 jobs worldwide.[2] Yet I cannot agree more with Elizabeth Becker, who in her book *Overbooked: The Exploding Business of Travel and Tourism* notes: while finance is serious, tourism is fun; while oil is serious, tourism is romantic.[3] This chapter concludes a series on international trade cultural services that we began to trace in the last two chapters. It returns to Nigeria to exemplify the opportunities and challenges of cultural tourism in development. And it suggests that understanding Africa's colonial history is important in paving a new path for African trade. Moreover, while cultural tourism has a promising role, the industry is a delicate dance that must be treaded carefully. The chapter recapitulates the need to consider nation branding, because as Haiti shows, a country with a poor image is less likely to grow its tourism sector effectively.

***

"An Igbo proverb tells us that a man who does not know where the rain began to beat him cannot say where he dried his body."[4] That line opens Nigerian writer Chinua Achebe's memoir, *There Was a Country: A Personal History of Biafra*. In keeping with Achebe's lead, let us return to Nigeria, where we began our analysis on trade in creative services. This return is necessary to consider tourism, our final conduit of supplying services (Mode II, consumption abroad; see Box 4.1). The analysis is also relevant for the rest of Africa and other parts of the developing world.

Suppose you have just finished reading Achebe's *Things Fall Apart*. Mesmerized by his cadences, you order his memoir *There Was a Country*. If this book is mailed internationally, in trade-speak, that is cross-border supply (Mode I) – this time not by internet, but in the mail. If it is shipped locally, that is domestic trade, or "in-border supply," as we decided to call it. Once the book arrives, you flip through the introduction and read about the "Scramble for Africa," when European powers gathered at the Berlin Conference in 1884–85 to create new African boundaries without either the representation of or consultation with Africans. That scramble contributed to the rough road of African trade, whose division baffles anyone concerned about Africa's development today. What is more, despite Africa's abundant creativity, the continent's "trade is overly dependent on a narrow range of primary products," as Valentine Rugwabiza, former deputy director-general of the World Trade Organization, notes.

As recently as 2010, two-thirds of Africa's total merchandise exports consisted of fuels and mining products:[5] a legacy of colonialism. The "infrastructure built during the colonial era was outward oriented with almost no internal networks to allow trade between African countries."[6] As you continue to read Achebe, you learn this: today's Nigeria was formerly an area of West Africa that was handed to Great Britain "like a piece of chocolate cake at a birthday party."[7] You note that Nigeria sits in an area that "was one of the most populous regions on the African continent, with over 250 ethnic groups." Since you are interested in cultural tourism, the following statement draws your attention: "The Middle Belt of Nigeria was the locus of the glorious Nok Kingdom and its world-renowned terra-cotta sculptures. The southern protectorate was home to some of the region's most sophisticated civilizations. In the west, the Oyo and Ife kingdoms once strode majestically, and in the Midwest the incomparable Benin Kingdom elevated artistic distinction to a new level."[8] These are things you rarely hear about Nigeria.

Intrigued, you decide you are going to visit Nigeria. You want to see the new cultural offerings, from Nollywood to cultural festivals.

You even expect to participate in the tradition and practice of making drums. This is because, with their encoded messages, as Steven Johnson writes, the "talking drums" of West Africa in Nigeria and elsewhere were the first long-distance wireless networks.[9] But you hesitate. There is the terrorist group, Boko Haram. And kidnappings. And corruption. And those e-mail scams? They remain as sly as ever.

Nonetheless, from your reading, you are convinced that there is more to Nigeria than its problems. You mull your options over. As you finish watching *Osuofia in London*, the advertisements that come flying across the screen include one by Nigeria's Federal Ministry of Culture Tourism and National Orientation. It offers a three-week package promising to show the true Nigeria, from music festivals to the *mbari*, the Igbo concept of "art as celebration."[10]

The moment you sign up for this trip, you have become a cultural tourist. On your trip to Nigeria, you will be traveling under the WTO's Mode II, consumption abroad, "where a service consumer" (in this case you, the tourist) moves from country A to country B "to obtain a service."[11]

TOURISM IN THE CHANGING GLOBAL ECONOMY

A long time ago, economists in the French school called physiocracy "energetically argued" that only "agricultural enterprise produced wealth, whereas merchants, manufactures, and other workers did not."[12] That idea seems ludicrous today. In our modern and ever-changing economy, development must fully court services.

Think about this: travel and tourism "generated $7.6 trillion (10 percent of global GDP) and 277 million jobs (1 in 11 jobs) for the global economy in 2014," according to the World Travel & Tourism Council. "Recent years have seen Travel & Tourism growing at a faster rate than both the wider economy and other significant sectors such as automotive, financial services and health care." In 2014, international tourist arrivals surged, "reaching nearly 1.14 billion, and visitor spending more than matched that growth. Visitors from emerging economies now represent a 46 percent share of these international arrivals (up from 38 percent in 2000), proving the growth and increased opportunities for travel from those in these new markets."[13]

Tourism has long been promoted for development. But within the framework of economic diversification, the tourism sector itself can be diversified, promoting offerings like those of the arts.

Although Africa is often associated with safaris, there is a need to ask how the culture could play a greater role in promoting local tourism. And in keeping with our leitmotif, how is Nollywood's Nigeria doing in this whole tourism business? Box 6.1 provides a snapshot.

BOX 6.1 A Snapshot of Nigeria's Travel and Tourism Sector

GDP: Total Contribution: "The direct contribution of Travel & Tourism to GDP was 1,861.4 [billion naira] ($7.4 billion), 1.7 percent of total GDP in 2016, and [was] forecast to rise by 1.1 percent in 2017, and to rise by 3.6 [annually], from 2017–2027, to 2,680.7 [billion naira] ($10.6 billion), 1.6 percent of total GDP in 2027."

GDP: Total Contribution: "The total contribution of Travel & Tourism to GDP was 5,124.3 [billion naira] ($20.3 billion), 4.7 percent of GDP in 2016, and [was] forecast to fall by 1.3 percent in 2017, and to rise by 4 percent [annually] to 7,507.7 [billion naira] ($29.7 billion), 4.5 percent of GDP in 2027."

Employment: Direct Contribution: "In 2016 Travel & Tourism directly supported 649,500 jobs (1.6 percent of total employment). This [was] expected to rise by 3.4 percent in 2017 and rise by 3.3 percent [annually] to 926,000 jobs (1.5 percent of total employment) in 2027."

Employment: Total Contribution: "In 2016, the total contribution of Travel & Tourism to employment, including jobs indirectly supported by the industry was 4.5 percent of total employment (1,793,000 jobs). This [was] expected to rise by 1.4 percent in 2017 to 1,818,500 jobs and rise by 3.6 percent [annually] to 2,598,000 jobs in 2027, 4.2 percent of total."

BOX 6.1 **(cont.)**

Visitor Exports: "Visitor exports generated 211.3 [billion naira] ($836.7 million), 1.9 percent of total exports in 2016. This [was] forecast to fall by 2.8 percent in 2017, and grow by 1.7 percent [annually], from 2017–2027, to 242.4 [billion naira] ($959.9 million) in 2027, 0.7 percent of total."

Investment: "Travel & Tourism investment in 2016 was 1,129.4 [billion naira], 7.2 percent of total investment ($4.5 billion). It [was expected to] fall by 5 percent in 2017, and rise by 5.4 percent [annually] over the next ten years to 1,821.5 [billion naira] ($7.2 billion) in 2027, 7.3 percent of total."

Source: WTTC 2017, 1. 2017 forecast. Values are in constant 2016 prices and exchange rates.

Cultural Tourism versus Creative Tourism

Some have suggested that it might be better to move beyond cultural tourism to creative tourism. This is because creative tourism has a wider agency in creating more jobs and other aspects people have a reason to value. Consider hands-on cross-cultural interactions. That said, whereas cultural tourism is related to anything cultural – from museums to dance festivals – what is creative tourism?

Creative tourism and cultural tourism are interrelated; in this book I use these terms interchangeably. According to Crispin Raymond and Greg Richards, however, creative tourism "offers visitors the opportunity to develop their creative potential through active participation in courses and learning experiences, which are characteristic of the holiday destination where they are taken." Examples include "blowing glass in Biot (French Riviera), dancing [the] Rumba in Barcelona, baking croissants in Paris, performing a concert in a church in Rome, participating in a cooking class in Bangkok, weaving according to Mayan tradition in Guatemala, or even producing chill out music in Ibiza."[14]

In line with those experiences, suppose on your trip to Nigeria you participate in *mbari*, that Igbo idea of "art as celebration." In the tradition and practice of *mbari* "[f]oreign visitors... are brought in as well, to illustrate the dynamic nature of life."[15] You are now not only a cultural tourist, you are also a creative one – even if you decide to just engage in drum-making, as we saw earlier, that is still the case. "This new way of discovering a foreign culture by experiencing it has been growing increasingly for the last decade," says the Creative Tourism Network. "Nowadays, the tourists no longer conform themselves in attending a traditional sightseeing tours, they need to feel involved into the destination's daily life. They don't want to be considered as 'tourists.'"[16]

Now, receiving tourists in daily life brings up the question of gentrification. Let me comment a little on this issue. Gentrification can be glorious, yet it can also have a negative impact financially struggling artists – if the cost of living goes up and drives them out, for example.[17] So in the name of gentrification, it is not difficult to see how places of cultural creation may face a danger of simply becoming places of cultural consumption. This production-consumption dichotomy deserves careful investigation.[18] Nonetheless, one could argue that creative tourism may have an edge in helping places preserve a sense of cultural creation, rather than remaining merely as corners of cultural consumption.

And while anyone who takes Economics 101 is drilled to remember the law of diminishing returns (or diminishing marginal utility), here, in an attempt to support the hypothesis of "more is better" (or nonsatiation), David Throsby observes that "cultural goods" (in this case, including cultural services) "have been described as experience goods, and as goods which are subject to rational addiction." If that premise holds, it "[means] that increased present consumption will lead to increased future consumption, such that demand is cumulative."[19] So, other things being equal, it is not unreasonable to suggest that if you are captivated with your creative tourism experiences, your interest in such services might increase rather than diminish.

Creative Tourism and Youth Employment

That this sector could create more employment for young people is not difficult to see. Creative jobs can be innovative, attractive, and enjoyable. So their very makeup provides ample reason why strategies to engage the youth should include such creative sectors. Indeed, the link between tourism and development deserves a hard look with this question in mind: What is the potential of this sector in addressing youth employment? "With almost 200 million people aged between 15 and 24," according to the African Economic Outlook, "Africa has the youngest population in the world. And it keeps growing rapidly. The number of young people in Africa will double by 2045."[20] As Throsby notes in *The Economics of Cultural Policy*, "Artistic and cultural activities at the local level can provide social engagement and employment-creation opportunities that may be useful, for example, as a means of re-engaging displaced social groups such as marginalized youth."[21]

In Nigeria, the cultural "attractions include traditional ways of life preserved in local customs; rich and varied handicrafts and other colourful products depicting or illustrative of native arts and lifestyle, and the authentic unsophisticated but friendly attitude of many in the Nigerian population,"[22] the country's High Commission in London boasts. Even so, with respect to cultural investments, trade, and development, it strikes a minor chord:

> [M]any of these [cultural] attractions are still largely untapped and even at their raw, undeveloped state, they are still being enjoyed by few outsiders, either very rich visitors in quest of exoticism or adventurous people in search of new challenges and experiences. The lack of required modern infrastructural facilities and in some parts of the country, acute conditions of underdevelopment and poverty can be seen. [And] many potential Nigeria bound [tourists] may not like to be confronted with [such scenes]. These are impediments to tourism, which the new administration has been tackling since assumption of office. Investors, both foreign and

> local, are therefore called upon to come and invest in the abundant tourism potentials [sic] in the country.[23]

Notice the call for investors. If you explore investing in Nigeria, what are the first steps? One of the first considerations is Nigeria's image. Even if we are told that besides Nigeria's cultural attractions the Nigerian people are authentic and friendly, Nigerians will be the first to tell you how their country is often viewed. As we noted in the discussion on national branding in Chapter 4, Daniel Kahneman observes this about human nature: People are prone to remembering "bad impressions and bad stereotypes." And in business, the "asymmetric intensity" to avoid losses[24] does affect investment decisions.

Certainly, from Nigeria to Tuva, the link between nation branding and tourism is natural. In fact, the "strongest country brands understand that the elements of Tourism combined with the infrastructural considerations of Heritage and Culture represent significant economic stimuli."[25] That explains why, in addition to courting investors, Nigeria would want to burnish its image in the most authentic way possible; this is true for other countries as well. In any case, if opportunities for investments are ripe, what does a creative tourism business model look like? Figure 6.1 presents a model, and it also connects to the economic links of the music industry in Nashville presented in Chapter 1.

Cultural Tourism in Urban and Regional Development

Cultural tourism has been advanced as a way to accomplish urban and regional development. This issue will be treated more thoroughly in Chapter 8, in the discussion on urban renewal. But to foreshadow it, let us take two points from David Throsby's *The Economics of Cultural Policy.*

First, "A single cultural facility or institution can on its own provide a stimulus to urban economic growth; the Guggenheim Museum in Bilbao, Spain, is often cited as a paradigm case of a cultural investment that has led to revitalisation of a depressed

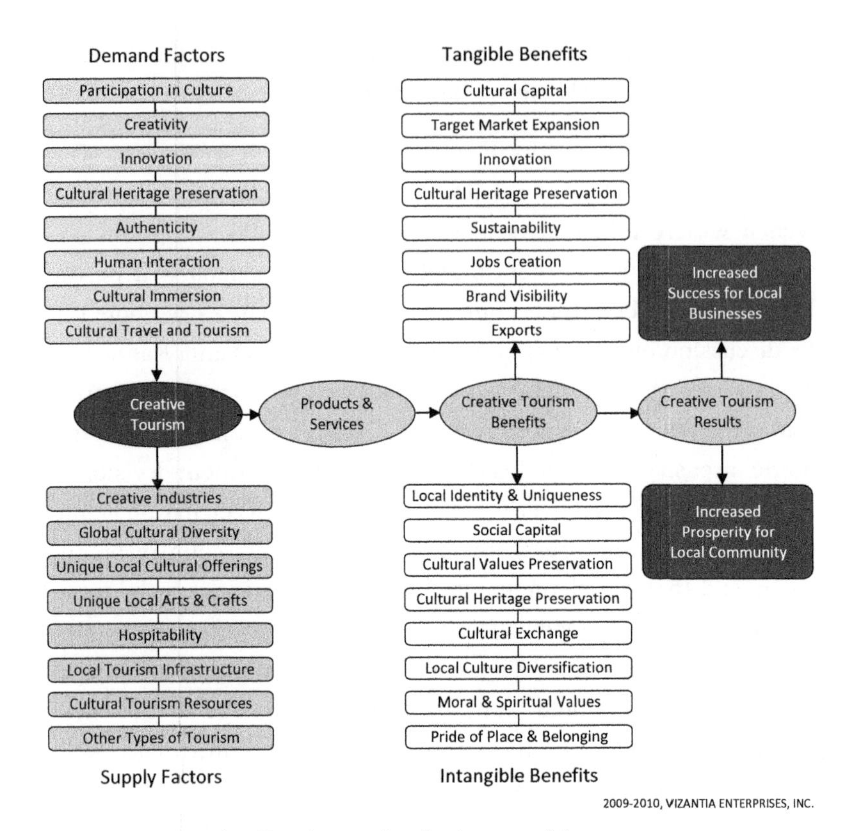

FIGURE 6.1 Creative tourism business model
Source: Ohridska-Olson and Ivanov 2010

urban area. Other iconic cultural buildings and structures, such as the Leaning Tower in Pisa, or the Taj Mahal in Agra, or the Great Wall of China are magnets for tourism, and over time, become important cultural symbols for local residents and overseas visitors alike."[26] Here recall the complementarity of the WTO's modes of supplying services.

Second, "Cultural industries can benefit from network and agglomeration externalities available in urban settings. The growth of 'creative clusters' in a number of cities – fashion in Milan, theatre in London, film-making in Hollywood" or in the Bollywoods and Nollywoods of the world – "reflects the economic advantage of co-location"[27] (see the discussion on Nashville in Chapter 1). At the risk of oversimplification, this perhaps connects to Paul Krugman's observation noted in Chapter 4: For historical reasons, regions that have enjoyed a head start as centers of production are likely to even attract more production.[28]

All well and good. Nevertheless, tourism is not without its problems. These need to be examined too.

THE UNCLEAR BENEFITS OF CULTURAL TOURISM

Tourism, as Adam Kaul notes, is a powerful lever in economic and social change, which he describes as being rife with irony, inequality, and essentialization.[29] In some cases, massive tourism can dilute local arts, confirming the doubts some have about modern globalization.[30] This happens, for instance, when local artists are coerced to adopt their performances to meet tourists' demands.

It should be no surprise if such consumer demand echoes foreign sentiments. This could occur even if a number of tourists may genuinely be interested in authentic traditional performances. In our contemporary world, for example, as Sen observes, the "power of Western culture and lifestyle in undermining traditional modes of living and social mores" is overwhelming. And for "anyone concerned about the value of tradition and of indigenous cultural modes this is indeed a serious threat. . . .The sun does not set on the empire of Coca-Cola or MTV."[31] This problem is not limited to diluting the cultures of the Tuvas of the world. Its tentacles reach far. In a 2015 *New York Times* article, "In Tourist Destinations, a Picture of Excess," Doreen Carvajal paints a portrait of what is increasingly becoming a dark image of tourism:

> From posing naked at Machu Picchu to filming their dives from hotel balconies into courtyard swimming pools, travelers across the world have been indulging in what officials and travel experts describe as an epidemic of narcissism and recklessness, as they try to turn vacation hubs and historic sites into their personal video and

> photography props ... [In this debacle,] tourists have insulted local sensibilities – and often caused extensive damage – in the course of taking enormous risks to try to capture themselves in a memorable travel moment that they can post on social media.[32]

For example, in Egypt, where tourism has long been a major export, in 2015 Russian tourists performed an act that was insensitive: They made a ten-minute video of nothing but pornography, an act that could have disquieted the tombs at Giza and the Sphinx – the shooting was done near these pyramids.[33] Egyptians authorities were outraged, even if tourism is a significant revenue earner for Egypt. Such insensitivities can nullify the touted benefits of tourism – from commerce to cross-cultural understanding. They are a form of cultural pollution.

What Is the Role of Policy?

Tourism is "arguably the biggest industry in the world," Elizabeth Becker argues in *Overbooked*. Yet "[f]ew foreign policy experts, economists or international policy gurus discuss the subject, much less ask whether tourism is enhancing or undermining distinct regional culture, a fragile environment, an impoverished country. Like any industry, tourism has winners and losers, and keeping it out of critical discussions about the direction of the economy or international debates about the environment is short-sighted."[34] Besides, in connection with the Artists Visa that was proposed in Chapter 5, there is the question of equity in mobility. For those tourists having trouble getting visas because of their countries of origin, or questionable middle-class status, for instance, this issue also deserves attention.

Regarding regulation, here is Becker again: One reason tourism is difficult to regulate is because, in addition to pastime and leisure, its positive associations are also associated with cultural prestige. Indeed, notwithstanding the utility of checks and balances, as Becker explains in "The Revolt against Tourism," tourism has its share of aversion to regulation. There are always exceptions, however. Consider France, where "Paris is, first of all, for Parisians":

> France is an exception, which is remarkable given that it is also the most-visited country in the world. In the 1950s, with American aid from the Marshall Plan, the French government used tourism to help rebuild the country. They discovered that tourism, when done properly, could underwrite the protection and nurturing of France's culture, landscape and way of life. In practical terms, that means tourism is promoted and subsidized, but also regulated, at all levels of government, in all matters of policy.[35]

From Nigeria to France and from Tuva to the Philippines, what Becker goes on to describe deserves attention: "Tourism is octopuslike, its tentacles reaching out to aspects of life that are diverse as coastal development, child prostitution, the treatment of religious monuments and the survival of a threatened bird species or native dancing." Yet the "very idea of describing tourism as a serious business is an oxymoron to many people ... The oil industry is serious. Finance is serious. Trade is serious" – hint, hint, trade in services, in which tourism falls, is not well understood as trade – "Manufacturing is serious. Foreign policy and economic policy are serious. Tourism is a frivolous pursuit: fun, sometimes educational in the lightest sense, often romantic, even exotic."[36]

Would such thinking induce much policy action? The first step in a strategy of economic diversification is recognizing the potential of cultural tourism. The larger point, however, is to make sure that tourism is carefully regulated. And since the nature of approaches is diverse, policies of course may differ from place to place. Whatever the case, learning from others informed by local observation could be the locus of balancing practical necessity with ethics and the realities on the ground. Here is France again: "France invented the first Ministry of Culture and then spread festivals around the country to send visitors far from Paris: music in Aix-en-Provence, film and advertising in Cannes; photography in Perpignan and dance in Montpelier."[37] It perhaps may have sounded better, if, like Nigeria, they called it the Ministry of Culture and National Orientation. For France has certainly scored in "orienting" people to French culture. Countries could take some tips from France. Not to copy and paste, but to see what might work in their own countries.

Green Growth and Tourism

The issue of sustainability as it relates to tourism also needs to be treated carefully. Broadly speaking, "sustainability means meeting the needs of today while preserving the resources for tomorrow," David Gelles observes. But, as he adds, the word "sustainable" can be nebulous: it "is sufficiently vague to mean quite a lot or nothing at all."[38] With respect to green growth and tourism, the claim that creative jobs (such as those in tourism) are greener than manufacturing deserves scrutiny. Some have argued that tourism is not as green as portrayed, and that serious attention is needed here. Becker explains:

> The United Nations World Tourism Organization projects that by 2030, global tourism will reach 1.8 billion trips a year. It is now so big that it will inevitably be part of conversations about climate change, pollution and migration. Without serious government attention, many beloved places will be at risk of being trammeled and damaged – what those in the tourism industry call being loved to death.[39]

If we venture further to discuss travel-induced pollution, tourism jaunts are not the only culprit, though. Citing a report by the Global Business Travel Association, the *Economist* reports that in 2015 "firms around the world [were projected to] spend a record $1.25 trillion" on work-related trips. "This largely reflects growing business confidence. In the downturn following the global financial crisis, suspending foreign jaunts was a quick way to cut costs. Now, firms are looking to grow, by sending staff out to hunt for deals."[40] In tabulating policies for green growth and tourism, concerned people may want to know: To what extent do business travelers combine their business trips with tourism? If no significant combination is apparent, does tourism travel pollute more than business travel? Such questions linger. In any case, we need responsible regulation, the kind that Becker signals, if benefits of tourism are going to be fully harvested in the long-awaited moment of meaningful development.

Tourism and Cultural Pollination

While environmental pollution and cultural pollution are certainly aspects of tourism, cultural cross-pollination is also possible for the better. From food to dance, the "image of regional self-sufficiency in cultural matters is deeply misleading, and the value of keeping traditions pure and unpolluted is hard to sustain."[41] Italian influences in opera across Europe are common, and so are African influences in American tap dance and jazz music. The peasant songs found in the remote villages of Hungary and Czech Republic that composer Béla Bartók incorporated in his work trace a rather intricate journey. "The songs," William Zinsser notes, " were based on old Greek ecclesiastical modes and on pentatonic scales from Central Asia, which Bartok said, freed him from 'the tyrannical rule of major and minor keys.'"[42] Who knows if some of these modes show up in Tuva's mighty throat songs discussed in Chapter 5?

Further evidence can be found in the spread of Irish music to the global stage: "If Irish music is a 'river of sound,' then it broke the geographic banks long ago and flooded into the many different parts of the world where it is listened to and played by people of very diverse cultural backgrounds," Adam Kaul writes. "Today, those floodwaters have also allowed other entities including people and other musical influences to flow back to the sonic river itself to become part of its current at the very core."[43]

Cultural influences do flow back and forth indeed. They sometimes take unexpected turns, though. Growing up in Uganda where I was somehow gripped by Bach's Two-Part Inventions, and thus copied these scores with abandon and even wondered how they would sound on an African fiddle, when the Ugandan organist Michaiah Mukiibi introduced me to Chopin's waltzes, I would discover another composer who left his mark on the Western musical canon. Playing Chopin meant mastering improvising waltzes and nocturnes in his style. And this model came in handy when I worked as a pianist at the Sheraton Kampala. There, I entertained guests, including tourists with whom the main language that brought us together was music. (That ballad "O Danny Boy" set to an Irish ancient tune of the Londonderry Air, moreover, was of those universal guests' favorites.) I can see why the influence of dance lessons shows up in Chopin's waltzes.[44] Until recently, however, I had no clue that this Polish composer, who lived in France and was fascinated with black keys, perfected and made the nocturne genre "uniquely his own, after the model established by the Irish composer John Field (1782–1837)."[45] Indeed, if it is at all is possible to account for "cultural value added" since ancient times, the cultural "geographical banks" were broken eons ago. And if individual artists continue to borrow from other cultures, then the Hollywoods of the world also do.

Tourism and Cultural Diversity

But as former World Bank President James D. Wolfenson pointed out, it is tremendously important that we "just don't have a Hollywood culture around the world," but that "we have indigenous cultures preserved and valued." He added something that was amiss at that controversial Berlin Conference in the1800s, a conference associated with the "Scramble for Africa": "I don't think that you approach different countries just based on a balance sheet analysis, because what is different about them is their culture." If you're "going to win the confidence of people in the countries, if you're going to be able to understand the people of the country; if you're going to make judgments about the people in the country about whether they trust you or not, what you have to do is to identify them in terms of their culture."[46]

Since we were seated in his Manhattan office overlooking the Avenue of the Americas, Wolfensohn delivered a rich metaphor: "If you come to New York and say the only way to judge New York is by the 100 richest business people, you will be missing out on what New York really is And I took the same approach in development." In other words, though New York is a global financial center, it is not only enriched by magnates; it is also enriched by the arts, the schools, the religious institutions, the immigrants, soccer in Central Park, you name it. Moreover, the wealth here is not only tangible. It is also intangible.

And speaking of intangible wealth, Robert S. Kaplan and David P. Norton pick up on this theme in their book *Strategy Maps: Converting Intangible Assets into Tangible Outcomes*: "All organizations today create sustainable value from leveraging their intangible assets" – the so-called "human capital; databases and information systems; responsive, high-quality processes; customer relationships and brands; innovation capabilities; and culture. The trend away from a product-driven economy, based on tangible assets, to a knowledge and service economy, based on intangible assets, has been occurring for decades."[47] As Kaplan and Norton go on to explain, "What's true of companies is even truer for countries." Generally speaking, as Creativeria realized, countries that "have high physical resource endowments but have made poor investments in their people and systems" tend to "produce far less output per person, and experience much slower growth rates," than those "that have few natural resources but invest heavily in human and information capital and effective internal systems." This point is surely not just about the arts. But whether or not we count arts education in stimulating imagination or pinpoint to the intangibility of services trade the larger point is this: "At both the macroeconomic and microeconomic levels, intangible assets drive long-term value creation."[48]

Yet, apart from paying lip service, development practice seems to be stuck in boxes that tend to exclude such thinking, despite the complementarity of fields in the ecology of meaningful development.

We have much to learn in the area of tourism, and the area of trade in services, as they relate to culture in development. The next section presents some policy recommendations.

CODA

Solicit and Fund Research Proposals on Tourism Related to the Arts

Since cultural tourism is understudied, countries that have long had a reputation for tourism related to the arts are worth serious study. Examples are diverse. They include Austria, Jamaica, Ireland, and Morocco. In the United Kingdom, music tourism boosts the economy by over £2 billion per annum.[49] But where do countries like Lao People's Democratic Republic stand? The recipient of the 2013 World Tourism Best Destination Award, Lao PDR is considered a cultural paradise.[50] Indeed, from my visit there in 2013, when I sailed from the Thai town of Chaing Khong to the Lao town of Luang Prabang via the mighty Mekong, called the "mother of waters," what I saw was no less a paradise.

In 2014, Lao's travel and tourism industry (directly and indirectly) contributed 12.8 percent of total employment, or 396,000 jobs.[51] While this sector is expected to continue to grow, how do such aspects as music tourism figure into Lao PDR's development (or tourism diversification) strategy? The central question is to see how developing countries with a comparative advantage in the arts can fully benefit from cultural (or creative) tourism. There is no ready formula. And there is no point in commissioning studies that will simply gather dust and not lead to action. But the following approach may prove helpful.

Engage Citizen Voices

Cultural tourism could be an area where citizen voices may play a greater role, especially on matters of cultural purity. As Sen argues, "it is up to the society to determine what, if anything, it wants to do to preserve old forms of living, perhaps even at significant economic cost. Ways of life can be preserved if the society decides to do just that, and it is a question of balancing the costs of such preservation with the value that the society attaches to the objects and the lifestyles preserved. There is, of course, no ready formula for this cost-benefit analysis, but what is crucial for a rational assessment of such choices is the ability of the people to participate in public discussions on the subject."[52] What we can learn from such public discussions deserves consideration in policy implementation.

Make a Concerted Effort to Improve Branding

There are more lingering considerations beyond discussions on cultural purity, though. Let us reflect on Haiti, another cultural paradise that has borne the brunt of such natural disasters as the devastating 2010 earthquake. Haiti already has community participation mechanisms in place; they include the *Table de Consultation* (the Communal Consultation Table). But Haiti's tourism attraction problem is instead often attributed to the issue we discussed earlier: nation branding. *Politically unstable, poor, violent, unsafe*, is that not what we often hear about Haiti? Such a narrative, as a World Bank document on Haiti's cultural heritage preservation and tourism puts it, stifles tourism development in this proud first black republic. Yet Haiti is much more than that.

I discovered Haiti's mystical rites and shots of spectacular beauty by chance. It took Wade Davis, whom the National Geographic Society has placed among the Explorers for the Millennium, to deliver that chance. The moment was profound. The photographs that accompanied Davis's lecture not only showed the cultural wealth of a Haiti I had never imagined. They also piqued me to consider the island's revolutionary history.

"That the revolutionary slaves of Saint Domingue defeated one of the strongest armies of Europe is a historical fact that, though often overlooked, has never been denied," as Davis writes in *The Passage of Darkness*. This is a land that Columbus once described this way, writing to his queen: "nowhere under the sun were there lands of such fertility, so void of pestilence, where the rivers were countless and the trees reached into the heavens."[53] Whether Columbus, who seemed to be more interested in exploiting the island's riches than describing natural beauty would give the same account today is another story. But what appears to be reaching the heavens these days is Haiti's crestfallen narrative.

It would be beyond peradventure to assume that if *politically stable, peaceful, safe* became the new synonyms for Haiti then things will suddenly change. There is a reason why there is a "to" in this headline: "In Haiti, Beauty That Plays Hard to Get (To)." Some of Haiti's stunning attractions like Belle Anse and Cascade Pichon are well-kept secrets – well kept partly because, as Dean Nelson observes, they have been hard to reach thanks to unsound infrastructure.[54]

Nevertheless, as Haiti tries to build itself from the tectonic shocks of natural disasters, not to mention piecing together what seem to be constant trappings of political and economic rubble, seeing Haiti from a place of strength rather than a place of weakness can make a difference.[55] At least that was my case after attending Davis's lecture, delivered at Phillips Academy. The profundity of Davis's images implanted in me such a rich portrait of Haiti that, a few years later, I was eager to join a student consulting team at The Fletcher School that worked to brand Haiti positively.

Such efforts have to be part of development policy, in addition to building infrastructure and the like. Think about the following point. Again, it confirms Kahneman's insights into the human mind, how our hardwired perceptions can be hard to change: The 2011 global study on homicide conducted by the United Nations Office on drugs and crime revealed that Haiti's homicide rates were much lower than those of its neighbors.[56] This fact, however, did little to deter tourists from visiting Haiti's neighbors.[57] We are told that the Haitian Ministry of Tourism takes tourists' safety seriously to the point that even new funds for a tourist police force were included in its 2014 budget. And initiatives to brand Haiti have generated promising outcomes. Still, if there is a pressing "need for more aggressive and targeted campaigns,"[58] then Haiti's evidence cannot but underscore the need to consider nation branding in development policy.

Since the arts can powerfully shape perceptions, this is another reason their positive contributions should be closely tied to development. On culture leading and trade following, moreover, consider the potency of music, an art form that Goethe called 'liquid architecture',[59] and whose rhythms from Haiti to Nigeria punctuate the legato and staccato of cultural beauty: "[music and other] visual images surrounding that music [can be] used in tourism campaigns to promote locations and attractions. Music then becomes a powerful soundtrack to television campaigns, a potent way of constructing authenticity."[60] Although the raised expectations could make music itself a tourist attraction, there is more to it: The "evocative qualities" of music can be "used to add credence to visual images, convey excitement, tradition, continuity with the past, elegance or escape."[61] Here we can see that the arts can add value within and yond each other.

Build on Pilot Work and Cultivate Meaningful Engagements

But if we believe that ideas can also be assembled like parts that make up a cellphone, or a car, or a pencil, that they can come from different disciplines and from different parts of the world, then the idea of "value added" is perhaps also germane in working together for collective good. I hinted at that idea in Chapter 5, and I will echo it again at the end of this book. But more immediately, here is why: In many cases, activities that bring about change do not originate from institutions like the World Bank. Indeed, successful "Brand Haiti" initiatives, for example, often stem from elsewhere. Nonetheless, while such institutions are "not the source of the transformation," they can help "scale up success," play as a "connector," and communicate "a successful experience." In a sense of noblesse oblige they can expand their "role as a platform to disseminate and/or scale up the impact of external development innovations with transformational potential."[62]

PART III Variations on a Theme

7 The Unsettled Question of Women in the Performing Arts

End all forms of discrimination against all women and girls everywhere.

Target 5.1, UN Sustainable Development Goals[1]

There is no doubt that progress has been made over the years in promoting gender equality. In fact, in nations like India and Bangladesh, women have held power in high office for long stretches.[2] But as former Indian Prime Minister Indira Gandhi said, you cannot shake hands with a clenched fist. Sometimes I feel we are trying to promote gender equality with a clenched fist. For example, we promote women's education but fall short on making sure that the cultural factors that might limit their absorption in the labor force are also addressed. We invite women to the table but fail to heed them in decision making. We benefit from women's contribution to economic and social progress yet we often turn a blind eye to the gender-pay gap. This is not always the case, to be sure. But if we are lax in combating all forms of discrimination against women, they are unlikely to reach their highest potential, and this is a cost to society.[3] This chapter considers gender inequality in the performing arts, a topic I find difficult to tackle, yet one that deserves attention in part because movies are so prominent in cultural trade, a topic we have considered in the previous Chapters 4, 5, and 6. Although the chapter highlights Bollywood, the problem is common across the world. Even Hollywood has yet to do better as such disturbing reports as the sexual harassment complaints against the producer Harvey Weinstein reveal.[4] Since the arts are a portrait of our lives, by perpetuating overt and subtle norms of female discrimination, the arts industry is likely to add to what holds back the full contribution of women. Yet the arts have the power to do more for gender equality.

***

The performing arts are riven with gender divides. Why does this matter for development? Since art is a portrait of our lives, when movies and other arts continue to reinforce female mistreatment, they also reinforce negative mental images, perpetuate norms of discrimination, and hold back development in all its forms. After all, "gender refers to the social, behavioral, and cultural attributes, expectations, and norms associated with being a woman or a man." And "gender equality refers to how these aspects determine how women and men relate to each other and to the resulting differences in power between them."[5]

To throw a spotlight on gender discrimination, let me start with India's Mumbai-based Bollywood, considered the world's largest movie industry (in terms of production). Bollywood is rife with gender concerns that are reflected in the global film industry.

The term "Bollywood" harkens to the days when Mumbai was Bombay, referring to the Hindi-language film industry there. It was coined relatively recently. But just as Hollywood is often used to refer to all movies made in America (even in New York and in New Jersey), Bollywood is often mistakenly used as a synonym for all of film production in India. "Strictly speaking," however, as Indian actress Nandana Sen told me, "one cannot call Bollywood the largest film industry in the world (as those statistics also include scores of regional-language films, which make up a long and rich tradition in India – much longer in fact than "Bollywood").[6]

In any case, in Bollywood – it supposedly generated $3 billion in 2011 and has been growing at about 10 percent per year[7] – top male actors can earn up to $16 million, compared to $1.5 million for their female counterparts, according to Palash Ghosh.[8] This is a pay gap of more than 90 percent. Of course, this issue is much more complicated than this; payments fluctuate over the years. Still, and even though the information here is limited, there is much reason to worry about such grotesque gender discrimination. The gap is as wide as the Indian Ocean itself.[9] This of course is not to say that there aren't any breakthroughs of female-oriented films that manage to become big hits and command big cash without a big male hero. For decades, this has been true every now and then, even more so these days.[10] And there are number of filmmakers who have challenged stereotypes set by the mainstream industry. These change makers dare to put the female perspective at the center, as Nidhi Shendurnikar Tere has argued.[11] But while such success can raise salaries of actresses, the increase would not come close to bridging the income gap between male and female stars.[12]

There are other grave concerns regarding female roles in Bollywood movies: notably, the issue of female sexualization. "In the first-ever study on how women are shown in popular films in the world's top 11 movie markets, India comes off poorly," Subodh Varma reported in the *Times of India* in 2014.[13] Nonetheless, there is a double standard here. Even though many popular Indian films may show more women in revealing clothes, or partially nude, than elsewhere, full nudity is still a taboo in India. And this is not a taboo for taboo's sake: It is held at a degree that is generally unprecedented across the world. This incongruity, one could argue, has to do with the representation and interpretation of female agency – both on screen and in the industry. The "heroine" of a top-grossing Bollywood film may wear revealing clothes, yet, of course, she must retain the image of a "good girl" at heart – a girl immersed in the world of goodness who cannot possibly take all her clothes off. "It's unsettling for most in India to face a woman (whether the actress, or the character) who has made a choice to be nude on screen," according to Ms. Sen. "She seems, ironically, to be far less objectified (and more subversive) by virtue of her agency than a partly nude actress, who more gingerly walks the line between the male gaze and pop moralism and is therefore not perceived as a threat."[14]

Again, why does this matter for development? India has over 1.2 billion people. In this huge and growing country, which swings between conservatism and modernization, sexual violence toward women is endemic. Consider this headline from *Forbes* magazine: "Rape Every 20 Minutes for the World's Largest Democracy?"[15] That was not in the 1900s; it was in the 2000s. So where does Bollywood come in? As the author of that *Forbes* story, Ruchika Tulshyan, notes, Bollywood cannot sidestep the responsibility of changing mindsets. This is obviously true elsewhere, but especially critical in a place where female mistreatment is pervasive, and where filmmakers normally decouple intellect and decision-making from female characters.[16]

It also bears adding that, just as Hollywood is not limited to the United States, Bollywood is not limited to India. It is a cultural staple elsewhere. From Kabul to Karachi, posters of Indian performers adorn the streets, as Humira Nooristani, a human-rights activist, writes in *Foreign Policy*. But, of course, they do not stay on the streets; they penetrate people's minds. And whatever you might think of intellectual property, "bootleg movies are widely available."[17] Whether watched legally or illegally, these films are likely to parade their purpose. Since Indian cinema is male dominated, as Nooristani and others conclude, the films too often portray women in Indian society in a male-centric way. In sum, they "mold opinions, and often encourage the poor treatment of women."[18] Moreover, it is not only the form that is problematic. It is also the content. From film to television, many Indian topics are overtly regressive to women's equality and freedom. Think about the celebration of child marriage. Think about the glorification of a man who pursues a woman relentlessly until she cannot help but say yes. And think about the projection of women as objects of desire rather than autonomous individuals.[19]

Now, this is not to imply that India is not doing anything about this. The country has recently passed some progressive measures. These include a Sexual Harassment Bill and the Protection of Children from Sexual Offences Act. But we should never forget that there is a difference between law and conduct. Writing in *Outlook* magazine about Jagruti, another precious young woman whose gang-raping brought focus on rape as a national crisis, Ms. Sen, who is also a children's book author and child-rights activist, went on to say: "Without doubt, the current focus on laws and law-enforcement is a positive outcome of Jagruti's tragedy, but let's not forget that our country has always showed an unsettling disconnect between what is legally permitted, and what is socially accepted and culturally projected." Furthermore, "the absence of consistent awareness-building renders it impossible for the legislation to translate into greater safety for our girls and women, who are largely uninformed about the new laws and their own rights."[20] And while the fate of some urban women is reported, there is much we do not hear – if we hear anything – about rural women and even those in slums and outskirts of urban centers.

On this point consider what Ammu Joseph, a journalist and author based in Bangalore, says in *Media and Gender*, a UNESCO publication prepared in cooperation with the International Association for Media and Communication Researchers: "As commentators have pointed out time and again, both the media and their target audiences tend to get particularly agitated when crimes, including sexual assault, affect 'people like us', while equally horrific crimes against the poor, the powerless and the distant tend to receive less media and public attention." Moreover, of all the prevalent forms of violence against women, rape is what often enjoys coverage, "almost always" with outrage, according to Joseph, whose books include *Whose News? The Media and Women's Issues* (co-edited with Kalpana Sharma). "Ironically, media fury over selected cases does not necessarily result in sensitive, responsible coverage."[21]

As Jean Drèze and Amartya Sen note in *An Uncertain Glory: India and Its Contradictions*, India has made remarkable progress; yet some of India's patriarchal norms, instead of waning, have spread like stubborn weeds. Why? Here is one possible reason: Over recent years, norms like the practice of dowry and a preference for male children have been emulated by people seeking higher social and economic status. This is a contrast from when these norms were not imitated, but were usually confined to those in the upper caste.[22]

Since this discussion is not intended to be a finger pointing exercise, what should be done? Here is Ruchika Tulshyan's take in her article, "How Bollywood Is Failing the Women of India":

> To effect any real change, we must bridge the chasm between the India that Bollywood portrays and the reality of the ordinary Indian woman in a slowly-modernizing, largely conservative society. I'm not at all suggesting that we should revert to the Bollywood of yesteryears, where chaste romances were portrayed as the norm. In fact, I find it encouraging when movies want to discuss truths that were shunned previously: from pre-marital sex to divorce. However, by simultaneously over-sexualizing women on screen, we sabotage any progress women are making towards equal opportunities, both in their personal and professional lives. It's time the powerful entertainment industry shouldered some responsibility for the India they're helping to shape.[23]

On the need to shoulder responsibility, Tulshyan amplifies this point: "Bollywood has a powerful role in shaping mindsets and behaviors in India. I would argue it's much more than just an entertainment industry. Movies have reflected the aspirations of many Indians for decades. Often, celebrities are revered in a manner akin to religious fervor."[24] But whereas religions can be rigid, media are flexible. They are fluid. This is particularly the case in countries with free markets and strong competition, as Miguel E. Basáñez writes in his book *A World of Three Cultures*. "In order to attract readers, listeners, and viewers, they try to appeal to the tastes of the majority; unfortunately in the battle for wider audiences, media often exploit the prurient interests and the fears of those people they seek to attract – horoscopes, vampires, and gossip about celebrities are hence common." What is new? Basáñez, who was a professor of mine and briefly served as Mexico's Ambassador to the United States, brings the point home: "While there are exceptions, such practices do not always serve the collective good."[25]

For the sake of collective good, I will submit that the entire global arts industry badly needs to do something about this. This is not just an Indian problem. It is a global problem.

A GLOBAL PROBLEM

The male versus female divide is apparent even in the most developed of nations. Consider the numbers in Figure 7.1 on the gender pay divide in Hollywood.

Pay, however, is only a part of the picture. In the nomination system for awards, things are also bleak.[26] Consider Figure 7.2. Since these figures do not even consider the issue of race, this is indeed a part of a complex picture.

The problem is not confined to Hollywood. A 2014 study, *Gender Bias without Borders: New Research into Female Roles and Characterization in Popular Films across 11 Countries*, examined a good 120 global films for almost three and a half years. The sample includes some top movie-making countries (in terms of profit): Australia, Brazil, China, France, Germany, India, Japan, the Republic

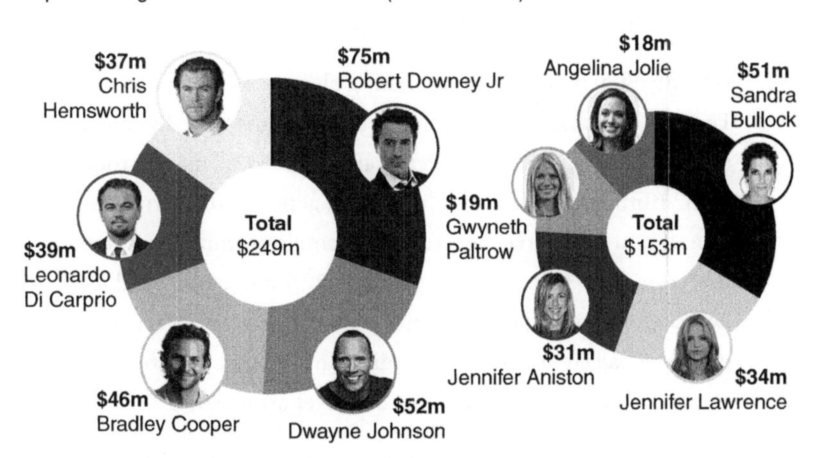

FIGURE 7.1 The male versus female pay divide in Hollywood
Source: Statista; McCarthy 2014.

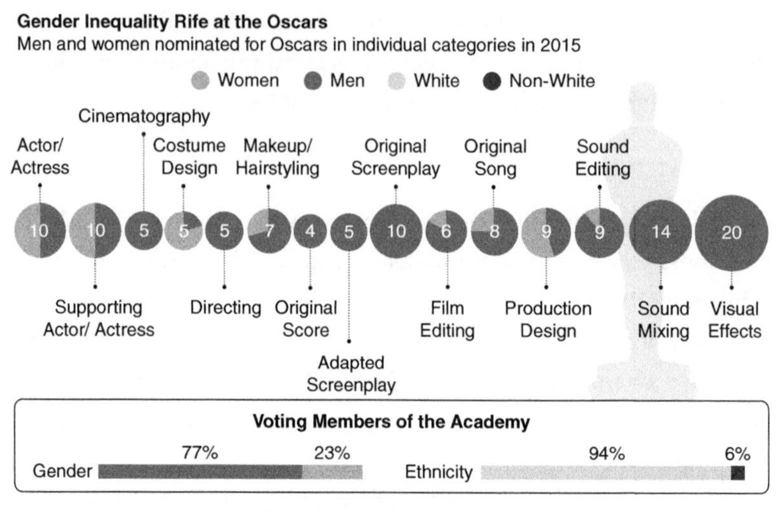

FIGURE 7.2 Gender inequality at the Oscars
Source: Statista; Swanson 2015

of Korea, Russia, United States, and the United Kingdom.[27] Commissioned by the Geena Davis Institute on Gender in Media, it received support from UN Women and The Rockefeller Foundation (see Annex 7.1). The study found "deep-seated discrimination and pervasive stereotyping of women and girls by the international film industry."[28] Here are a couple of points from the study:

> (1) Only 30.9 percent of all speaking characters are female. . . . (2) Females are missing in action/adventure films. Just 23 percent of speaking characters in this genre are female. (3) Out of a total of 1,452 filmmakers with an identifiable gender, 20.5 percent were female and 79.5 percent were male. Females comprised 7 percent of directors, 19.7 percent of writers, and 22.7 percent of producers across the sample. (4) Films with a female director or female writer attached had significantly more girls and women on screen than did those without a female director or writer attached.[29]

Point (4) should not come as a surprise. Yet "as with so many other aspects of social, cultural and economic life in the 21st century" women are still poorly represented in decision-making positions in media industries – that is the case if you consider the relative proportion of the female labor force in the sector, according to Karen Ross in *Media and Gender*. Moreover, despite the increasing numbers of women trained in media and those entering the industry, few secure the top jobs; many are trapped in middle management jobs.[30]

Of course, there are many organizations working to change that picture. In the cultural dimension, UNESCO, for one, seeks to ensure that, inter alia, women "share their creativity with audiences," that they "reach senior management positions," that they "participate in decision-making processes," that they overcome "negative stereotypes and limitations on freedom of expression based on gender," and that they "access technical and entrepreneurial training." Talking of access to training, education remains one of the most effective investments that point directly to development that is not only sustainable, but also equitable. But although progress has been made, women tend to have less access to education. And since inequality takes many forms, "addressing gender inequalities in education is a complex task," as UNESCO observes.[31]

But the challenge at hand is not just about providing more education to more women. It also includes dealing with societal norms that may limit women's absorption in the labor force,[32] not to mention their excellence and passage to participate in the processes of decision-making. This is why in realizing the "culturally neglected needs of women across the world,"[33] such cultural sectors as the movie industry have a special calling. After all, from transmitting cultural knowledge and skills to protecting and safeguarding heritage, gender relations often come into play. This is also the case for the "emergence and strengthening of vibrant cultural and creative sectors."[34]

I have concentrated on movies, because as noted in the prelude to this book, the architecture of the arts is intertwined. (And it is not difficult to find such gifts of dance, drama, and music within one artist.) But I feel compelled to say a word or two about sexism in the world of dance and sexism in the world of music. For these two worlds surely do not count for little in the movie industry and the arts community at large.

Regarding the former, dance is not immune from the gender divide. Although females are welcome to become ballerinas, they face their own glass ceilings; or rather "dance ceilings." Consider choreography. Writing in the *Guardian*, the dance critic Luke Jennings notes that while there are prominent female choreographers in the United Kingdom, it is always the men who are likely to get the killer commissions – even if they are less experienced:

> "It's a nightmare for those of us who watch as men get given chances they are simply not ready for while we graft away at our craft and take smaller-scale opportunities," says Janis Claxton, an Edinburgh-based choreographer. "Women quit because they don't get the support that their male colleagues get, and having to push constantly against this outrageous gender inequality is infuriating."[35]

Should we just sit back and let some sort of "invisible hand" – or perhaps "invisible dance" – take care of the business here? Should we be dismissive because this is anecdotal evidence?

In music, a portrait from history is also telling. As an organ student who had a predilection for Bach and Mendelssohn, I feasted on Mendelssohn's organ sonatas, which, to my delight, manifested Bach's influences. And I vividly recall the moments we would debate how Mendelssohn was instrumental in promoting Bach.[36] It was in these discussions that I would learn that Mendelssohn had an extremely gifted sister named Fanny. When Fanny was born, her father Abraham Mendelssohn Bartholdy wrote a rather prophetic statement. In a letter to his mother-in-law, he reported what Fanny's mother Lea Salomon saw in Fanny: the child had "Bach-fugue fingers." And what Bach-fugue fingers they were![37]

An impeccable pianist and composer, Fanny would go on to compose more than 400 pieces of music. Fanny was not living in

India trying to write scores for Hindi cinema. She was living in Germany. Yet the common denominator of being a woman meant that she would only managed to publish a few of her pieces. And guess what? Those pieces (six of them), according to Eugene Gates's article about women in music in the *Kapralova Society Journal*, were published under the name of her brother, Felix Mendelssohn.[38]

You hear similar stories about Mozart's musically gifted sister Maria Anna (nicknamed Nannerl). As we sing the praises of Mozart's music as a "pinnacle of human achievement," what happened to Nannerl? *The Geography of Genius* says she has an Austrian liqueur called Apricot Schnapps named after her. Female geniuses are often forgotten. This is because if we are all like plants, as the Austrian classical-music radio host Friederike of Vienna may put it, women often do not get the water they need. "Historically," as Weiner concludes, "women were denied the resources required for creative excellence: access to mentors, rewards (intrinsic and extrinsic), patronage, an audience."[39]

We are no longer living in the ancient days of Fanny and Nannerl. And certainly progress has been made in supporting women's creative agency. Yet even today what the choreographer Claxton of Edinburgh described still lurks as a "theme and variations" in the arts. In the orchestral world, it was not until the introduction of "blind auditions" that women gained greater acceptance into orchestras. When they auditioned behind a screen, the number of women players in the top five orchestras in the United States increased from 5 percent in 1970 to 25 percent in the mid-1990s.[40] In a stunning finding, two female economists, Claudia Goldin and Cecilia Rouse, uncover what they found:

> The screen increases by 50 percent the probability a woman will be advanced out of certain preliminary rounds. The screen also enhances, by several fold, the likelihood a female contestant will be the winner in the final round ... The switch to "blind" auditions can explain between 30 percent and 55 percent of the increase in the proportion female among new hires and between 25 percent and

> 46 percent of the increase in the percentage of female in the orchestras since 1970.[41]

That incremental change since 1970 is welcome, and should be further encouraged. But there is a need to take a closer look at orchestral leadership. "Discouraged by ingrained prejudice and arguments that they don't possess what it takes to command an orchestra," as Michael White explains, "successful female conductors still have the rarity of a protected species."[42] Indeed, while things may change, if you look at the 2012–2013 data on American orchestras (about 800 of them), 80 percent of conductors were male and 20 percent were female.[43] If that is not enough, when Elim Chan won the 2014 Donatella Flick Conducting Competition, of the 225 entrants, guess how many women competed? Only five.[44]

Elsewhere, while "images and ideas in songs are not always degrading, much of [the] music industry over the past few years has built its identity on the ability to objectify, degrade, and outright insult women with lyrics and pop culture images."[45] Whether that picture will change any time soon that remains to be seen.

THE GREAT QUESTION: WHY DOES THIS MATTER FOR DEVELOPMENT?

Choreographer Karole Armitage's take on the role of art in society, noted in Chapter 3, is germane here: Art is often a portrait of life in our time. If I may add, it can be a portrait of the kind of world we want to live in: the future we want to create. As noted repeatedly in this book, the arts can be transformational.

We should never forget how important the contributions of women are to the world's economic, political, and social wellbeing. The equal rights of nations are not only for men; they are also for women. Likewise, the wealth of nations is not only for men; it is also for women, generated not only by men but also by women.

Drèze and Sen note that gender inequality is among the issues that keep a great many people in the "new India" on the margin – "not only women themselves, but also men and children who would benefit from a more active, informed and equal participation of women in social and public life."[46]

That is true elsewhere. So surely there is a need not to just consider what the world can do for women (even though that remains important); there is also a need to consider what women can do for the world, and the potential they can unleash.

Is there a way to change gender bias working with new economists' models? Muhammad Yunus, economist and founder of Grameen Bank, has demonstrated that investing in women is a smart investment. Through the microcredit network he launched that has helped millions of women, he saw this with his own eyes. He noted this, about so-called "human capital": If you read most economics textbooks, good luck finding such things as: "A man." "A woman." "A child." Since "economic theory doesn't recognize that 'labor' is made up of both men and women," the Nobel laureate goes on to lament, "its view of the world is male-dominated (treating 'male' as the 'default value' between male and female)."[47]

Earlier, we traced how this "male-dominated" portrait affects the movie industry. It continues to do so, and the effects are large. The physical and emotional effects of stress take a deep toll[48] (see Box 7.1). Meanwhile, when those in the arts industry are challenged about sexism, they say that is the "nature of the business"; "sex sells." When economists are challenged as to the sexist basis of their terminology and concepts, they say they do this "for the sake of 'simplicity.' "[49] Sometimes this simplicity becomes too simple – to a shocking degree. And while *ceteribus paribus* (all other things being equal) is a useful assumption – indeed, this book has benefited from it – it cannot be a way to hide simple truths in complex mathematical models.[50]

Economists need to simplify things. As Dani Rodrik argues in his book *Economics Rules: The Rights and Wrongs of the Dismal Science*, "simple models of the type that economists construct are absolutely essential to understanding the workings of society. Their simplicity, formalism, and neglect of many facets of the real world are precisely what make them valuable. These are a feature, not a bug. What makes a model useful is that it captures an aspect of reality. What makes it indispensable, when used well," as Rodrik emphasizes, "is that it captures *the most relevant aspect of reality in a given context.*"[51]

"Different contexts – different markets, social settings, countries, time periods, and so on – require different models. And this is where economists typically get into trouble. They often discard their profession's most valuable contribution – the multiplicity of models tailored to a variety of settings – in favor of the search for the one and only universal model."[52] Consider this last point: "When models are selected judiciously, they are a source of illumination. When used dogmatically, they lead to hubris and errors in policy."[53]

At Grameen, Yunus and group realized what economic models and development policy often miss: "to think about men, women, and children not as units of 'labor' but as human beings with varying capacities and needs."[54] What is more, even in the context of the Bollywoods of the world, the women we are talking about are a diverse group. While some belong to religion A, others belong to class B. While some exhibit ambition B, others exhibit desire A. In sum, they lead different lives. Moreover, as actress Nandita Das, who has dealt with the industry's dark-skin prejudices attests, some deal with multiple challenges at once. So any policy for the representation of women in a progressive manner cannot be a monotone.[55] It has to be holistic.

As part of this more complete picture, the noninstrumental justification of gender equality is equally important. Note this point in *Getting to Equal*, a 2016 World Bank report on *Women, Business and the Law*: "We cannot forever remain victims of the idea that the agenda of inclusion and equality (pertaining not just to women but to any group) has to be justified as a means toward the end of higher economic growth. Indeed, what we need to argue is that, even if we

BOX 7.1 On Demeaning Women and a Call for Empathy from None Other than Adam Smith

"The personal stories you hear out of Bollywood – or indeed any competitive industry – include stories of failure only when they are followed by stories of great success," Diksha Basu notes.[58]

Adam Smith, as far-ranging a moral philosopher as they come, sheds light on this tendency in *The Theory of Moral Sentiments*: "It is because mankind are disposed to sympathize more entirely with our joy than with our sorrow, that we make parade of our riches, and conceal our poverty."[59]

But what about the stories of those who face setback after setback, like many women in the face of gender discrimination and sexual violence?

And what about those who twist Smith's words, and find economic justification sexualizing women in films or engaging young girls in brothels: After all, sex sells, and the women are economic agents. In Smith's own words, we can "parade their riches."

Smith himself, though, calls for empathy: "though our sympathy with sorrow is often a more pungent sensation than our sympathy with joy, it always falls much more short of the violence of what is naturally felt by the person principally concerned."[60]

had to sacrifice some economic growth in order to achieve inclusion and greater equality, the trade-off would be well worth it."[56]

Gender equality is too important to be a seen as only a problem for women. But here is the thing: Some female colleagues confided to me that some women *are* the problem. They marginalize fellow women, and abuse men, playing the gender card. A male colleague stressed another concern: There are communities now where the group at risk is boys. But because they are not girls, not much is done about it.

These observations highlight the point that many female colleagues have made: Some women are not into the gender debate.

To some, this whole gender agenda seems a Western thing, imposed on locals. These are not new concerns. That is why considering the diverse parts that make up development is essential. And it is also why the gender issue cannot be "dumped" on women. More men need to be on board. In the arts, more "creative men" need to be part of the solution.

Indeed, what George A. Akerlof and Rachel E. Kranton show in *Identity Economics* deserves attention: "Ethnographic studies indicate that people continue to view some jobs as appropriate for men and others for women. Those who violate these norms are often ambivalent about their work and subject to harassment and even violence."[57] Is the arts community ready to help improve that portrait? Concerned people want to know.

8 The Arts in Mental Health, Social Healing, and Urban Renewal

> Determinants of mental health and mental disorders include not only individual attributes such as the ability to manage one's thoughts, emotions, behaviours and interactions with others, but also social, cultural, economic, political, and environmental factors such as national policies, social protection, living standards, working conditions, and community social supports. Exposure to adversity at a young age is an established preventable risk factor for mental disorders. . . . Depression alone accounts for 4.3 percent of the global burden of disease and is among the largest single causes of disability worldwide . . . particularly for women.
>
> World Health Organization[1]

If the first wealth is health, as Ralph Waldo Emerson put it, then we have yet to fully harvest the benefits of a healthy society when it comes to mental disorders. Mental health does matter. When Margaret Chan, the former World Health Organization's director-general, says that, she is not out of her mind. But why is it that, annually per person, less than $2 is spent on mental health globally, and less than $0.25 in low-income countries? And why is it that almost 70 percent of this money is allocated to standalone mental hospitals that are often notorious for human rights abuses, whose healing powers seem to be negligible?[2] This issue is largely ignored. And it is all the more neglected because many mental disorders are invisible. If you think the world lacks enough doctors, the situation is much worse for pediatric psychologists. Moreover, just as individuals can be depressed, communities can also get depressed. The arts are therapeutic, as they help us get in touch with our inner selves and can help heal our societies. This chapter describes how the arts have been instrumental in healing trauma from Rwanda to Uganda, and renewing cities from Newark to Rio. The stories here are a testament for the need to invest in the arts for mental health, social healing, and urban renewal.

***

"POUNDING THE PAIN": MENTAL CATHARSIS AND SOCIAL HEALING IN RWANDA

Much has been said about the Rwanda's 1994 genocide. Yet we will perhaps never fully know the mental toll this slaughter took on people. When I visited Rwanda fourteen years after the fact, what I saw at the Kigali Memorial Centre continues to haunt me; it was simply horrific. If you are up to it, here is a sample: clothes soaked in dry blood, skulls with ferocious holes, machetes with sharp tongues. I wondered how the Rwandan people could move on.

One group of women has decided to help themselves in a creative way. Besides their ice cream business, they are pounding their pain with nothing but drumming. I am not going to debate the efficacy of this troupe, called Ingoma Nshya. This is because many of us are good at finding one story and then lionizing it as if it were the next New Testament. But the drumbeats of Ingoma Nshya, which is now featured in a documentary, *Sweet Dreams*, deserve a sharp ear.

That ear should especially be attentive, because, seen in a purely instrumental dimension, Rwanda's economic recovery has been impressive. But since human beings are not like roads or buildings, as Rwandan humanitarian Odile Gakire Katese observes, how do you rebuild a person?[3]

Ten years after the genocide, Katese, whose talents ran from acting to writing, started Ingoma Nshya, to help Rwandese women overcome the trauma of genocide. The troupe would also alter the face of Rwanda's male-dominated drumming culture, and lead to the creation of the country's first national drum festival.[4] Katese had researched at Rwanda's ethnographic museum only to discover that one reason why drumming was male-dominated was because it was thought that drums were too heavy for women to carry. Carrying drums is, of course, not the same as playing them. But still, there was another catch: The drums were to be played exclusively for the king.[5]

Overcoming such barriers makes Katese's work multidimensional. First, besides taking a swipe at physical and psychological gender barriers, in equity of cultural expression, women can also be good drummers. This is tenable whether they are playing for the king, for the commoner, or for themselves. Second, Ingoma Nshya, which means "new era," "new kingdom," or "new drum" (depending on which source you consult), illustrates the powerful beat of cultural catharsis. "For the women – orphans, widows, wives and children of perpetrators – the group has been a place to begin to live again, to build new relationships, to heal the wounds of the past."[6]

The historical circumstances of Rwanda's genocide are beyond the scope of this book. But the brutality depended on mental manipulation and twisting human identity: "A person being recruited to join the Hutu killing mob in 1994 was being asked, if only implicitly, not to see himself as a Rwandan, or as an African, or as a human being (identities the targeted Tutsis shared), but only as a Hutu who was duty bound to 'give the Tutsis their due.'"[7]

The butchery was coupled with tens of thousands of rapes. As if that were not enough:

> Assailants sometimes mutilated women in the course of a rape or before killing them. They cut off breasts, punctured the vagina with spears, arrows, or pointed sticks, or cut off or disfigured body parts that looked particularly "Tutsi," such as long fingers or thin noses. They also humiliated the women. One witness from Musambira commune was taken with some 200 other women after a massacre. They were all forced to bury their husbands and then to walk "naked like a group of cattle" some ten miles to Kabgayi. When the group passed roadblocks, militia there shouted that the women should be killed. As they marched, the women were obliged to sing

> the songs of the militia. When the group stopped at nightfall, some of the women were raped repeatedly.[8]

Amidst that orgy of rapes documented by Alison des Forges and others, this recital did not escape my attention: "Women were obliged to sing the songs of the militia." Indeed, the arts can be used for bad purposes. Yet, as I have tried to stress, they can play a vital role in advancing the full dimensions of human wellbeing. One can only pray that Rwanda's economic performance will continue to march from strength to strength, that its benefits will tickle the poorest of the poor. Nonetheless, there is much reason to consider that genocide perhaps still haunts people, and to note what can be done about it.

I focused on the plight of women here, but there are men who also are in the camp of sorrow. This haunting hurts nations in ways that the strategic application of economics may fail to heal. That is why, regardless of their instrumental contribution, the arts do matter. If they continue to aid mental health and social healing, as Rwanda's drumming women show, then they should be hailed for that. And it is not unreasonable to suggest that the arts should go hand in hand with all that matters in building the true wellbeing of nations. After all, "Many sad things become worse because we feel we are alone in suffering them," as Alain de Botton and John Armstrong write in *Art as Therapy*. "We experience our trouble as a curse, or as revealing our wicked, depraved character. So our suffering has no dignity; it seems due only to our freakish nature. We need help in finding honour in some of our worst experiences, and art is there to lend them a social expression."[9]

IF PHYSICAL HEALTH IS THE FIRST WEALTH, IS MENTAL HEALTH THE LAST HEALTH?

In his *Principles of Economics* N. Gregory Mankiw stresses a familiar issue: the link between workers' health and productivity. As he notes, poor health takes a toll on productivity.[10] This problem is especially acute in developing countries. From HIV/AIDS to Ebola, diseases devastate economies in ways impossible to imagine. Health concerns are often linked to physical health. That, however, does not erase the problem of mental health, "a state of well-being in which an individual realizes his or her own abilities, can cope with the normal stresses of life, can work productively and is able to make a contribution to his or her community."[11] Given the diversity of stress around the world, demand for treatment is high, yet supply and prevention are piecemeal. Despite the obviousness of this problem, it is largely ignored.

Consider what Margaret Chan, the former director-general of the World Health Organization, has to say: "Mental health matters, but the world has a long way to go to achieve it."[12] Globally "annual spending on mental health is less than US$2 per person and less than US$0.25 per person in low-income countries, with 67 percent of these financial resources allocated to stand-alone mental hospitals, despite their association with poor health outcomes and human rights violations."[13] There is also a gap in mental specialists. On average, there is one psychiatrist for 200,000 people or more in countries where almost half the world's population lives. Even worse, "mental health care providers who are trained in the use of psychosocial interventions are even scarcer."[14]

In my own Uganda, less than 1 percent of the doctors specialized in psychiatry as of 2010.[15] Pediatric psychologists and other trauma specialists are rare. Part of the problem is the global indifference to this whole menace. In some parts of West Africa, for example, desperate families simply place mental health victims in chains.[16]

As it happens, there is a growing literature on the arts and mental health. There is a need to analyze this literature. For example, the "20 Surprising, Science-Backed Health Benefits of Music" are worth scrutiny. They range from relieving symptoms of depression to elevating moods, to putting people in touch with their feelings.[17] Can these benefits be applied to address the concern of posttraumatic disorder?

AN ARMY OF ARTISTS

In war-torn northern Uganda, posttraumatic disorder is a major problem. Yet the country does not have the capacity to supply psychiatrists. The arts – a tool rarely used – could provide a practical and affordable supplement to therapy. Although they are not a panacea, they could play a prominent role in repairing the torn social fabric in places like northern Uganda.

I became more familiar with the ills of northern Uganda and the enormity of the child-soldier problem on a teaching and performance tour of Uganda and Kenya in 2000. After one organ performance in Kampala, Carl Peeters, then the Belgian consul to Uganda, told me that I needed to visit the Belgian-funded Laroo Boarding Primary School for War-Affected Children.

The so-called Lord's Resistance Army, led by Joseph Kony, which shoulders much of the blame for this conflict, had many stratagems. Here is one: It recruited and rewarded boys with wives for each egregious act they executed. You hear stories that are difficult to believe: A 19-year-old with numerous children from several wives; a 15-year-old young woman who was impregnated by a 17-year-old young man. For girls, it is often unclear who the fathers of their children are; aside from being assigned as wives to teenage boys, they were also raped or made mistresses of older commandos. In addition to accidental parenthood, engaging in killing, raping, maiming, and torturing members of their own community has caused unimaginable emotional damage.

In their posttraumatic state, when many victims return to their communities, they are likely to become enmeshed in crime, in stealing, murder, drugs, and sex slavery. No government in such a society should simply imprison young people who break the law. Building special schools and providing reparations to former child soldiers are welcome actions. But rehabilitating the minds and convincing communities to accept victims are crucial.

In 2009, Randy Kennedy reported on the first United Nations mission that engaged the arts in rehabilitating northern Uganda. UN goodwill ambassador Ross Bleckner[18] traveled to northern Uganda to paint and draw with former child soldiers.[19] When I learned about this story, my exchange with Bleckner confirmed what was reported: Through what Bleckner calls "microcreativity," these children open up by creating something that brings them pride as they struggle to restore their self-worth.[20] Although northern Uganda has rich cultural traditions, during prolonged conflicts, communities are likely to lose their cultural practices. So, in addition to providing catharsis, the arts could help revive the region's cultural heritage, and through mentorship, connect young people with tribal elders.

The "Ugandan government recognizes mental health as a serious public health and development concern, and has recently implemented a number of reforms aimed at strengthening the country's mental health system."[21] Though the government's reforms include developing community mental health services and providing equity of access to such services across different groups, the government is just scratching the surface. An army of artists, armed with art, should be taken seriously in this endeavor. And here, we should avoid the temptation of sprinkling the arts as an add-on. They should be fully integrated in mental health services. At a minimum, artists, collaborating with the ministry of health, could have rotating residencies of, say, three months in districts they are most needed. While I have focused on Uganda, this would be helpful around the world.

HEALING THE SOCIAL ILLS OF DEPRESSED URBAN AREAS

> Cultural policy has much to contribute towards re-revitalising depressed urban areas, improving livability and stimulating urban and regional economic growth.
>
> David Throsby[22]

When we think about mental health and social healing, we should recognize that disorders are not limited to individuals. Cities and regions can also be "depressed." From the favelas of Rio to the inner cities of America, this plight is all too familiar. To focus more on "urban healing," I proceed to America, a place whose GDP is in the trillions of dollars, but that could use a lot more renewal in cities with persistent crime and other social ills. Moreover, as has often noted, even many affluent Americans in good neighborhoods could use a better quality of life.

In his book *Rich, Free, and Miserable,* John Brueggeman points out something that has baffled even Nobel prize-winning economists who are not hostile to markets: "The logic of the market – that everything is for sale and we should strive to get as much as we can – has pushed beyond the economic sphere into other parts of our lives. The most important consequence is a deteriorating capacity for meaningful relationships."[23] You need not have experience in solitary confinement to realize that it can take a toll on people's mental and social wellbeing. In fact, it can be argued that the lack of meaningful relationships (between individuals and communities) also fuels all sorts of inequality.

NEWARK: REPAIRING A CITY'S PSYCHE

A few years ago, I had the opportunity to consult for the New Jersey Performing Arts Center in Newark, New Jersey. While my assignment was in the "digital space" – it was concerning digital technology in arts education – I had to physically move to Newark. Trying to find quick and affordable housing was no breeze. *That park is dangerous, you cannot live near there. That neighborhood is dangerous. Forget that street.* Those are some of the warnings I received. No wonder the New Jersey Performing Arts Center "was the arts center that was never supposed to be built."[24] The tales of caution went on and on. I ended up staying in New York, and then commuting to Newark. Although Newark is just across the harbor from Manhattan, the two cities are almost worlds apart when it comes to such problems as stubborn crime rates.

So when Thomas H. Kean, New Jersey's governor at the time voiced the belief that New Jersey should have its own performing arts center, renewal was a theme. "Ultimately it was decided there was no better place for a Jersey arts center to take root than in Downtown Newark; a building that would not only host the world's greatest performers, but also act as a catalyst for revitalizing the state's largest city."[25] The project cost, as you might guess, was in the millions of dollars: a proposed $300 million for "the complex and four proposed regional centers"[26] for dance, theater, music, and arts education. The plan ended up with one center in Newark at the cost of some $180 million.[27]

The center, which opened in 1997 (the idea had "started in 1986 as a grand plan" by Governor Keane)[28] struck a chord that reached the business community and amassed impressive public and private support. Here is what Robert E. Brooks, then Prudential Insurance Company's vice president of corporate and social responsibility, told the *New York Times*: "'This is the greatest single piece of news we've heard in this city in the past 10 years.' He said Prudential would be 'a strong supporter of this project.'"[29]

Now, I must submit that the arts are not the only tool that can revitalize places. Sports and other activities also count. And whatever the case, good political leadership also plays a role. A drop in crime and soaring real estate prices across the river in New York "helped polish the city's appeal."[30] But the election of Cory A. Booker as mayor of Newark in 2006, some say, enhanced the spirit of change.[31] This goes to show that the arts are one of many ingredients needed to revitalize a city. The arts are useful agents: part of the ecosystem of what makes a city livable, attractive, and even likable. Nonetheless, even with all the improvements, problems persist – and this is the case even if we discount the issue of gentrification and how it can negatively impact artists as noted in Chapter 6.

In a *Business Insider* article entitled "New Jersey's Largest City Is a Mess," Ellen Wulfhorst makes you rethink all what we have said: "A handful of streets in New Jersey's largest city boast glistening apartment towers with floor-to-ceiling views of the Manhattan skyline, but much of the rest of Newark bears the scars of stubbornly high crime rates and persistent poverty."[32] In addition to having one of the highest murder rates in the United States, one in four residents lives in poverty.[33]

Things were not always that way. Newark once was not only a bustling port; it was also a manufacturing center, fixed on a steady march to prosperity. But according to some accounts, events like the 1967 race riots changed all that. They tore the city's social fabric asunder. Moreover, the city experienced its share of political corruption and the so-called white flight. And make what you will of the fact that in 2008, Sharpe James, Newark's five-term mayor, ended up in federal prison for fraud.[34]

In rebuilding the ark of Newark, Booker's successor as mayor, Ras Baraka, son of poet and activist Amiri Baraka, has a difficult journey to navigate. Since coming to office in 2014, he has tackled some tough urban issues: from efforts to "improve public health" and "defuse gangs" to improving the often strained relations between the community and the police. "Supporters see signs of success," according to Wulfhorst. Besides all else that is happening, "the city's performing arts center and sports arena are regularly packed." But "Baraka has a long way to go to mend the city's infrastructure and psyche, which have suffered since Newark was torn apart by race riots a half-century ago."[35] In our context, this last observation is of particular interest. Renewal is not all about building infrastructure; it is also about repairing the people's psyche.

This is because the character of any place is a reflection of people who dwell within it. And it is in building character, and healing psyches, that the positive application of the arts can play a role. While the arts are not a panacea, there is reason to acknowledge the diverse contribution of the New Jersey Performing Arts Center to Newark: In addition to attracting millions of visitors since its opening, the center has reached more than 1.6 million children.[36] When I worked there, the idea to tap into digital technology was to do more, and reach more.

These children need not become professional artists. Nonetheless, given all the troubles that Newark faces, there is much reason to celebrate how the arts can show these children a more hopeful hometown. I say this because in my own Uganda, I grew up at a time when political violence rocked the country. Music at the church (for me, the music center) secured a better existence. Newark and Kampala are worlds apart in many respects. Yet I would bet that children involved in the arts can see a great light, as I did in Kampala. Since the arts enrich people and places, they should be celebrated for their own sake. Equally important, however, they should be tapped for the diverse cultural transformations they can make.

To take quick a look at Asia (I shall comment more on this region later), rapidly urbanizing China faces the challenge of improving lives and livelihoods in its thousands of urban areas. One approach is being taken by the Wanda Group, China's largest cultural enterprise to date (see Chapter 1). According to Wanda Cultural Industry Group President Zhang Lin, Wanda's investments of 50 billion yuan in the Wuhan Central Culture District are expected to contribute over 1 billion yuan in taxes annually and also create more than 30,000 urban jobs. Those instrumental targets notwithstanding, Wanda recognizes that investing in culture can be good for business and also induce notable social benefits, as put forth at the beginning of this book: Cultural industries are greener, because they are not resource guzzlers like manufacturing; they provide higher employee satisfaction; and they can help build social capital and social equality effectively. Indeed, as noted in the discussion on social capital in Chapter 1, the arts have immense potential to induce an environment where gender and other forms of social inequality can be discussed.[37] To expand on such discussions, the next example turns to Brazil. In this place culture is presiding over attempts to build communities in Rio de Janeiro, one song at a time.

BUILDING "HOUSES OF CULTURE AND MUSIC" IN THE MIDDLE OF VIOLENCE IN RIO

It was the Brazilian Grammy-winning song "The Girl from Ipanema" that introduced me to Brazil. The song caught my attention in the early 1990s not at a beach in Rio but at the piano bench at the Sheraton

Kampala, where as noted in Chapter 6, I worked as a pianist. (It was one of those songs that also made the list of guests' favorites.) If music can be interpreted as liquid geography, this bossa nova jazz number captures the rhythms and beauty of the idyllic beach of Ipanema, in Rio de Janeiro.

The description in *The Rio de Janeiro Reader* edited by Daryle Williams, Amy Chazkel, and Paulo Knauss de Mendonça captures the tenor of this glorious city: "The Atlantic Ocean crashes down upon a spectacular coastline that extends across the mile-wide entrance to Guanabara Bay. Oceanic tides pulse throughout a great natural harbor covering more than four thousand square kilometers, but steep mountain ranges flanking the oceanic canal shield coves, islands, marshes and mangrove forests along the bay's inner shores." Levitating like cathedrals of nature, the islands are something else. They "are blessed with unobstructed views of inland mountain ranges (*serras*) of varying heights and shapes, including the Serra dos Órgãos, where the peaks evoke the form of organ pipes." No wonder André Filho's song "Marvelous City," written in 1934, has inspired "the nickname "Marvelous City" and variants such as "Wonder City" and "A Marvel of a City." These labels "have served as shorthand for all that is extraordinary" about Rio de Janeiro's glory.[38]

That glory notwithstanding, Rio has its share of challenges – challenges that cannot be easily abbreviated. For one, Brazil is no stranger to sharp inequality. The juxtaposition of the favelas or shantytowns, filled with narcotics, violence, and biting poverty amidst Rio the marvelous, is hard to comprehend. There are more than 6,000 favelas, and they shelter about one-third of Rio's more than 6 million people.[39] Imagine raising children under such circumstances, where drug dealers are like warlords, command more control than the police, and are more present than parents.

When the American musician and producer Quincy Jones first beheld the favelas, there were "more than three thousand kids with no parents." That was way back in 1956, when he was touring Brazil with Dizzy Gillespie's group on a US State Department tour. So what is the picture today? Regardless of the time span and the changes in numbers of children, "the ghetto is the ghetto." That conclusion comes from no less an artist than Jones, who "grew up in the South Side of Chicago during the Great Depression." The social canvas of ghettos, whether in Newark or Rio, is punctured by the same problems worldwide.[40] Against the backdrop of poverty and inequality of Rio, "AfroReggae, a movement that uses music and culture to provide hope and opportunity to young people, is taking the favelas back – one song at a time."[41]

In their book, *Culture Is Our Weapon*, Patrick Neate and Damian Platt note that AfroReggae, a nongovernmental organization, almost had no choice but to get started: "If it was a punch-up that conceived AfroReggae, it was a tragedy that gave birth to the movement." In 1993, thirty police officers shot and killed twenty-one innocent citizens in the Vigário, a large favela in Rio; this was in retaliation for the murder of four officers. This so-called Vigário Geral Massacre drew a symphony of outcry worldwide.[42] As the documentary based on AfroReggae, *Favela Rising*, confirms, the massacre triggered an artist movement. Here is how things unfolded:

> Among the residents killed was the brother of Anderson Sá, a former drug-trafficker who as a response to his personal tragedy became a social revolutionary. Anderson began to search for ways to end the violence in Vigario Geral. On his search, he met Jose Junior, another resident who had been campaigning for a change in the favela. Together, they formed AfroReggae, a movement was to counteract violence through music and dance.[43]

By 1994, "AfroReggae had established their first Núcleo Comunitário de Cultura." (Community Nucleus for Culture). Whether offering workshops in recycling or percussion or dance, the objective was simple: to provide "an alternative to drug trafficking and *subemprego* – underemployed."[44] Through such projects as the Conexões Urbanas (Urban Connections), AfroReggae has connected with the city government to engage the favelas with amity. This event provides free concerts in favelas, featuring guests and local stars. Be it bringing in Gilberto Gil, a musician with trumpets of political activism who served as minister of culture in Lula da Silva's administration, or funk DJ Marlboro, or hip-pop crew Racionais MCs of São Paulo, Urban Connections has tried its best to revitalize the worst of Rio.[45] But what is in this for the children?

Another Brazilian artist and political activist, Caetano Veloso, known for his participation in Brazil's Tropicália musical movement, shares what he saw: "I have seen for myself very young children handling heavy weapons and it's still unbelievable to me. But AfroReggae? These guys teach younger children how to play and, in doing so, they keep them out of trafficking. They have built houses of culture and music right in the middle of all this violence."[46] Neate and Platt further explain:

> Every AfroReggae nucleus has a different approach that has been designed over time and tailored to the needs of the parent community. Whereas the organization's presence in Vigário, for example, is primarily cultural, with emphasis on music, theater, and dance, in Lucas they have a computer technology center, bringing state-of-the-art equipment and training to the favela. Contagalo, on the other hand, part of a complex of three favelas high on the hillsides above Copacabana and Ipanema, is where the circus project is based.[47]

The program not only courts poor communities. In 2004, for example, AfroReggae decided to engage military police battalions with "cultural invasions." This was in the neighboring state of Minas Gerais. From percussion to dance, streetball, graffiti to theatre, for some four months, these "invasions" targeted the police – but in a good way, to integrate them into the community.[48] It was a prime example of using culture to establish meaningful relationships.

These activities put people at the center of development. They are investments in the cultural capital of the community. Denise Dora of the Ford Foundation – which has supported AfroReggae under the aegis of its human-rights initiative – observes: "'The killing of young people is one of the main human rights problems in Brazil; both in terms of impunity and the public acceptance that allows the police or others to carry out these killings. Unfortunately, they are so common now that people just accept them without being made to feel in any way uncomfortable.'" As she goes on to say, "This is a key problem for Brazilian society as a whole."[49] But you need not look far to realize that even the United States has not escaped this problem.

There are no universal answers to fix this problem, one that has increasingly become an invisible war between the police and young people. Yet in the need to restore trust, equity, and human rights, as initiatives like AfroReggae demonstrate, artistic interventions have a role to play. They respond to the whole person – their sense of community, their creativity, and their sense of worth. They demonstrate to the residents of the favelas (and elsewhere) that they are important and worthwhile.

They are also immediate and tangible. "'If you see the right thing to do,'" as Dora concludes, "'you just have to do it. That's what AfroReggae does and that's why they're so effective and so important.'"[50]

Rio's beauty is also immediate and tangible – the stunning backdrop to the scenes played out every day on the streets of the favelas. Looming over the city is the world's largest Art Deco statue, the Christ the Redeemer that invites visitors to Corcovado Mountain.[51] And on the whole, the place seems to be ornamented by mountains of beauty. It comes as no surprise therefore that in 2012, UNESCO designated Rio's "Carioca Landscapes between the Mountain and the Sea" as a World Heritage Site, noted for "Outstanding Universal Value":

> The dramatic landscape of Rio de Janeiro has provided inspiration for many forms of art, literature, poetry, and music. Images of Rio, which show the bay, Sugar Loaf and the statue of Christ the Redeemer have had a high worldwide recognition factor, since the middle of the 19th century. Such high recognition factors can be

> either positive or negative: in the case of Rio, the image that was projected, and still is projected, is one of a staggeringly beautiful location for one of the world's biggest cities.[52]

Rio's sweeping beauty, though, is not the end of the story. Indeed, beauty or "high recognition factors" can be either positive or negative. As with any big city, Rio's problems go beyond the problems of its ghettos. There are mountains of problems elsewhere, even in Rio's waters. While Rio has much to celebrate for hosting the 2016 Olympics, consider this: In August 2015, scientists found that a "2016 Rio Olympics water venue is full of human waste and teeming with viruses."[53]

Of course, a variety factors contribute to why human waste and viruses were in these Olympic waters. Is it the poverty in the favelas? Is it people's attitudes? Is it the government's sustained indifference? Is it a combination of all the above? Whatever the case, as Throsby notes, cultural policy has much to contribute to the renewal and livability of places and even stimulate economic growth.[54] This, in turn, fuels the complementarity of social and economic progress. And if we put human beings at the center of development, the linkages between mental health, social healing, and urban renewal are not hostile to one another. They dance together.

MENTAL HEALTH AND THE ARTS IN ASIA AND THE PACIFIC: A BRIEF INQUIRY

We have roved from Uganda to Rwanda, and from Newark to Rio, touching on how the arts can ignite healing and renewal. But before closing this chapter let me recapitulate the issue of mental health. I will do so by commenting a little on the situation in the Asia-Pacific region. After all, mental disorders that can arise from the pressure to succeed as noted in the Overture are not limited to Taiwan.

Across the world, having people reach their highest potential is a prime development objective. Yet according to an Economist Intelligence Unit study sponsored by Janssen Asia Pacific, "Mental illness is the second largest contributor to years lost due to disability (YLDs) in the Asia-Pacific region." This echoes the link between health and productivity, not to mention other aspects of wellbeing people have reason to value. "Nowhere, though, do more than half of those affected receive any medical treatment. This is not some temporary crisis. It is business as usual."[55] What is new?

In the instrumental bearing, which no doubt enjoys broad policy attention, the economic hits are mega: Between circa 2016 and 2030, economic growth in India and China is expected to suffer a reduction of some $11 trillion due to mental health. In Australia and New Zealand, the problem presently knocks 3.5 and 5 percentage points off GDP, respectively. And because "the effect of suicide – a particularly large problem in South Korea and Japan – is not included in these calculations, the real human and financial cost of mental illness is likely far worse."[56]

Fortunately, from Japan to Indonesia mental health policy is gaining traction. This is the case even at such bodies as the Asia-Pacific Economic Cooperation and the Association of Southeast Asian Nations. Yet this malaise is not the easiest to contain. First of all, there is the issue of stigma. Even here, it is not unusual for patients to find themselves chained. Other issues include rural-urban divides, the complexity of the illness itself, and access to treatment.[57] How can the arts help?

As is the case elsewhere, in the Asia-Pacific region the arts have played a prominent role in the deliverance of people from mental sorrow.[58] The act of ink brush painting in Asia, for example, has been attributed to calming people's moods – and this is not only as they paint, but also as they view their final creation. (This takes us back to northern Uganda and Bleckner's theory of microcreativity.) Besides visual arts, the tradition and practice of qigong and bell chimes are also prominent in the Asian catalog of arts-based therapy.[59]

These Asian arts-based therapies are not just for the ill. Unlike contemporary Western models, they are important in maintaining health and wellbeing in people's daily lives. "Given the traditional use of the arts in the service of self-cultivation, relaxation and meditation," moreover, "it's not surprising that the field of art therapy has made tremendous gains in Asia," according to *Art Therapy in Asia*, a volume edited by Debra L. Kalmanowitz and others.[60] That is a strong statement. But to consider Amitav Gosh's *Dancing in Cambodia, At Large in Burma*, for example, is to allow that the arts can indeed revive a people.[61] This is so, because even the "sudden and spontaneous bouts of joy only strengthen the belief that artistic heritage is the very life and soul of a nation."[62]

A UK study called "Quantifying and Valuing the Wellbeing Impacts of Culture and Sport" seems to collaborate the above conviction: "Arts engagement was found to be associated with higher wellbeing. This is valued at £1,084 per person per year, or £90 per person per month."[63]

Such quantification aside, here is the thing: across the world, the determinants of mental health go beyond individual attributes. There are also "social, cultural, economic, political and environmental factors such as national policies, social protection, living standards, working conditions, and community social supports."[64] So "promoting mental health and preventing mental disorders extends across all sectors and all government departments."[65] It is a shared responsibility. Although the arts are not panaceas, they are powerful agents that drive progress, even in mental health and social renewal. I will insist on that, even as I acknowledge the goodness of art for art's sake.

CODA

The organization called FundaMentalSDG, which petitioned the United Nations to include mental health in the Sustainable Development Goals, proclaims: "We are committed to the belief that there can be no health without mental health, and that there can be no substantial development without including mental health into the UN Development Agenda 2030."[66] The Sustainable Development Goals indeed mention mental health. Consider target 3.4: "By 2030, reduce by one third premature mortality from non-communicable diseases through prevention and treatment and promote mental health and well-being."[67]

Whether mention in the Sustainable Development Goals is sufficient or not, that is another matter. On that note, it remains to be seen whether people, cities, countries, and even organizations such as the World Health Organization will fully engage the arts in "promoting mental health and preventing mental disorders."[68] I particularly mention the World Health Organization because in its *Mental Health Action Plan 2013–2020*, you will be hard pressed to find any reference to the arts and mental welfare. Yet the plan trumpets the need for shared responsibility. While promoting mental health is good for its own sake, mental illness carries a high price tag as we have seen – from loss of productivity and crushing health bills to unsafe types of behavior and poverty. These consequences amount to billions of dollars worldwide.

Since cost-benefit analyses are revered by some economists as if they were catechisms, I am not sure if any of the arts programs mentioned here has been evaluated. Maybe economists and statisticians will one day take on that thankless task. My simple reading is that at the practical level, such analyses could sharpen the debate of what works and what does not, and what is exaggerated and what is implicitly accepted. In fact, since we have hinted at measuring things impossible to measure, get set for Chapter 9, which considers some numbers behind the story here. Meanwhile, the arts are not waiting for data to make a difference. They continue to heal and renew, one beat at a time, one place at a time. The choice of whether to fully tap them is ours.

PART IV Rondo: A Round-Up of Data

9 Creative Data Collection

> I sometimes feel that seeing the world through the eyes of an economist is like seeing the world through the ears of a bat. We notice a lot that others miss, and we miss a lot that others notice.
>
> Tim Harford, Undercover Economist[1]

Data collection is a hot-button issue in the arts and development debate. I have been concerned about this for a while, because I am often challenged to find numbers to support anecdotal evidence or intriguing examples of the arts' role in development. In some circles, for example, you can easily be seen as a snake oil salesman when you suggest that the arts are good for mental health without having an iota of data to back that claim. The debate is further complicated by the fact that many in the arts community, for good reason, are not into data collection. This chapter suggests that we should try to collect "creative data" where we can. Numbers, like pitches, are not the problem. But just as pitches can be off tune, numbers, too, can be off base. In his candid book, *Poor Numbers,* Morten Jerven reminds us that data too often determines the allocation of resources. Yet statistical capacities of countries like those in Africa are in a sorry state.[2] The issue, then, is that even statistics on areas like the rate of economic growth have to be improved and assessed in a holistic manner. Along that path, this chapter considers the collection of cultural data, even as it allows that we cannot really capture all of what the arts can offer in numbers.

***

A few years ago, when Craigslist was "the" list, a friend circulated an ad posted on Craigslist Vancouver. It went like this:

> We are a small & casual restaurant in downtown Vancouver. We are looking for solo musicians to play in our restaurant to promote their work and sell their CD. This is not a daily job, but only for special

> events, which will eventually turn into a nightly event if we get positive response. More jazz, rock, & smooth-type music around the world and mixed cultural music. Are you interested in promoting your work? Please reply back ASAP.

One musician found it necessary to reply as follows:

> I am a musician with a big house looking for a restauranteur to promote their restaurant and come to my house to make dinner for my friends and me. This is not a daily job, but only for special events, which will eventually turn into a nightly event if we get positive response. More fine dining & exotic meals and mixed ethnic fusion cuisine. Are you interested in promoting your restaurant? Please reply back ASAP.[3]

It is perhaps unfair to conclude that the restaurateurs did not mean well. But even without making any quick judgments, what does this picture tell you? How are the arts normally valued, consciously or unconsciously, in our social order?

What is true at the micro level – as captured in the exchange between the musician and restaurateurs – is also true at the macro level. National accounts severely undervalue the arts and culture.[4]

This gap touches on what the legendary pianist Vladimir Horowitz noted: "The notes in the score did not tell you what the music was. The music was *behind* the notes." The performer's job is to search for this music.[5] Likewise, data do not tell us the complete story. Data, like a music score, are just there to guide us. It is our job to search for the human story behind the data.

Finding that story means we need more effective emphasis on analysis, for data on their own are not enough. Although the quest for data may help us answer questions, in connection to what I alluded to in the Prelude to this book, that is not enough. We also need to assess the answers we get in a genuine and holistic manner.[6] That habit by another legendary Vladimir named Vladimir Nabokov, author, chess problem composer, entomologist, and lepidopterist, is especially pertinent when dealing with data and their diverse manifestations. Moreover, as Nobel-economist Angus Deaton has argued, even the basic economic development facts, such as GDP growth rates, ought to be deeply debated much more than is the case.[7]

This is all the more important when you ponder what Morten Jerven writes in *Poor Numbers*: Data demand and dependence continue to march onward and upward. And "evidence-based-policy" has become a buzzword in development circles, as if evidence is for evidence's sake. In the stampede to find evidence, Jerven goes on to say, scholars are increasingly employing complex econometric methods, borrowing techniques from medical sciences. Yet while scholars borrow methods and metaphors from such disciplines – this borrowing is actually fine if used judiciously – the accuracy of lab experiments is surely not the same as economic development observations. What is more, bordering on that line "lies, damned lies and statistics," a great many times what is called evidence based is not evidence based at all. It is a patchwork "based on educated guesses, competing, and debatable assumptions," dressed as figures of objective data. "Leading scholars know that the data are weak," Jerven assures us, "but most data users are incapable of judging exactly how weak and how this weakness affects policy analysis."[8] This is why the art of assessing the answers we get is important.

In many ways, this assessment is not the same thing as a teacher ticking off right or wrong answers from an answer sheet. It requires constant adaptation, holistic interpretation, and even unlearning bad habits. Jerven cites that in some cases experts have made a ritual of training local statisticians on how to use the latest software. Yet the real challenge – how to deal with "absent or deficient data" – is not emphasized.[9] If we are lax in assessing answers the latest software churns out, we are unlikely to know how to deal with absent or poor numbers.

Even more important, when we are earnest in assessing outcomes we are more likely to ask the right questions. Here historians of science have much to teach us. As they often observe, "asking the right question is more important than producing the right answer." Leading myrmecologist Edward O. Wilson makes that point clear: "The right answer to a trivial question is also trivial, but the right question, even when insoluble in exact form, is a guide to major discovery."[10]

And in the search for major discoveries, just as the absence of notes does not mean that the music is not there – recall that a lot of music around the world is not the easiest to notate (as noted in Chapter 2) – the same can be said of data. Its absence does not mean that the story is not there. Echoing that point in her book *Big Data, Little Data, No Data*, Christine L. Borgman, author of the award-winning monographs *Scholarship in the Digital Age* and *From Gutenberg to the Global Information Infrastructure*, has this to say: "Having no data is all too often the case, whether because no relevant data exist; they exist but cannot be found; exist but are not available due to proprietary control, embargoes, technical barriers, degradation due to lack of curation; or simply because those who have the data cannot or will not share them."[11]

Above all, "Data are neither truth nor reality." (*Poor Numbers* should remind us of this.) "They may be facts, sources of evidence, or principles of argument that are used to assert truth or reality." No wonder when it comes to defining data, a term that has enjoyed five centuries of usage, the only agreement that enjoys broad consensus is this: there is no single definition. The term *data* is not "a pure concept nor are data natural objects with an essence of their own," according to Borgman. And in isolation, data do not function. "The most inclusive summary is to say that data are representations of observations, objects, or other entities used as evidence of phenomena for the purposes of research or scholarship."[12]

To allow that the term "data" is synonymous with "statistics," moreover, is to note that historically statistics did not always involve churning out numbers. Take Germany, where the term *Statistik* originated in the late eighteenth century. In this land of Bach, "the challenge was to map disparate customs, institutions and laws across an empire of hundreds of micro-states," according to William Davies. "What characterized this knowledge as statistical was its holistic nature: it aimed to produce a picture of the nation as a whole. Statistics would do for populations what cartography did for territory."[13]

Fast-forward to today: Statistics have undoubtedly evolved. All the same, this process even now has been mostly concerned with what we make it a priority to measure. In that sense, biased priorities lurk in our minds. So, how can we blame national statistical accounts for lacking cultural data without checking our mindsets? Consider the following story. It might be called a master class on cultural valuation, because in a way, it recapitulates the Craigslist exchange in the preamble to this chapter.

In 2007, the *Washington Post* performed an experiment on context, perception, and priorities that involved world-renowned violinist Joshua Bell playing incognito. The experiment was at the L'Enfant Plaza Metro Station in Washington, DC, during morning rush hour. For a virtuoso who can command compensation of $1,000 a minute, playing masterpieces on a Stradivarius violin that cost about $3.5 million, you would think that Bell would take the metro station by storm, even during rush hour.[14]

But the experiment proved otherwise. More than 1,000 people passed by, many of them rushing to work. The most Bell could make for his forty-three-minute performance was $32 and some change.[15] If commuters knew about this performance, the results of this experiment would probably have been different. Indeed, when the event was announced and repeated seven years later at another venue, in Washington's Union Station, Bell's reception was different. "Just by announcing it and having people ready to listen, you saw the difference," Bell said. "It was actually pretty electric, with a lot of people packed in. It was a nice bookend, the exact opposite of what happened the first time."[16]

If we are ready to listen, if we pay attention, the narrative of the human experience is bookended by culture. If anything, the Joshua

Bell experiment should remind us of this. Culture and the arts have a huge and vibrant economic and social story to tell. In fact, if you use this story as a yardstick for assessment, our use of the term "developing countries," as some argue, should perhaps be retired. As we have seen, even the poorest of nations have immense cultural wealth. Yet the arts are often dismissed on the premise that they cannot be measured, or that their data are nonexistent or "invisible." In cartography it is like saying that one established territory is not there because we cannot draw or read its map. This does no good to the arts community. It does no good for data-driven policy makers. And this thinking marginalizes the poor whose livelihoods may depend on (or benefit from) their artistic activities, or those whose voice is amplified through the arts.

Complicating measurement is the fact that cultural activities span a variety of sectors, including education; trade and competitiveness; poverty; and urban, rural, and social development. To deal with this range, cross-cutting solutions must be considered, in such areas as jobs; gender; and fragility, conflict, and violence.

An even further complication is the fact that "there are purists who shirk at the mention of art and commerce in one breath,"[17] as Kaushik Basu puts it.

More than twenty years ago the Danish economist Trine Bille Hansen asked a question that touches on the gist of the issue that we have been examining in this book: "How can the economic value of the arts be calculated?" She argued that in this calculation, numerous analyses tend to focus on how the arts contribute to the baskets of consumption and income, balance of payments and employment. "On this basis it has been said that it is 'good for business' for the government to invest in the arts – because the money comes back again in the form of industrial development, employment, tourist earnings, direct and indirect taxes," et cetera.[18] No doubt. And since this book pivots on the complementarity and the diversity of the arts' contribution to development, I have not shied away from such analyses. Hansen's point, however, is that the basis of such analyses is incorrect because "the *purpose* of the activity" is not accounted for. She suggests that it is essential to evaluate the arts by their contribution to creativity and innovation and to the quality of life.[19]

Surely, recognizing such an approach has implications for arts policy and research.[20] In fact, with respect to enriching people's lives, the arts and subjective wellbeing measurements should be encouraged more.[21]

That said, much has changed since Hansen made those remarks. The arts' contribution to employment, income generation, international trade in cultural goods and services, and so on, is becoming part and parcel of government policy formation, as are questions of intellectual property.[22] No doubt there is more to be done. But why should calculating the arts' contribution to innovation and creativity or to the quality of life be seen as excluding accounting for their contribution to employment, income, and the like?

To some extent, the points above take us back to Chapter 2 on the role of arts education. For artistic pedagogy, even for its own sake, can be a locus for creativity, innovation, and overall wellbeing. But as we saw in Chapter 1, we can find creativity and innovation at work even in the instrumental wings of clusters like Nashville. And focusing on mental health, social healing, and urban renewal, Chapter 8 attempted to place the people's quality of life at the center – even if this is provided in tandem with both social and economic welfare.

Whether you agree with Hansen's position or not, do we not need to do a better job understanding and measuring the dimensions of culture and the arts in the economy and in society? Do we not need better partnerships to gather data? And do we not need creativity to capture data fully? This chapter explores those questions.

THE COMPLEX SYMPHONY: CREATIVE DATA COLLECTION

According to the World Bank, only one-quarter of its member countries "have adequate capacity and data to assess progress in poverty reduction and shared prosperity, and to account for sustainable development."[23]

The case for a sound arts policy in development is often weakened by the lack of data. The reasons for this border on what Borgman has observed, as we saw earlier, and they include the difficulty in measuring the true value of the intangible and tangible aspects of the arts in purely quantitative terms; the reluctance of some in the arts community to push for what they see as the "commodification" of the arts; the political and development priorities at hand; and the fact that a lot of arts services are cash-related transactions, if reported at all. With respect to the performing arts, the United Nations explains: "Income from [the] performing arts derives from box-office revenues, national and international touring, performance royalties and taxation, for which data are seldom collected or reported nationally" even in developed countries; "consequently, it is impossible to conduct a global comparative analysis. Performing arts are a special case, since their products are expressed as an intangible or immaterial service, unlike other creative industries where figures for tangible goods (such as a piece of sculpture in the case of visual arts) serve as the basis for a quantitative analysis."[24]

Even the data available on the arts can raise questions about the methodology used. There may be huge gaps that are impossible to identify readily, making standardization and compatibility difficult to achieve.

For example, if the music industry's contribution for one city in one country – Nashville – has been estimated in 2013 at over $5 billion (see Chapter 1), even if the time span is over a decade, how come the estimates for the performing arts exports worldwide are much lower: only about $2.7 billion as of 2002 (see Table 9.1)? In Chapters 4, 5, and 6, we saw that African countries, which make up a huge chunk of developing countries, have yet to do better in trade. Yet according to the United Nations data presented in Table 9.1, about a half of creative-goods exports were from developing countries.

It could be that the way the data are collected and interpreted varies greatly from region to region, even within rich countries. For instance, audio-visuals and dance, drama, or music lessons could be

Table 9.1 *Exports of creative goods by economic group, 2002 and 2011 (in millions of US$)*

	World		Developing		Developed		Transition	
	2002	2011	2002	2011	2002	2011	2002	2011
All creative goods	198,240	454,019	73,890	227,867	123,169	222,597	1,181	3,555
Art crafts	17,503	34,209	9,201	23,383	8,256	10,653	45	172
Audio-visuals	455	492	35	90	417	400	3	2
Design	114,694	301,262	53,362	172,223	60,970	127,239	362	1,800
New media	17,506	43,744	4,412	14,607	13,071	28,918	23	219
Performing arts	2,754	–	250	–	2,478	–	26	–
Publishing	29,908	43,077	3,157	8,106	26,061	33,650	690	1,321
Visual arts	15,421	31,127	3,474	9,456	11,916	21,631	31	40

Source: UN 2013, 161.

Note: "Transition" means from moving from one economic system to another, such as ex-socialist countries moving to market-based economies. And "goods" here probably include services given the composition of the items listed.

seen as part of the performing arts, to some extent, and not solely as education. But how are such distinctions captured in data and statistical analyses across the world? And if many cultural goods and services are also composed of inputs from diverse parts of the world, then how is this captured in the final tabulations of cultural trade data? Is there no need to consider such questions?

Moreover, if we take a step back, the great problem of dubious accounting is not limited to statistical deficiencies in poor countries. It is a longstanding problem even in rich countries. Consider the so-called Hollywood accounting or Hollywood bookkeeping. A movie such as the 1983 *Return of the Jedi,* which made almost half a billion dollars against a budget of $32 million, has been deemed "unprofitable." The reasons for this might be various. But are they difficult to decouple from corporate greed? Does the mendacity of such practices not render it difficult to trust the industry's data, not to mention the issue of fair pay for artists? "Most corporations try to make a profit by limiting costs," as Derek Thompson, the author of *Hit Makers* observes, but in Hollywood economics, movie "corporations manage to record a loss by maximizing costs."[25] The movie industry may provide statistical evidence for these losses. But to what extent are these data "evidence-based," or are they "evidence-baked" instead?

Even beyond Hollywood economics, in *The End of Accounting and the Path Forward for Investors and Managers,* Baruch Lev and Feng Gu write that companies' financial reports have largely deteriorated, to the detriment of investment and credit decisions. These reports no longer reflect the essential factors that confer on businesses a sustained competitive advantage and that create corporate value.[26] The authors maintain that the major drivers of value have shifted from such areas as property, plant, machinery, and inventories to brands, patents, human resources, information technologies, and other intangibles.[27] Given the transition from the industrial age to the information age, this is not difficult to see.

Yet, entrenched in the past, the so-called generally accepted accounting principles (GAAP) continued to march to the beat of their own drum, treating these new value creators as ordinary expenses. "That accounting, say Lev and Gu, distorted both the balance sheets and the income statements of intellectually based companies, rendering reported financial information increasingly irrelevant."[28] This is not the moment to go into the debate about what Lev and Gu propose should be done (they also discuss media and entertainment). But acknowledging their argument opens up a need to look into what actually creates a company's true value today, and whether data on this phenomenon is up to date with the latest realities of valuation. This is especially important because, as Diane Coyle, founder of the "Enlightenment Economics" group in Great Britain, has argued, economics has yet to give us the tools for valuing intangibles. And there are even fewer tools for valuing intangibles with public good characteristics and social externalities.[29]

The already intricate creative economy is under constant transformation, propelled by unrelenting technological advances. Therefore, it is critical to emphasize the value of partnerships in collecting data. Here the World Bank's pledge to "promote a call to action for all development actors to work in concert" is a welcome signal. It is welcome precisely because no single agency can act alone in realizing the momentous process of development. "Partnerships need to operate on every scale, from multibillion dollar programs with global constituencies to village cooperatives."[30]

PUBLIC AND PRIVATE PARTNERSHIPS FOR CREATIVE DATA COLLECTION

The need to forge partnerships in the quest for data on the creative economy is apparent. After all, the interactions of the arts range from multibillion-dollar global agencies to minute village cooperatives. Nonetheless, these partnerships should not be limited to such agencies. As I will argue in the finale of this book, an effort of collaboration across disciplines, between economists and noneconomists, between artists and nonartists, is also crucial. This is the case even though partnerships themselves are not panaceas immune from freeriding, competition, unaligned interests, and other challenges.[31] In any event, here are some possibilities.

Develop a National Database on Cultural Assets

Since most developing countries lack even simple databases on cultural assets, Japan's statistics on cultural properties provide a blueprint of what could be done (see Table 9.2). Counting such properties may provide an entry point to the inquiry of how many jobs they

Table 9.2 *Japan's cultural properties designated by the national government (as of June 1, 2017)*

Type of cultural properties	Number	
Designated important cultural properties	13,119	a) 1,101
Fine arts and crafts	10,654	a) 878
Structures	2,465	a) 223
Historic sites, places of scenic beauty and natural monuments	3,210	b) 172
Historic sites	1,784	b) 61
Places of scenic beauty	402	b) 36
Natural monuments	1,024	b) 75
Important tangible folk cultural properties	220	
Important intangible folk cultural properties	303	
Important intangible cultural properties		
Recognized individuals	76	
Performing arts	37	
Craft techniques	39	
Recognized holding groups	27	
Performing arts	13	
Craft techniques	14	
Traditional building preservation areas	114	

a) National treasures only; b) Specially designated places only.
Source: Ministry of Education, Culture, Sports, Science and Technology.
Source: "Statistical Handbook of Japan 2017" (Statistics Bureau, Ministry of Internal Affairs and Communications) www.stat.go.jp/english/data/handbook/pdf/2017all.pdf#page=197.

provide, revenue and taxes they generate (or absorb), and so forth. Organizations and countries could work with the public and private sectors to count the cultural properties of given countries, including assessing intangible properties like the performing arts. Recognizing the value of these cultural properties could lead to important spin-offs in the areas of education and cultural preservation, as in Japan:

> As of June 1, 2017, 13,119 items were assigned as designated important cultural properties, of which 1,101 were classified as national treasures. In addition, the government has provided support for such activities as theatrical performances, music, handicrafts, and other important intangible cultural properties. It also has worked to preserve important folk-cultural properties, such as annual cultural events and folk performing arts, as well as to train people to carry on such traditions.[32]

For this type of exercise to be effective, however, there is a need to move away from thinking that accounting for cultural assets is a luxury, which only rich countries like Japan can afford.

Build on Efforts by UNESCO, the World Bank, and the World Trade Organization to Measure the Contribution of Culture to Economic Development

In 2013, UNESCO approved the Hangzhou Declaration, "Placing Culture at the Heart of Sustainable Development Policies."[33] "In this context," as UNESCO explains, "understanding the contribution of cultural employment to the economy is vital. Without appropriate methods of measurement and reliable statistics, countries lack the tools necessary to evaluate the extent and characteristics of cultural employment in a comparable way."[34]

UNESCO's Institute for Statistics (UIS) has reported "developing a global survey on cultural employment statistics using the methodology of the 2009 UNESCO Framework for Cultural Statistics. The results will shed light on the contribution of culture to economic and social development, as well as the conditions of those engaged in cultural activities."[35] Partnerships between UIS and other organizations may help answer questions that UIS is raising: What is "the size of the cultural labour force in the economy"? What is the "social status of women in cultural employment"? And "how many artists are employed as performers"?[36]

The framework for such a partnership could be similar to one the World Bank and the World Trade Organization inaugurated in 2013, when the two institutions agreed to develop and maintain a database on trade in services.[37] It could extend to include the United Nations Statistics Division, taking into account the dimension of trade in cultural services.

Make an Effort to Measure Cultural Trade in Value Added

As we saw in Chapter 4, many goods and services we buy include inputs from various corners of the globe, as the Organization for Economic Co-operation and Development and the World Trade Organization note. That composition notwithstanding, conventional measures of international trade do not always reflect this phenomenon. The joint OECD-WTO initiative, "Measuring Trade in Value Added" (TiVa), "addresses this issue by considering the value added by each country in the production of goods and services that are consumed worldwide. TiVA indicators are designed to better inform policy makers by providing new insights into the commercial relations between nations."[38]

Here, Pascal Lamy observes an issue that echoes the need to see beyond the immediate answers we get: "The statistical bias created by attributing commercial value to the last country of origin perverts the true economic dimension of the bilateral trade imbalances. This affects the political debate, and leads to misguided perceptions."[39] In trying to correct those perceptions TiVa estimates are not short of shortcomings. And, at the moment, as Timothy Sturgeon, a contributor to Global Value Chain theory, has argued, TiVa's shortcomings should not escape treatment with great caution.[40] All the same, as improvements get made, how can TiVa or similar exercises be expanded to include effective measurement of value added in cultural trade?

Even more ambitious, if the arts fuel imaginations, which then contribute to value chains in unexpected ways, if at all possible, how can such artistic value added be captured effectively in global trade statistics?

Team Up with Regional Development Banks

Other partnerships could be forged with regional development banks – such as the African Development Bank, the Asian Development Bank, and the Inter-American Development Bank (IDB) – to collect and share data on the creative economy and cultural assets.

For instance, the IDB has prepared a report on "The Economic Impact of the Creative Industries in the Americas," a "collation of existing quantitative data on the economic performance of the creative and cultural industries."[41] It "surveys forty-four countries – including thirty-four countries in the Americas and ten benchmark countries from other regions around the world. It also recommends ways to improve and standardize national measurement frameworks to better track trends within and across countries and support more evidence-based policymaking."[42] The database that accompanies the report could be expanded.

Commission Groups to Collect and Standardize Data on the Cultural Sector

IDB's approach provides a feasible example of what other development banks, organizations, and countries could do. The World Bank and others could commission a study on "cultural data" for certain regions or countries. This could be done with such entities as Oxford Economics; the Living Standards Measurement Study under the World Bank's Development Economics Research Group; or the World Bank's Development Economics Data Group (DECDG). For instance, select countries could be encouraged to apply for grants from DECDG to collect data on their cultural industries.

This approach may contribute to the standardization (or harmonization) of the cultural sector's statistical codes from region to region in the long term. Imperfect as it may be, it may be better than nothing. And it may also help the creation of *The Little Data Book on Cultural Industries*.

Update the System of National Accounts

The System of National Accounts, "the internationally agreed standard set of recommendations on how to compile measures of economic activity,"[43] could be updated to more completely reflect the creative economy. Along those lines, updating the Standard Industrial Classification and the Standard Occupational Classification to truly account for services and culture would be a huge step forward.[44] As things stand, these codes deal with manufacturing in detail. For services, however, that is hardly the case. Even more important, cultural activities are more likely to cross several sector headings. So, while culture is as big or bigger than finance, it is invisible for this reason.[45]

Another area of attention and collaboration are the satellite accounts, which "[focus] on a certain field or aspect of economic and social life in the context of national accounts," such as the environment, or and tourism.[46] Coyle, who has advised the UK Treasury, argues that accounts labeled "satellite" might have a hard time becoming influential as long as political debates continue to focus on economic growth.[47] Whether that picture will change anytime soon remains to be seen. In any event, the European Commission's manual on tourism provides a model for a cultural satellite account.

Three points from this manual merit attention. First, instead of just focusing on evident components, define the bits and pieces of the whole economy linked to the cultural sector. Second, consider adopting methodologies used to measure other sectors in national accounts, but bear in mind that the cultural sector has multiple linkages. Such methodologies of course need to be rigorous and comparable. Nonetheless, as noted a few paragraphs ago, lab experiments, for one, are not the same as real life observations in economic development. So, even in this case, any adoptions have to be used judiciously. The third point relates to a major point Jerven makes in *Poor Numbers*: Even beyond the cultural sector, improvements on data accuracy, reliability, and dissemination are badly needed. Such improvements could inform processes that make comparisons between national economies where possible.[48]

Forge Other Creative Partnerships

Creative partnerships to collect data could extend to companies such as YouTube. That YouTube, a video-sharing service started in 2005, now has more than one billion users[49] speaks volumes about the power of visual content delivery platforms. Many of YouTube's videos, whether commercial or otherwise, have some artistic component to them. The short movie or film character of many of the clips presented suggests that this channel should be further studied with respect to the arts, commerce, and technology. This analysis could expand the discoveries in which data on the arts can be captured in the digital world.

"YouTube and Vevo, another popular site, now pay labels a small royalty when punters watch a music video," the *Economist* reports.[50] But with respect to development, one wonders: How many music, dance, or dramatic videos from Asia, Africa, Latin America, or the Middle East are downloaded each month? Are these upcoming artists or well-known stars? How much revenue (from adverts, for instance) is collected in relation to such videos? And what percentage is distributed to the artists? This is an area of inquiry that data groups may have reason to consider.[51]

Gather Data via Google, Radio Stations, Streaming Platforms, and Other Agencies

Google, UN Global Pulse, radio stations, and streaming platforms (like Spotify) provide another approach for which data on the creative arts like music could be gathered. And various agencies could also be useful in collecting and aggregating cultural data industry globally.

These may include: Fair Trade organizations; the International Confederation of Societies of Authors and Composers; the International Federation of the Phonographic Industry; MIDiA Consulting; PricewaterhouseCoopers; Universal Music Group; and the World Intellectual Property Organization.

A number of regional arts organizations serve as supporters or conveners of local talent and royalty collection agencies. These organizations could also be helpful in collecting data on income and commercial and social activities related to the arts. Here is a sample: the Association of Asian Performing Arts Festivals; the Association of Caribbean Copyright Societies; the African, Caribbean and Pacific Group of States; the Arab Fund for Arts and Culture; the Arterial Network; the New Zealand International Arts Festival; the Pacific Arts Association; Southern African Music Rights Organization; and the World Culture Festival. In many countries, places of worship and educational institutions have a number of artistic activities going on. The question is whether the quest for data should include these institutions. Moreover, new technologies have potential to help us develop more tools of inquiry.

It must be remembered, however, that more data is not always better data. Small data can be equally as valuable. Although "Big Data" has come to acquire star status, covering front pages of major and minor publications and enjoying policy pronouncements, as Borgman notes, it is usually better to have the right data than having more data. And while we have been told that big data is "the oil of modern business," "the glue of collaborations," and "a source of friction between scholars," Borgman occasions a crucial reminder: "Data do not flow like oil, stick like glue, or start fires by friction like matches. Their value lies in their use," as noted in the 1997 National Research Council report entitled *Bits of Power*.[52]

OTHER QUESTIONS TO CONSIDER

(1) What is the average budget for ministries of culture in the developing world?

(2) How many cultural diplomacy initiatives take place, say, between Africa and China, per year?
(3) How many cultural tourism laws have been issued lately due to the increasingly bad behavior of the newly rich tourists?
(4) How many arts and urban revitalization programs provide feasible examples of what can be done at the national and the international level?
(5) How many radio stations are dedicated solely to non-Western music, at least in the United States, the world's leading music market today?

The list could surely be greatly lengthened. And since earlier I insisted that we have to assess the answers we get, the process of evaluation would surely need constant adapting.

ESTABLISHING A CULTURAL TRADE INDEX

The creation of measures such as gross domestic product, the human development index, and gross national happiness has enriched the development debate. Against this backdrop, it is worth exploring the development of an index that would track patterns of trade in cultural goods and services. The index could be called the Cultural Trade Index (CTI). A sample is shown in Table 9.3 on the 2011 art crafts total trade of Egypt, Ghana, and South Africa.[53]

Such an index is not all encompassing. First and foremost, the data feeding into this index will need to be improved. Moreover, as noted earlier, some items captured in the CTI may also comprise of inputs from all over the world. Consider musical instruments. Statistics for China's recent rise as a leading exporter of instruments such as pianos and violins could be reflected in the CTI. That said, where do the inputs that go into these instruments originate?[54] Such questions are relevant. But the index could facilitate the debate on the outcomes of creative trade and its contribution to human development, at least in the instrumental dimension.[55] Besides the CTI, a Cultural Exchange Index (CEI) could also be created to show how countries participate in international cultural exchanges—and this idea, in a way, connects to Edward Pearlman's proposed Cultural Exchange Free Trade Agreement described in Chapter 5. The CEI could look like this:

Table 9.3 *A proposed Cultural Trade Index Example of index computation | Art crafts total trade, 2011 | Figures in millions (USD)*

Country	Egypt, Arab Rep.	South Africa	Ghana	Rank (based on result in Step 3)	
Step 1: Country's art crafts trade ÷ total trade between the 3 countries (Egypt, South Africa, and Ghana; i.e., 47 053+126 798+14 596) = 188 447	759÷188 447 = 0.0040276576	175÷188 447 = 0.0009286431	$126 ÷$188 447 = 0.000668623	Egypt, Arab Rep.	#1
				Ghana	#2
Step 2: Base country chosen: Ghana. Country's total trade/Ghana's total trade	47 053÷14 596 = 3.2236914223	126 798÷14 596 = 8.6871745684	14 596÷14 596 = 1	South Africa	#3
Step 3: Outcome in Step 1 divided by outcome in Step 2.	0.0040276576÷ 3.2236914223 = **0.001249393**	0.0009286431÷ 8.6871745684 = **0.0001068982**	0.000668623 ÷ 1 = **0.000668623**		

[a] Includes carpets, celebration, other, paperware, wickerware, and yarn. [b] Includes art crafts, audio visuals, design, new media, performing arts, publishing, and visual arts. So "goods" here probably implies goods and services given the composition of the items included. [c] Balance of Payments and International Investment Position Manual Sixth Edition (BPM6). The total trade of Ghana is the base chosen for illustrative purposes, but even if the base were Egypt or South Africa, the result would not shift as such. Sources: UNCTADstat 2014 and Kabanda 2016g.

Table 9.4 *A proposed Cultural Exchange Index*

Global cultural exchange, sending			Global cultural exchange, receiving		
Country	Number of artistic exchanges sent abroad	Rank	Country	Number of artistic exchanges received from abroad	Rank
A	50 events	#1	A	40 events	#1
B	40 events	#2	B	30 events	#2
C	30 events	#3	C	20 events	#3

Source: Kabanda 2016g.

As noted in a working paper introducing this idea, the above exercise could be weighed against population, GDP, or the percentage of government expenditure on cultural exchanges, or the budgets of ministries of culture. It should nonetheless be noted that, as often the case, cultural exchanges might also promote commerce in other areas as countries learn more about each other's cultures and build amity. David Throsby has argued that point by reminding us of that old adage cited in the overture to this book: "where culture leads, trade follows."[56]

CODA: A CAVEAT

These days, it seems as if where numbers lead, development follows. But as the saying goes, not everything that counts can be counted, and not everything that can be counted counts.[57] Along those lines, consider this observation by the Nobel-economist Wassily Leontief:

> The structure and the operation of the entire national economy is typically described by a relatively small number of aggregative variables (and a correspondingly small number of indirectly estimated, aggregative structural parameters). Actual measurements of such variables as 'total GNP', the level of total employment, the price levels of all consumers' and producers'

> goods, that is, the computation of appropriate aggregative index numbers, is usually delegated to hard-working economic statisticians.
>
> It is a rather thankless task. The long history of search for an ideal index number formula has only demonstrated that aggregation is inevitably bound to yield a blurred picture of observable reality. It also frequently conceals the lack of detailed factual information.
>
> Modern social and economic statistics fall very short of what would be needed to implement a realistic, working model of a complex modern economy.[58]

Indeed, modern social and economic statistics do not tell us all there is to know. And this has generally shortchanged the contribution of the arts to economic and social progress. That does not take away the contribution of creative work to the economy, though. Again, just consider the recent American and Nigerian GDP revisions (Chapter 1). That fact remains, even if many artists themselves struggle to make ends meet, arts programs lack adequate funding, and many more impediments plague the creative economy. In development, the basis to support the arts often begins with a request for data, as part of evidence-based policy making. That being the case, there is a need to embrace "creative data" collection to generate more and better data. Moreover, given GDP's cachet, if such data help to show how the arts contribute to GDP, well and good. Nevertheless, if GDP is "too important to be ignored," as Jerven concludes, "numbers are too poor to be trusted blindly." An inquiry into the nature and causes of development therefore "cannot be limited to the use of economics and statistics. Interdisciplinary approaches are required."[59] There is therefore a pressing need for economists, statisticians, and even politicians to make an effort to understand the nonmeasurable aspects of the arts. Data, after all, like science, whether pure or dismal, "can give us knowledge, but it cannot give us wisdom."[60]

Finale

On Imagination and Choice

It's Not How Good You Are, It's How Good You Want to Be.

Paul Arden[1]

Now when the people began to search for the wisdom behind progress, in the end it was not whether development came first and then the arts followed, or some sort of miraculous statistical formula. Much of it was imagination in thought and deed. Imagination was the future, and the future was imagination. It was the cradle of progress. That is why nations like Creativeria started to embrace the arts in their development agendas. But to build on Creativeria's vision there has to be collaboration between institutions and disciplines. In realizing that collaboration, this finale is a call to imagine the future we need. As the old adage says, where there is a will, there is a way. What often holds back the application of the arts in development is that we often do not comprehend their diverse contributions to improving people's lives. In the stampede to promote our narrow interests and hail the next development celebrities, we fail to meet the development objectives we care so much about. Of course there are exceptions. But if we want to expand the role of the arts in development, that choice is ours.

***

An adage ascribed to many people, including Peter Drucker, Abraham Lincoln, and Forrest C. Shaklee, is not only worth a bumper sticker; it is also worth a minder sticker: "The best way to predict the future is to create it."[2] In this book, I have tried to show how we might create a future we need via the creative wealth of nations. The call is clear. We need development that puts all human beings at the center, one that emancipates the potential of each person. I am not saying that by promoting the arts, poverty and other global challenges will suddenly vanish. But again, I venture to insist that culture, a global symphony in which the arts are prominent notes, is integral to what drives human progress and quality of life.

Nevertheless, one could insist that arts can be misused. And that is undeniable. Indeed, who knew, for example, that Islamic militants "believe poetry converted to chants will help them recruit new fighters and inspire existing ones"?[3] But often for the best, the arts can transform us. Through monetary and nonmonetary dimensions, they can contribute to development in diverse ways. These ways, as I have argued in this work, include emancipating creativity and innovation – vehicles that drive human capabilities and modern economic progress – promoting environmental stewardship; inducing creative commerce that stretches from music and movies to crafts and tourism; enabling green jobs, promoting nation branding, cultural democracy, and cross-cultural understanding; working to close the gender gap; and aiding mental health, social healing, and urban renewal. These are precisely among the bits and pieces that drive meaningful development, development needed to carry the poor along.

Now, I must acknowledge that arts are picking up some steam here and there. In fact, this work would have been difficult to analyze and to defend without any practical examples to show. Development, however, tends to be replete with competing doctrines, which stymie innovative thinking, as I noted earlier in this book. And these doctrines are often excited by the best way we think we should achieve development. Inevitably there is a temptation to rush to convenience.[4] This has implications. It can, for example, turn the means to achieve objectives into propaganda. And when the arts march in, they can harp the hype with dazzling flair. Instead of questioning how they can help the poor to make livelihoods, for instance, their goodness is turned into a show. This cannot but make working together difficult as we strategize to steal the stage.

That brings me to the point of cooperation (or lack thereof). As President Barack Obama says in *The Audacity of Hope,* to consider a related example, "most people who serve in Washington have been trained either as lawyers or as political operatives – professions that tend to place a premium on winning arguments rather than solving problems."[5] Likewise, development is full of smart people with a marginal propensity to cooperate, especially across disciplines. Why? This is because we have a predilection to compete instead.

This, one could argue, is a byproduct of the tendency to promote our own doctrine rather than solve problems. But even if we mean well, by failing to lend an earnest ear to others and to venture into unfamiliar territory, we fall short of reaching the development objectives we care about. "A united system of knowledge is the surest means of identifying the still unexplored domains of reality,"[6] E. O. Wilson concludes in *Consilience: The Unity of Knowledge.*

Modern economic thought has perforated trade and development in unimaginable ways, ways that might even baffle maestro Adam Smith. Nevertheless, as Buchholz notes in his *New Ideas from Dead Economists,* "Economics is the study of choice. It does not tell us what to choose. It only helps us understand the consequences of our choices."[7] Likewise, the arts exhibit creative wealth. But they do not tell us to choose them. That choice is ours.

If we want to realize a future that is creative, innovative, sustainable, tolerant, and peaceful – one that cares not to leave the poor drowning in poverty and living undignified lives, as Drucker, Lincoln, Shaklee, and others would say – we need to create it. That creation is about choice, as Creativeria in the overture to this book reckoned. Consider what Einstein, who took refuge in music whenever he was stuck,[8] said: "Logic will get you from A to B. Imagination will take you everywhere." The current logic in development has surely driven progress from point A to point B. And that should be acknowledged. But is this progress equitable? Is it sustainable?

Remember: It is not about how good we are; it is about how good we want to be. If development wants to dance in a better way, there is not just more to be done. There is more to be done differently.[9] This requires vision. Since modern economics is driven by creativity and innovation, a couple in steady courtship with the arts, let me recapitulate that mighty question posed in Chapter 1: Would you rather bet on a country that banks on natural resources, or one that banks on creativity and innovation?[10] Even beyond the instrumental bearing, should culture not be tapped for its contribution to people's quality of life? If my thoughts can induce interest in *fully* considering culture in development, I will have much reason to tap dance.

Annexes

Annex 1.1

United Nations Education Science and Culture Organization (UNESCO)

The cultural and creative industries are those that combine the creation, production, and commercialization of creative contents that are intangible and of a cultural nature. These contents are usually protected by copyright and can take the form of a good or a service. Besides all artistic and cultural production, they include architecture and advertising.

United Nations Conference on Trade and Development (UNCTAD)

The creative industries are at the core of the creative economy, and are defined as cycles of production of goods and services that use creativity and intellectual capital as their main input. They are classified by their role as heritage, art, media, and functional creations.

World Intellectual Property Organization (WIPO)

The copyright-based industries are those that are dedicated, interdependent, or that are directly or indirectly related with the creation, production, representation, exhibition, communication, distribution or retail of copyright-protected material.

Department of Culture, Media and Sports of the United Kingdom (DCMS)

The creative industries are those activities based on creativity, individual talent, and skill, and that have the potential to create jobs and wealth through the generation and exploitation of intellectual property.

Economic Commission for Latin America and the Caribbean (ECLAC)

The content industries are: publishing, film, TV, radio, phonographic, mobile contents, independent audiovisual production, web contents, electronic games, and content produced for digital convergence (cross-media).

Source: Márquez and Restrepo 2013, 37.

Annex 1.2 Cultural Industries and Creative Industries

Cultural industries	Creative industries
"The term *'cultural industries'* traces its genealogy back to earlier work in the Frankfurt School in the 1930s and 1940s, which scathingly decried the commodification of art as providing an ideological legitimization of capitalist societies and the emergence of a popular *culture industry*. Such pessimistic views of the relation between culture and capitalist enterprise are still held by some. This is notably the case of the Left, and particularly today in the context of the debate on the threat of global cultural homogenization. In these views, culture and the economy are seen as mutually hostile, each driven by logic so incompatible that when the two are made to converge, the integrity of the former always suffers. By the early 1960s, however,	"The term *'creative industries'* is applied to a much wider productive set, including goods and services produced by the cultural industries and those that depend on innovation, including many types of research and software development. The phrase began to enter policy-making, such as the national cultural policy of Australia in the early1990s, followed by the transition made by the influential Department for Culture, Media and Sport of the United Kingdom from cultural to *creative* industries at the end of the decade. This usage also stemmed from the linking of creativity to urban economic development and city planning. It was given a first significant boost by the important work carried out by the British consultant Charles

(*cont.*)

Cultural industries	Creative industries
many analysts had begun to recognize that the process of commodification does not always or necessarily result in the degeneration of cultural expression. Indeed, often the contrary may be true, for industrially (or digitally) generated goods and services clearly possess many positive equalities. Hence, by the 1980s the term *'cultural industries'* no longer carried the pejorative connotations of the earlier term and began to be used in academia and policy-making circles as a *positive* label. This referred to forms of cultural production and consumption that have at their core a symbolic or expressive element. It was also propagated worldwide by UNESCO in the 1980s and has come to encompass a wide range of fields, such as music, art, writing, fashion and design, and media industries, e.g. radio, publishing, film and television production. Its scope is not limited to technology-intensive production as a great deal of cultural production in developing countries is crafts-intensive. Investment in the traditional rural crafts, for example, can benefit female artisans by empowering them to take charge of their lives and	Landry on the 'creative city.' A second and highly influential force internationally was the work of Richard Florida, an American urban studies theorist, on the 'creative class' that cities needed to attract in order to ensure their successful development. This 'creative class' is a very capacious grouping of many different kinds of professional, managerial and technical workers (not just creative workers in the cultural and creative industries), producing innovation of various types. Together they form a 'class' that Florida took to be the fountainhead of innovative energy and cultural dynamism in present-day urban societies. In this perspective, cultural activities were seen primarily as amenities in the urban infrastructure that would serve to attract a mobile, professional labour force and provide an outlet for their highly focused and purposeful leisure time. After an initial wave of great enthusiasm, notably among mayors of cities in the United States, northern Europe and East Asia, the appeal of the 'creative class' paradigm declined markedly. Scholars found that Florida's thesis was not supported by empirical

(*cont.*)

Cultural industries	Creative industries
generate income for their families, particularly in areas where other income opportunities are limited. All of these productive domains have significant economic value, yet also are vectors of profound social and cultural meanings."	evidence and did not provide sufficient guidance on the necessary and sufficiently durable conditions under which such skilled and creative individuals would congregate and remain in any given place to become key agents in local and regional development. In addition, Florida himself recently admitted that even in the United States, the rewards of his strategy 'flow disproportionately to more highly-skilled knowledge, professional and creative workers' and added that 'on close inspection, talent clustering provides little in the way of trickle-down benefits.'"[a]
Cultural economy	
"The perspective that centers on the interplay between Culture and economy has also been expressed in the notion of "cultural economy." This way of seeing is important because it also encompasses the broader way of life-understating of culture by revealing how identities and life-worlds are intertwined with the production, distribution and consumption of goods and services. It also recognizes that what we refer to as the "economy" is bound up with processes of social and cultural relations. In this sense it reminds us the economy is part of culture.[b]..."	

Source: UN 2013, 20–21, 24.
Note: a. Florida 2013. b. See Pollard et al. 2011.

Annex 1.3 Economic linkages of the music industry

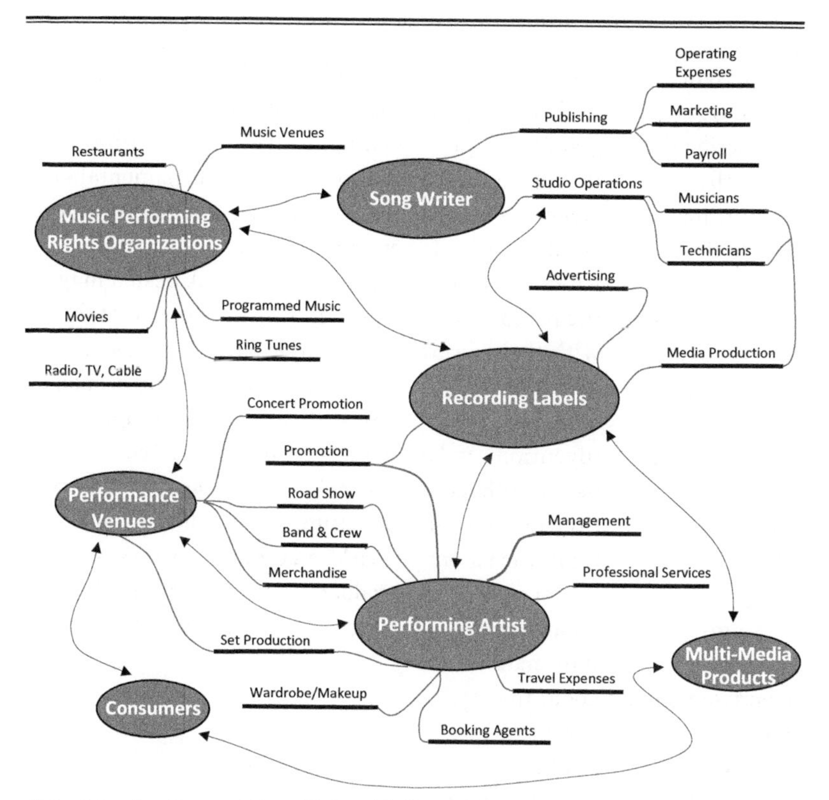

Note: Arts education could be added to this illustration.
Source: Raines and Brown 2006.

Annex 4.1

A – Definitions related to intellectual property

"Intellectual property (IP) refers to creations of the mind, such as inventions; literary and artistic works; designs; and symbols, names and images used in commerce.

"IP is protected in law by, for example, patents, copyright and trademarks, which enable people to earn recognition or financial benefit from what they invent or create. By striking the right balance between the interests of innovators and the wider public interest, the IP system aims to foster an environment in which creativity and innovation can flourish."

(*cont.*)

Copyright	Patents	Trademarks	Industrial designs
"Copyright is a legal term used to describe the rights that creators have over their literary and artistic works. Works covered by copyright range from books, music, paintings, sculpture and films, to computer programs, databases, advertisements, maps and technical drawings."	"A patent is an exclusive right granted for an invention. Generally speaking, a patent provides the patent owner with the right to decide how – or whether – the invention can be used by others. In exchange for this right, the patent owner makes technical information about the invention publicly available in the published patent document."	"A trademark is a sign capable of distinguishing the goods or services of one enterprise from those of other enterprises. Trademarks date back to ancient times when artisans used to put their signature or "mark" on their products."	"An industrial design constitutes the ornamental or aesthetic aspect of an article. A design may consist of three-dimensional features, such as the shape or surface of an article, or of two-dimensional features, such as patterns, lines or color."
"**Geographical indications** and appellations of origin are signs used on goods that have a specific geographical origin and possess qualities, a reputation or characteristics that are essentially attributable to that place of origin. Most commonly, a geographical indication includes the name of the place of origin of the goods."			

Source: WIPO n.d.

B – Definitions related to copyright industries
"The **core** copyright industries which are wholly engaged in the creation, production and manufacture, performance, broadcasting, communication and exhibition, or distribution and sale of works and other protected subject matter."
"**Interdependent** copyright industries are industries which are engaged in the production, manufacture and sale, and renting or leasing of equipment. Their function is wholly or primarily to facilitate the creation, production, or use of works and other protected subject matter."
"The **partial** copyright industries are industries in which a portion of the activities is related to works and other protected subject matter and may involve creation, production and manufacture, performance, broadcasting, communication and exhibition, and distribution and sales."
"**Non-dedicated** support industries are those in which a portion of the activities is related to facilitating broadcast communication and the distribution or sale of works and other protected subject matter whose activities have not been included in the core copyright industries."

Source: WIPO 2015, 51 59, 60, 62.
Note: Copyright industries may also include creative industries.

Annex 5.1 The Proposed Artist Visa versus the Existing O-1B Visa

The United States grants an O-1B visa to "individuals with an extraordinary ability in the arts or extraordinary achievement in motion picture or television industry."

Evidentiary criteria for O-1B	Evidentiary criteria for artist visa
"Evidence that the beneficiary has received, or been nominated for, significant national or international awards or prizes in the particular field, such as an Academy Award, Emmy, Grammy or Director's Guild Award, or evidence of at least (3) three of the following:	"Evidence that the beneficially has" recognition in country of origin or whose artistry can be construed as adding significant value to the national and international cultural scene. Must meet "evidence of at least (3) three of the following":

(cont.)

Evidentiary criteria for O-1B	Evidentiary criteria for artist visa
• Performed and will perform services as a lead or starring participant in productions or events which have a distinguished reputation as evidenced by critical reviews, advertisements, publicity releases, publications, contracts or endorsements.	• Will perform services in a group, or "as a lead or starring participant in productions or events ... evidenced by critical reviews, advertisements, publicity releases, publications, contracts or endorsements."
• Achieved national or international recognition for achievements, as shown by critical reviews or other published materials by or about the beneficiary in major newspapers, trade journals, magazines, or other publications.	• Achieved national recognition "for achievements, or cultural contribution as shown by critical reviews or other published materials by or about the beneficiary in newspapers, trade journals, magazines, or other publications."
• Performed and will perform in a lead, starring, or critical role for organizations and establishments that have a distinguished reputation as evidenced by articles in newspapers, trade journals, publications, or testimonials.	• Will perform in cultural festivals or other venues such as schools "as evidenced by articles in newspapers, trade journals, publications, or testimonials."
• A record of major commercial or critically acclaimed successes, as shown by such indicators as title, rating or standing in the field, box office receipts, motion picture or television ratings and other occupational achievements reported in trade journals, major newspapers or other publications.	• Occupational achievements "as shown by such indicators as" previous performance record like itineraries, ticket sales "or reported by newspapers or other publications" or evidenced by CD or video recordings.

(cont.)

Evidentiary criteria for O-1B	Evidentiary criteria for artist visa
• Received significant recognition for achievements from organizations, critics, government agencies or other recognized experts in the field in which the beneficiary is engaged, with the testimonials clearly indicating the author's authority, expertise and knowledge of the beneficiary's achievements.	• Recognition or endorsements "from organizations, critics, government agencies or other recognized experts in the field in which the beneficiary is engaged, with the testimonials clearly indicating the author's authority, expertise and knowledge of the beneficiary's" cultural contribution.
• A high salary or other substantial remuneration for services in relation to others in the field, as shown by contracts or other reliable evidence."	• "[Remuneration] for services in relation to others in the field, as shown by contracts or other reliable evidence."
• Duration: Up to 3 years	• Duration: 3 months

Source: USCIS 2017. Kabanda 2013.

Annex 7.1 Gender Bias Without Borders[1]: Facts and Figures

"• Only 30.9 percent of all speaking characters are female.
- A few countries are better than the global norm: U.K. (37.9 percent), Brazil (37.1 percent), and Korea (35.9 percent). However, these percentages fall well below population norms of 50 percent.
- Two samples fall behind: US/UK hybrid films (23.6 percent) and Indian films (24.9 percent) show female characters in less than one-quarter of all speaking roles.
- Females are missing in action/adventure films. Just 23 percent of speaking characters in this genre are female.
- Out of a total of 1,452 filmmakers with an identifiable gender, 20.5 percent were female and 79.5 percent were male. Females comprised 7 percent of directors, 19.7 percent of writers, and 22.7 percent of producers across the sample.

(cont.)

- Films with a female director or female writer attached had significantly more girls and women on screen than did those without a female director or writer attached.
- Sexualization is the standard for female characters globally: [G]irls and women are twice as likely as boys and men to be shown in sexually revealing clothing, partially or fully naked, thin, and five times as likely to be referenced as attractive. Films for younger audiences are less likely to sexualize females than are those films for older audiences.
- Teen females (13–20 years) are just as likely as young adult females (21–39 years) to be sexualized.
- Female characters only comprise 22.5 percent of the global film workforce, whereas male characters form 77.5 percent.
- Leadership positions pull male; only 13.9 percent of executives and just 9.5 percent of high-level politicians were women.
- Across prestigious professions, male characters outnumbered their female counterparts as attorneys and judges (13 to 1), professors (16 to 1), medical practitioners (5 to 1), and in STEM [Science Technology Engineering Math] fields (7 to 1)."

Source: Smith et al. 2014, 24–25.

Notes

OVERTURE

1. World Bank n.d., 3. "Cultural Heritage."
2. "Gross domestic product (GDP) is the monetary value of all the finished goods and services produced within a country's borders in a specific time period. Though GDP is usually calculated on an annual basis, it can be calculated on a quarterly basis as well. GDP includes all private and public consumption, government outlays, investments and exports minus imports that occur within a defined territory. Put simply, GDP is a broad measurement of a nation's overall economic activity" (Investopedia n.d.a.). See also Callen 2012. GDP is different from GNP (gross national product). "GNP includes, and GDP excludes, income owned by residents but generated abroad, and GNP excludes, and GDP includes, incomes generated domestically but owned by foreigners. The difference is usually small, but it is very important for some countries" (Deaton 2013, 30–31).
3. See Luke and Igoe 2015. NB: Even though the Sustainable Development Goals mention culture, they fall far short from a full-fledged acknowledgment of culture's potential role in development.
4. On measuring the health of a country and its economy, we surely need strength and security. But again, "strength isn't just military might, it's also the spiritual strength to make it through tough times, the strength to find new solutions to old problems, and the strength to do what's right. And security isn't just the idea that we can protect ourselves and keep our families safe and well fed – it's the ability to educate ourselves to be leaders in a world that is changing faster than a growing baby" (Rodale 2009).
5. UN 2015, 8.
6. See Sen 2000, 297.

7. Inspired by Rachel Carson's "A Fable for Tomorrow" in *Silent Spring*, problem sets in my fall 2011 law and development course with Jeswald W. Salacuse at The Fletcher School, and Paul Collier's *The Bottom Billion*.
8. Kabanda 2015c.
9. The terms "creativity" and "innovation" are becoming trite these days, because they are over used. But since they will appear often in this book, I must immediately point out that they do not mean the same thing as they are often inadvertently used to mean. In brief – and this is but one way of looking at these terms – creativity is the capability to conceive something new. Innovation, meanwhile, is the capability to put ideas into action. (For more on this see Kabanda 2015e, 5.)
10. Throsby 2010, 52.
11. For a related discussion, see Adams 2011; Helft 2014.
12. Throsby 2010, 39–40.
13. UN 2010, 24.
14. Throsby 2010, 40. On a related point, there is no doubt that social isolation and loneliness can take a toll on public health and general welfare broadly speaking. But the following point warrants attention: "[A]lthough loneliness and social isolation entail equivalent levels of risk, they are not interchangeable," according to the psychologist-researchers Julianne Holt-Lunstad and Timothy B. Smith. "Social isolation denotes few social connections or interactions, whereas loneliness involves the subjective perception of isolation – the discrepancy between one's desired and actual level of social connection. Although social isolation and loneliness may co-occur, individuals can be isolated without feeling lonely or feel lonely despite having others present" (Holt-Lunstad and Smith 2016, 987). At any rate, as social isolation and loneliness increasingly become debated as public health issues (see Brody 2017, Holland 2017, and Holt-Lunstad and Smith 2016), how often are the arts considered in public policies to address the risks they pose?
15. Putnam n.d. 1.
16. Cultural democracy "comprises a set of related commitments," according to Webster's *World of Cultural Democracy*: "protecting and promoting cultural diversity, and the right to culture for everyone in our society and around the world; encouraging active participation in community cultural life; enabling people to participate in policy decisions that affect the

quality of our cultural lives; and assuring fair and equitable access to cultural resources and support" (WWCD n.d.).

17. UNESCO 2001.
18. Tichy and Bennis 2007, 14.
19. Basu 2010, x. "It is the translation of directly observable reality into international terms at one end of a mathematical argument and the translation of the mathematical symbols into observable facts at the other end that really counts. And such translation can be given only in ordinary non-mathematical language" (Leontief 1992, 143).
20. Tim Johnson is of "the opinion that almost all of the criticism of the use of mathematics in economics stems from a lack of understanding of what mathematics is, reflecting a general ignorance in economics that has led to the failure of mathematics in economics." See "Why Mathematics Has Not Been Effective in Economics" (T. Johnson 2017).
21. Sen 2000, 132.
22. Heilbroner 1971, xv. Also see "When It Comes to the Economy, Math Isn't Magic" (Livio 2009). See also T. Johnson 2017.
23. Heilbroner 1971, xvii.
24. Okeowo 2015, 36.
25. Xiao 2013.
26. Indo Asian News Service 2012.
27. Sui 2016.
28. Sen 2004, 37.
29. Fraser 2008.
30. UN 2013, 16.
31. UN 2015, 24, 27.
32. UN 2015, 9.
33. "Aspects of cultural policy that currently figure in government policy agendas include: the prospects for the creative industries as dynamic sources of innovation, growth and structural change in the so-called new economy; the role of the arts and culture in employment creation and income generation in towns and cities, especially those affected by industrial decline; the appropriate means by which governments can support the creative and performing arts; legal and economic questions concerning the regulation of intellectual property in cultural goods and services; and the possibilities for public/private partnerships in the preservation of cultural heritage" (Throsby 2010, ix). See also UN 2013.

34. Kabanda 2013, 9.
35. World Bank 2014b, 5. Kabanda 2014b, 2–3.
36. Speaking of "systematic understanding," "There are at least two different senses in which we popularly use the term understanding," according to Kaushik Basu. "When people say that they 'understand general equilibrium theory or Brouwer's fixed point theorem,' and when they say that 'they understand music or human psychology,' in both cases they are referring to cognitive processes in the brain, leading to some acquisition of information, but in different ways" (see Basu 2010, 13 for more on this point.)
37. World Bank n.d.b, 3.
38. See Kabanda 2007.
39. Haecker 2012, 1
40. European Commission 2015.
41. Also see Kabanda 2014b, 2.
42. Sen 2000, 3.

1 AN UNTAPPED AND UNMEASURED ECONOMY

1. Sen 2001, 1.
2. Some have suggested that it may be better to move away from the notion of "intrinsic vs. instrumental" benefits to "direct vs. indirect" contributions of the arts to wellbeing. See Ingersoll and Carnwath 2015.
3. See Fuentes 2017, Wilson 2017, Johnson 2016, and Weiner 2016. One Sunday morning in 2015, I caught a program on National Public Radio called "Mysteries of an Expanding Universe." The conversation was between *On Being*'s host Krista Tippett and Mario Livio, a senior astrophysicist at the Hubble Space Telescope Science Institute. It centered on Livio's book entitled, *Is God a Mathematician*? As I listened along, this thought stood out: Math is neither invented nor discovered; it is both. Since this involves imagination in a self-reinforcing cycle, I wonder if a moral philosopher like Adam Smith would have asked, "Is God an Artist?" After all, in Genesis, to consider a spiritual bearing, we are told that God *created*; not that God *modeled*. Whereas this is not a religious debate, it challenges us to consider that math, from which economics likes to religiously draw, also connects to art and nature. As Livio concludes, to a large extent, math is part of the square roots of human imagination that have led us where we are in human progress. It is therefore important that, as part of the human

culture of imagination, science and math communicate like literature and poetry. (For more on this see Livio 2015.)

4. BEA 2013.
5. Imasogie and Kobylarz 2013.
6. O'S. 2014.
7. British Council n.d.
8. Jung 2016. Some people, including Leonel Kaz, who was among those who helped create the Ministry of Culture, suggest that the ministry may be better served by staying under the Ministry of Education. This is because the latter's budget is "100 times bigger" than that of culture. Moreover, there is a need to introduce cultural education into less privileged schools, as culture tends to be usurped by the elite (Jung 2016). But given its importance, one could argue that why then not increase public funding for the arts and work to improve the effectiveness of the cultural ministry?
9. Almino 2016.
10. Reuters 2016. See also Abrams 2016.
11. Weiner 2016.
12. The Endogenous Growth Theory, whose introduction is attributed to Paul Romer and Robert Lucas in the 1980s, may also be relevant here. The theory provides that "economic growth is developed from within the system as a direct result of exogenous or internal processes. The endogenous growth theory, as opposed to its direct counterpart the exogenous growth theory, holds that economic growth is primarily a result of those endogenous variables like investment in human capital, knowledge, and innovation rather than external forces." (Moffatt 2015). See also Romer 1994. As usual, theories are not without criticism. Here is an except by Paul Krugman: "The reasons some countries grow more successfully than others remain fairly mysterious, with most discussions ending, as Robert Solow remarked long ago, in a 'blaze of amateur sociology.' And whaddya know, business cycles turn out still to be important" (Krugman 2013).
13. Buchholz 2007, xviii.
14. Harris 2017.
15. Seabrook 2012.
16. Wanda Group. n.d. a. On culture and green jobs, see UN 2013, 69.
17. Wanda Group. n.d. b.

18. See Brzeski 2016 and Kokas 2017.
19. Kabanda 2014a.
20. Ratha and Kabanda 2015.
21. Iyengar and Hudson 2014.
22. Throsby 2010, 40.
23. Throsby 2010, 29.
24. Lehrer 2011.
25. For example see Rothman 2015.
26. Isaacson 2011, xxi.
27. Hiskey 2011.
28. Hiskey 2011.
29. Hiskey 2011.
30. Hiskey 2011.
31. Hiskey 2011. See also NPR 2014.
32. Weiner 2016. For example, see 224, 236, 268, and 322–323.
33. Franz 2008, 9–10
34. Franz 2008, 9–10.
35. S. Johnson 2016, 12. Interpreted more broadly, development could also use some play and delight. This is because it tends to put a premium on toughness, as if we need more blood, sweat, and tears for development. The usual attitude submits that wisdom demands toughness, hence the calculated neglect for concerns that are deemed "soft-headed" (Sen 2000, 35). I make this connection because the arts are likely to be neglected in this view, for they are seen as luxuries. "This hard-knocks attitude," as Sen has argued, "contrasts with an alternative outlook that sees development as essentially a 'friendly' process." Because it is not fixated on 'toughness and discipline,' a friendly attitude is more likely to induce play and delight, and thereby stimulate creative buds or improve collaboration. "Depending on the particular version of this attitude, the congeniality of the process is seen as exemplified by such things as mutually beneficial exchanges (of which Adam Smith spoke eloquently), or by the working of social safety nets, or of political liberties, or of social development – or some combination or other of these supportive activities" (Sen 2000, 35–36).
36. Franz 2008, 9.
37. Smith 1994, 11 – BK. 1, ch 1. See also Franz 2008, 9.
38. Franz 2008, 10.

39. Bar 2016.
40. Bar 2016. For technical details see Baror and Bar 2016.
41. Root-Bernstein and Root Bernstein 2001, 30. See also Isaacson 2017.
42. Franz 2008, 10.
43. Weiner 2016, 42.
44. Isaacson 2017, 519.
45. De Botton and Armstrong 2016, 107.
46. Read 1999; original emphasis.
47. Weinstein 2007, 70. The son of Joyce Ellen, an artist and high school teacher, and Mark Weinstein, a philosopher and jazz flute-player, Weinstein's books include *Adam Smith's Pluralism: Rationality, Education, and the Moral Sentiments*.
48. Márquez and Restrepo 2013.
49. UN 2013, 19–20.
50. *World Policy Journal* 2011.
51. Liberalizing property rights does not generally mean shared prosperity, or for that matter, poverty reduction. In some cases, such provisions make the poor worse off, especially when they are duped into signing unfair legal contracts. This exploitation is common in property and intellectual rights.
52. See McKinley 2013.
53. Nashville Convention & Visitors Corp n.d. "The Story of Music City."
54. Penna, Thormann, and Finger 2004, 97.
55. World Bank 2001.
56. Harper, Cotton, and Benefield 2013, 17, 77; Nashville.gov/Mayor's Office 2013.
57. B. Johnson n.d.
58. B. Johnson n.d.
59. Nashville Area Chamber of Commerce n.d. "Colleges & Universities."
60. B. Johnson n.d.
61. Nashville Convention & Visitors Corp n.d. "The Story of Music City."
62. Innovation Nashville n.d.
63. I am grateful to Maelle Noe for bringing this point to my attention.
64. Juma 2011, 63.
65. Lee and Tee 2009, 88.
66. Lee and Tee 2009, 88.
67. Lee and Tee 2009, 90, 91. For example: (i) Singapore "made significant strategic investments for key scientific and economic contributions to

its biomedical industry cluster through the provision of grants, funding and tax incentives to catalyze growth within this industry." (ii) "Besides establishing a strong biomedical research infrastructure, the Singapore state has put in place a supportive environment for commercial exploitation of intellectual assets created within the public research institutes. Regulatory policies have been introduced to protect intellectual property (IP) and risk-taking" (Lee and Tee 2009, 90, 91).

68. Scott 1997, 334.
69. Scott 2004, 7.
70. Gálvez-Nogales 2010, 12.
71. Robinson 2013, 36.
72. Throsby 2010, 18.
73. For more on the valuation of cultural products, consider Throsby's book, *Economics and Culture* (2001).
74. Economists describe such goods as "*non-excludable* (once they are produced they are available to everyone and no one can be excluded from them) and *non-rival* (one person's consumption does not diminish the amount available to others)." Since there is no market "on which the rights to them can be exchanged," and that "their benefits arise outside of conventional market processes," public goods – and this definition can also include services – are classified as *non-market goods*. Examples include "national defense and a free-to-air broadcast television signal." When assessing the economic value of cultural products, "three sources of non-market benefits can be identified" and taken into account: *existence value* (people value the arts simply because they exist); an *option value* (people wish to retain the option that they may wish to consume the arts at some time in the future); and the *bequest value* (people think it is important to pass the arts on to future generations)" (Throsby 2010, 19).
75. Throsby 2010, 20.
76. Sen 2001, 1.
77. And that should not be a surprise. This is because, as we saw at the beginning of this chapter, even in the instrumental dimension countries are just starting to capture the contribution of the creative sector to GDP. In any case, just because the arts' role is not well quantified, that does not diminish their contribution to social inclusion.
78. El Sistema is not without its critics. But overall, the program has been highly regarded for what it attempts to do.

79. Bayly 2004, 371.
80. Smith 2000–2009.
81. Putnam 2001, 19. See Smith 2000–2009 for more definitions of social capital and Coleman 1988 and Bourdieu 1983. NB: Social capital can be a "private good" and a "public good" simultaneously (see Putnam 2001, 20).
82. Bowlingalone.com n.d., "About the Book."
83. Smith 2000–2009.
84. Putnam 1993, 169.
85. Such experiences are also common in other areas, from sports to religious affiliations.
86. Sen 2001, 1–2.
87. Putnam n.d.
88. World Bank Group 2014b.
89. Ruble 2017, 526. On "weak ties" see Weiner 2016, 302–303.
90. Putnam 1993, 183.
91. Putnam 1993, 177.
92. By all means social capital can be positive or negative. "Therefore it is important to ask how the positive consequences of social capital – mutual support, cooperation, trust, institutional effectiveness – can be maximized and the negative manifestations – sectarianism, ethnocentrism, corruption – minimized," as Putnam has argued. "Toward this end, scholars have begun to distinguish many different forms of social capital."In this effort, perhaps the most important is the distinction between *bridging* social capital and *bonding* social capital; the former is *inclusive,* whereas the latter is *exclusive.* Putnam goes on to explain: "Some forms of social capital are, by choice or necessity, inward looking and tend to reinforce exclusive identities and homogeneous groups. Examples of bonding social capital include ethnic fraternal organizations, church-based women's reading groups, and fashionable country clubs. Other networks are outward looking and encompass people across diverse social cleavages. Examples of bridging social capital include the civil rights movement, many youth service groups, and ecumenical religious organizations.

    "Bonding social capital is good for undergirding specific reciprocity and mobilizing solidarity. Dense networks in ethnic enclaves, for example, provide crucial social and psychological support for less fortunate members of the community, while furnishing start-up financing, markets, and reliable labor for local entrepreneurs. Bridging networks, by contrast, are better for linkage to external assets and for information diffusion . . ."

Bridging social capital "can generate broader identities, whereas bonding social capital bolsters our narrow selves" (Putnam 2001, 22–23.) For more on this see citation.

93. Basu 2010, 98.
94. World Bank 2013, 16.
95. De Laat 2010, 3.
96. Lallanilla 2013.
97. World Bank 2013, 55.
98. Sen 2013, 4.
99. Sen 2013, 4.
100. Sen 2013, 4; original emphasis
101. World Bank n.d. "Mali."
102. Human Rights Watch 2013.
103. Raghavan 2012.
104. Raghavan 2012.
105. Sen 2013, 3.
106. World Bank 2014b, 18.
107. Basu 2011, 113.
108. World Bank 2013, 55.
109. Algan and Cahuc 2007.
110. Scott 1997, 324.
111. OECD and UN 2011, 14.

2 ARTS IN EDUCATION

1. See K. Robinson 2001, for example.
2. See Nordland 2015.
3. Sen 2000, 297.
4. World Bank n.d. "Afghanistan."
5. Radio Free Europe/Radio Liberty 2009.
6. Baily 2001.
7. Radio Free Europe/Radio Liberty 2009.
8. ANIM and Ministry of Education, Afghanistan (July 2014). E-mail exchange between author and ANIM.

9. ANIM and Ministry of Education, Afghanistan (July 2014).
10. Smith 1994, 842 – book V, ch. 1, pt. III, art. 2d.
11. WQXR 2013.
12. History 1998.
13. Mehr et al. 2013.
14. Mehr et al. 2013. Still, there is research that suggests otherwise. For example, see Lipman 2014 and B. Ehrlich 2015.
15. Schultz 1992, 133. While education and knowledge are not necessarily the same thing, we use this term in this case to mean education.
16. Schultz 1992, 131.
17. Milanović 2015a. Milanović's analysis has generated debate. But consider this excerpt from his piece called "On 'Human Capital' One More Time": "You can be the best pianist in the world, or the best brain surgeon, with, in both cases, huge amount of 'human capital,' but that 'capital' will bring you zero income if you do not work: perform in concerts, or operate in your hospital. You can be, of course, a very rich worker, as our violinist and brain surgeon are, while a poor widow may depend only on the income from the meager savings left by her deceased husband. But [the] violinist will still make his income through labor and the widow through ownership." For the rest of the discussion, see Milanović (2015b). In his piece called "People Aren't Androids," Paul Krugman (2015) had this to add: "Branko says that the essential difference between skills and physical capital is that the former aren't worth anything unless you work, and that is certainly an essential difference. I would, however, also emphasize the flip side: if you think of capital as something that rentiers can own, which is surely one of the important things we connote when we use the C-word, then labor force skills are not capital in that sense. Children of the wealthy can inherit or buy factories and buildings; absent indentured servitude or the coming of androids, they can't buy worker skills."
18. "Human capital" and "human capability," as Sen puts it, "cannot but be related, since both are concerned with the role of human beings, and in particular with the actual abilities that they achieve and acquire. But the yardstick of assessment concentrates on different achievements" (see Sen 2000, 293–297).
19. Sen 2000, 294.
20. Sen 2000, 296.
21. Sen 2000, 294.

22. Weiner 2016, 76–77.
23. Weiner 2016, 77.
24. Root-Bernstein and Root-Bernstein 2001, 46.
25. Weiner 2016, 77.
26. Weiner 2016, 77.
27. K. Robinson 2001, 188.
28. Blair A. Ruble, e-mail message to author, March 31, 2017.
29. Root-Bernstein and Root-Bernstein 2001, 12.
30. Davis 2009, 35, 59–60.
31. Huizenga 2013.
32. Blair A. Ruble, e-mail message to author, March 31, 2017.
33. S. Jonhson 2016, 68–69.
34. Diop 2013. See Kabanda 2014b.
35. Iyengar and Hudson 2014.
36. Iyengar and Hudson 2014.
37. Iyengar and Hudson 2014.
38. Iyengar and Hudson 2014.
39. Landrieu 2016, 11:12–21:11.
40. Landrieu 2016, 11:12–21:11.
41. Landrieu 2016, 11:12–21:11.
42. Consider Lipman 2013. Gardner's theory of multiple intelligences is also worth exploring. See Smith 2002, 2008.
43. Root-Bernstein and Root-Bernstein 2001, 36–39. And here, such polymaths as Leonardo da Vinci have much to teach us about observation. "Leonardo's greatest skill was his acute ability to observe things." So writes Isaacson of this diversely talented individual. "It was the talent that empowered his curiosity, and vice versa. It was not some magical gift but a product of his own effort" (Isaacson 2017, 520).
44. Root-Bernstein and Root-Bernstein 2001, 43–44.
45. Root-Bernstein and Root-Bernstein 2001, 46.
46. Gardner 1999.
47. S. Johnson 2016, 15, 72–74.
48. S. Johnson 2016, 73–74.
49. S. Johnson 2017, *IA* 00:00–29:52.
50. S. Johnson 2016, 73–74.
51. S. Johnson 2016, 72–76.

52. S. Johnson 2016, 83.
53. Algan, Cahuc, and Shleifer 2013, cited in World Bank 2015, 70.
54. World Bank 2015, 70.
55. World Bank 2015, 71.
56. MacGillis 2007.
57. MacGillis 2007.
58. Peters and Woolley 2007.
59. *Newsweek* 2007.
60. Stewart 2017.
61. Center for American Progress 2008.
62. MacGillis 2007.
63. Palca 2015.
64. Gardner 1999.
65. Sanskriti Centre for Theatre of the Oppressed. n.d.b, 2. See also www.janasanskriti.org/aboutus.html.
66. La Ferrara, Chong, and Duryea 2012 and Jensen and Oster 2009, cited in World Bank 2015, 76.
67. Mockus 2015.
68. Caballero 2004.
69. Mockus 2015.
70. Mockus 2015.
71. Kabanda 2015d.
72. Mansfield and Yohe 2003, 34.
73. Davis 2005, 200.
74. Goldblatt 2006, 17–18.
75. Davis 2005, 200–201.
76. Davis 2005, 180.
77. Kolbert 2014.
78. UNEP et al. 2013.
79. Kabanda 2014b.

3 THE ARTS AND ENVIRONMENTAL STEWARDSHIP

1. Kelaher 2017.
2. Economist 2013b.
3. All quotations and background information from *Landfill Harmonic.*
4. Tierney 2015.

5. Kabanda 2016h.
6. CBS News 2013.
7. Lee 2006.
8. The New Orleans Jazz & Heritage Festival and Foundation, Inc. 2013.
9. The New Orleans Jazz & Heritage Festival and Foundation n.d.
10. Palca 2015.
11. Palca 2015.
12. The Crossroads Project n.d.
13. Palca 2015.
14. Carson 2002, 113–114.
15. Duggan 2013.
16. Pérez-Peña, Richard 2014.
17. Imagine 2020 n.d.
18. The Green Belt Movement. n.d.b.
19. Nobelprize.org. n.d.b.
20. Nobelprize.org. n.d.a.
21. The Green Belt Movement. n.d.b.
22. Taking Root 2015.
23. My Hero n.d.
24. The Green Belt Movement. n.d.a. See footage here: www.greenbeltmovement.org/get-involved/be-a-hummingbird.
25. PBS 2009.
26. PBS 2009.
27. Carson 2002, inside front cover.
28. Carson 2002, 287–288.
29. Carson 2002, 287–288.
30. See Lihs 2009, 1.
31. American Museum of Natural History n.d.
32. Brooks 2015.
33. Ehrlich and Ehrlich 2010, 481.
34. Ehrlich and Ehrlich 2010, 482.
35. World Bank 2015, 162.
36. Brooks 2015.
37. Karole Armitage, e-mail message to author, December 13, 2015.
38. Brooks 2015.
39. Brooks 2015.
40. Ehrlich and Ehrlich 2010, 489.

41. When the MAHB was born at the beginning of the twenty-first century, "it was known as the Millennium Assessment of Human Behavior, making the point that it was following the Millennium Ecosystem Assessment (MEA) but focusing on human behavior and collective actions leading to global collapse. But that name led to considerable confusion, especially because another global behavioral assessment was underway, and because MAHB activities range from research related to how behavioral, cultural, and institutional change toward a sustainable path can be accomplished to generating fora to discuss and illuminate that path." It was therefore decided that MAHB would retain its acronym and re-focus its name to a more accurate description: the Millennium Alliance for Humanity and the Biosphere (MAHB n.d).
42. Ehrlich and Ehrlich 2010, 489.
43. Brooks 2015.
44. Brooks 2015.
45. Lihs 2009, 3.

4 INTERNATIONAL TRADE IN CULTURAL SERVICES

1. The theoretical and political opposition to "free trade" is not new. "As early as the 1830s," C. A. Bayly has written, "the German economist Friedrich List had begun to argue against uncontrolled free trade. Its proponents, he implied, had forgotten that, as a global phenomenon, free trade would inevitably damage the economies and livelihoods of numerous national systems of political economy. It was all very well for the British, whose eighteenth-century commercial efficiency was increasingly supported by the great savings created by industrial production. But in a country like Prussia or Piedmont, free trade would only wipe out local manufactures and squander existing national resources" (Bayly 2004, 301).
2. Krugman 1993, 23–26.
3. University of Wisconsin-Madison 2009.
4. The WTO "is the only global international organization dealing with the rules of trade between nations. At its heart are the WTO agreements, negotiated and signed by the bulk of the world's trading nations and ratified in their parliaments. The goal is to help producers of goods and services, exporters, and importers conduct their business" (WTO n.d.b).

Even Agreements for culture-related commerce can be negotiated at the WTO. But as Tania Voon (2007) notes, the rhumba between the WTO rules and cultural trade can be divisive. And the WTO itself is often misunderstood. As Simon Lester et al. explain, "Reading about the WTO in the popular press, it is sometimes easy to come away with misconceptions about how the organization operates." Given the misconceptions, here is a quick explanation: The WTO is a "Member-driven organization, in that most of the decisions that come out of the WTO are the result of an agreement among all of the countries or customs territories that are WTO Members." It "is not a global parliament with legislators making decisions that national governments must follow. Rather, it is a tool of the governments themselves, through which they make joint decisions" (Lester et al. 2008, 65). See also Kabanda 2016b. All the mystery aside, there is cultural trade potential even in the poorest of nations. The question is how such trade can gain greater application in development.

5. Lester et al. 2008, 597–601. The "everything you cannot drop on your foot" saying is from the entry called Public Citizen News: *Trade Negotiators Push Agreement on Health Care, Education, and Other Services* by Chris Slevin (under "Public Citizen's Lori Wallach and EU Trade Commissioner Pascal Lamy Sound Off on GATS"). See Public Citizen n.d.
6. WTO n.d.b. See also Kabanda 2015b.
7. The inclusion of services "in the Uruguay Round of trade negotiations led to the General Agreement on Trade in Services (GATS). Since January 2000, they have become the subject of multilateral trade negotiations" (WTO n.d.c.). For the Agreement's scope, definition, and other articles see www.wto.org/english/docs_e/legal_e/26-gats.pdf.
8. See UNESCO 2009; Onishi 2016.
9. This section draws heavily from Kabanda 2016f.
10. "This Is Nollywood" n.d.
11. Nsehe 2011.
12. Omanufeme 2016.
13. "This Is Nollywood" n.d.
14. Onishi 2016. See also Kabanda 2016f, 13.
15. Moudio 2013.

16. O'S. 2014.
17. Onishi 2016.
18. Onishi 2016.
19. There are cases where more than one part could come from the same country, which happens to also make the final product, but that is not the point. See Lamy 2011.
20. Investopedia n.d.b. "The measure of imported inputs that are embedded in exports for a typical industry is also known as vertical specialization" (see Maurer and Tschang 2011, 22). "At the microeconomic level," "value added" "is defined as 'the amount by which the value of a good . . . increases at a specific step in a production process.' [Measured in monetary terms, this excludes initial costs.] At the macroeconomic level, in the context of measuring exports, it is defined as 'the value of national work performed (i.e., the contribution of all national factors of production) in a country's exports.' Export values calculated using the value-added method differ from official reported export values, which do not distinguish between 'national' (domestic) inputs into a product and foreign inputs into that product" (Allen n.d.). For our purposes let us consider another dimension: One could conjecture that if a Brazilian band is based in New York, for example, its presence there could add to its value. In another instance, if Brazilian music is produced and exported by an eminent Japanese label, one could also argue that this adds to its value (in terms of international recognition). These scenarios could be reversed, if not mutually reinforcing, and value here may extend beyond monetary accounting.
21. OECD-WTO n.d.
22. Investopedia. n.d.b.
23. Lamy 2011.
24. Adapted from Read 1999.
25. Maurer and Tschang 2011, 14–15.
26. FutureBrand n.d., "2011–2012 Country Brand Index."
27. Morrison 2017, 104, 100–101; for an extended discussion see pp. 100–111.
28. Kahneman 2011, 302. If development experts or others have weak perceptions of certain countries in which they work, it is easy to see why they may have patronizing attitudes toward these countries. This could be true even if these practitioners have good intensions.

29. It could be argued that the lack of confidence in the economic future of their countries is a major reason why many Africans have risked their lives to cross the Mediterranean for greener pastures in Europe. While Europe might provide better opportunities, life is not as easy there as portrayed (or branded) in the media.
30. FutureBrand n.d., "2011–2012 Country Brand Index."
31. Kahneman 2011, 304.
32. FutureBrand n.d. "2011–2012 Country Brand Index."
33. Lester et al. 2008, 633.
34. UN 2015, 24.
35. As the term "soft power" "moved into common usage, [it] has been stretched and twisted, sometimes beyond recognition," according to Joseph S. Nye (2006), who coined the term.
36. Nye 2008, 31.
37. Mansfield and Yohe 2003, 31.
38. Recent arts-related purchases include Apple's acquisition of Beats, a headphone maker that also offers a music-streaming service. See Karp and Barr 2014.
39. Throsby 2010, 52.
40. Polgreen 2015.
41. Kishtainy et al. 2012, 312.
42. Weiner 2016.
43. Weiner 2016, inside cover.
44. L. Thompson 2013.
45. A Systematic Country Diagnostic is meant to employ "data and analytic methods to support country clients and teams in identifying the most critical constraints to, and opportunities for, reducing poverty and promoting shared prosperity sustainably, while explicitly considering the voices of the poor and the views of the private sector" (World Bank 2014b, 25).
46. In relation to backward and forward linkages, these activities may also help stimulate voices of the poor, build social unity, and boost domestic confidence, including that of local investors.
47. De Botton and Armstrong 2016, 200.
48. FutureBrand n.d. "2012–2013 Country Brand Index," 84. See also Kabanda 2014b, 54–55.
49. This section draws heavily from Kabanda 2016f.

50. Berman and Saliba 2009, 4. They paraphrase George Clemenceau.
51. WIPO 2008.
52. Merges 2011, 1.
53. Mackay 2009.
54. Mackay 2009. See also Kabanda 2016f, 14.
55. These figures are from a study by PricewaterhouseCoopers cited in the *Times of India* 2010.
56. BEA 2017.
57. See Galloway 2012.
58. BEA 2013.
59. Timberg 2015. See also Kabanda 2016e.
60. Alain Ruche, e-mail message to author, May 23, 2016.
61. Jewell 2016, 3.
62. Sen 2012. See also Kabanda 2016a, 16.
63. ARIPO n.d.
64. See Kabanda 2016f.
65. Seabrook 2012.
66. See WIPO 2008, 163. "The Role of Intellectual Property in Development and WIPO's Development Cooperation Program."
67. Lohr 2002.
68. Lohr 2002. See also Kabanda 2016f, 9.
69. United States History n.d.
70. Kabanda 2007, 8.
71. See Kabanda 2016f, 11.
72. See Kabanda 2016f, 11.
73. SAMRO n.d.
74. See Kabanda 2016f, 11.
75. Kabanda 2007, 13–14. See also Kabanda 2016f, 11–12.
76. Larcarte 1984.
77. SAMRO 2015.
78. See Kabanda 2016f, esp., 12.
79. See Kabanda 2016f, 12.
80. See Kabanda 2016f, 12.
81. See Kabanda 2016f, 12–13.
82. Musinguzi 2010. See also Kabanda 2016f, 13.
83. Musinguzi 2010. See also Kabanda 2016f, 13.
84. Fowler 2004, 127. See also Kabanda 2016f, 9.

85. Olian 1974. See also Kabanda 2016f, 9.
86. Stiglitz 2009, 141.
87. Faris 2013.
88. Meeks-Owens 2013.
89. See AFDB Group 2014.
90. Davis 2009, for example, see 64–74.
91. Whether this knowledge is in the public domain or not is another matter. But complaints here are all but familiar. For example, see Faris 2013.
92. African Musicians Profiles n.d.
93. Sanneh 2009.
94. Sanneh 2009.
95. Gollin 2008, 26–27.
96. Gollin 2008, 28. See also Kabanda 2016f, 3-4.
97. May and Sell 2005, 44. See also Kabanda 2016f, 4.
98. May and Sell 2005, 45. See also Kabanda 2016f, 4.
99. Negotiated between 1986 and 1994, TRIPS débuted into a multilateral trading system at the Uruguay Round in 1995 (see Kabanda 2013, 66–67). The Agreement invites members, including developing states, to enforce intellectual property as a means of encouraging innovation. Article 7 highlights TRIPS' objectives: "The protection and enforcement of intellectual property rights should contribute to the promotion of technological innovation and to the transfer and dissemination of technology, to the mutual advantage of producers and users of technological knowledge and in a manner conducive to social and economic welfare, and to a balance of rights and obligations" (WTO 2017; see also Kabanda 2016f, 3).
100. Yusuf et al. 2009, xiv.
101. Stiglitz 2009, 141.
102. Finger 2004, 1.
103. J. Michael Finger, interview by author, Somerville, MA, November 28, 2011; see also Kabanda 2016f, 3.
104. *This Is Nollywood* n.d. See also Kabanda 2016f, 13–14.
105. In this case, one could suggest that the state should shoulder the bulk of the responsibility to subsidize such creative endeavors, providing a truly adequate enabling environment on all fronts, including generous financial assistance.
106. Kabanda 2014b, 40.

107. Commission on Intellectual Property Rights 2002, 15. See also Kabanda 2014b 40 and Kabanda 2016f, 10–11.
108. James D. Wolfensohn, interview by author, New York, January 14, 2013.
109. Recent measures to fight piracy include the Copyright Alert System (CAS), which "was developed to help consumers understand the importance of respecting copyright and to alert them of possible infringing activity that has taken place using their Internet connection. . . . [Users] may receive up to six Alerts culminating with a Mitigation Measure. . . . The measures defer for each Internet Service Provider (ISP) but may, for example, take one of the following forms: A temporary reduction of Internet speed; Redirection to a landing page until the primary account holder of your account contacts your ISP; Redirection to a landing page where the primary account holder must review and respond to educational information" (Center for Copyright Information n.d.). Needless to say, these measures are more likely to make sense in places where internet infrastructure is sound. Also, in many developing countries, piracy is still common via physical CDs, cassettes, or DVDs (Kabanda 2014b, 40).
110. Sen 2001, 1.
111. Kabanda 2014b.
112. "Unlike Tort Law or Criminal Law, IP deals not only with Patents, Copyrights, Trademarks and Trade Secrets but also with Unfair Competition, Right of Publicity and more. Moreover, IP interacts with many other areas of law such as Antitrust, Torts, Property Law, [Customary Law], and Contracts. Yet the legal aspects of IP are only one part of the story. To get a thorough understanding of IP, one should also have a good grasp of its economic rationales, political ideology and the prevailing theories that brought this area to life. Furthermore, theoretical knowledge alone is not enough in order to teach IP – practical skills are of an essence and teaching them is not an easy task" (WIPO 2013, 5).
113. For a comprehensive analysis on teaching intellectual property and development policy options, see WIPO 2013.
114. TIPA. n.d. See also Kabanda 2014b, 58–59
115. TIPA n.d. See also Kabanda 2014b, 58–59.
116. The proceedings from this project are documented in the World Bank's "Workshop on the Development of the Music Industry in Africa" (World

Bank 2001), and in the book called *Poor People's Knowledge* (Finger and Schuler ed., 2004).

117. J. Michael Finger, interview by author. See also Kabanda 2016f, 15–16.
118. See related example in Burnett 2013.
119. Lohr 2002.
120. Lohr 2002. See also Kabanda 2016f, 9–10.
121. See www.iprcommission.org/home.html; Commission on Intellectual Property Rights 2002.
122. Ghosh 2013.
123. DI International Business Development 2012, 5.
124. See also Kabanda 2014b, esp. 59–61.
125. Annan 2013, 7.
126. ICIJ 2017.
127. Resource Matters 2017, 2.
128. Fitzgibbon 2017. Resource Matters 2017.
129. See Zucman 2015.
130. CKU 2016, "The Right to Art and Culture 2013–2016."
131. Asia-Europe Foundation 2010.

5 ARTISTS WITHOUT BORDERS IN THE DIGITAL AGE

1. See World Bank 2016.
2. Tamkivi 2014. BBC 2010.
3. UN News Centre 2014.
4. UN 2010, 136.
5. IFPI 2016, 8, 17. See also Kabanda 2016d.
6. ITC and WIPO 2008 in UN 2010, 144–145. For more information, see www.intracen.org or ifcreg@intracen.org.
7. UN 2010, 144–145.
8. UN 2010, 144–145.
9. Kabanda 2014b.
10. UN 2010, 145.
11. Ingham 2015.
12. UN 2010, 145–146.
13. In music, online platforms (or Digital Service Providers) include Amazon, Deezer, Google Play, Medianet, Pandora, Rhapsody, Spotify, and iTunes. Others like Fuga take an integrated approach, working with labels and artists, distributors and aggregators, and Digital Service Providers. In Asia,

besides China's streaming services controlled by such companies as Tencent, Alibaba, and China Mobile (Cookson 2014), there also are emerging startups like KKBOX that are making inroads in the Asian digital music market. Such technologies are now seen as the likely hope for an industry that has suffered persistent losses. Although worldwide revenues for music labels fell by 4 percent to $15 billion in 2013, this reversal of the slight rise in 2012 was "due to Japanese consumers finally giving up on CDs, as much as the rest of the world had already done. A closer look shows that streaming services are starting to bring the business back into profit in countries that have suffered steady declines, such as Italy." Moreover, aside from worries "that streaming may cannibalize downloads," streaming helps independent labels enjoy "the double market share they had on CDs." International trade in this medium is also expanding: via streaming, music easily travels beyond national boundaries, tapping into revenues from far-flung markets (*Economist* 2014, 63). In the GATS this may fall under Mode I, cross border supply (Kabanda 2014b).

14. Kramer 2015. Some may argue otherwise, but Kramer is not entirely off key.
15. IFPI 2015, 19. See also Kabanda 2016d, 9 and 2016e.
16. iROKO n.d.
17. iROKO 2015.
18. iROKO Partners n.d.
19. O. 2012.
20. O. 2012.
21. O. 2012.
22. iROKO Partners n.d.
23. Pham 2009.
24. Merges et al. 2012, 713. Napster was sued by members of the Recording Industry Association of America (A&M Records, Inc. v. Napster, Inc., 239 F.3d 1004) (9th Cir. 2001) for contributory infringement and vicarious infringement of copyright. This legal battle drove Napster into bankruptcy. "During the pendency of this litigation," however, "a new generation of peer-to-peer software providers entered the market, prompting another legal battle" (Merges et al. 2012, 714). These were Grokster, Ltd. and StreamCast Networks, Inc. StreamCast developed promotional materials to market its service as the best Napster alternative. It came up with its own program, called OpenNap,

"engineered 'to leverage Napster's 50 million user base.' One proposed advertisement read: 'Napster Inc. has announced that it will soon begin charging you a fee. That's if the courts don't order it shut down first. What will you do to get around it?'" (Merges et al. 2012, 716).

25. Enigmax 2009.
26. Ernesto 2015.
27. IFPI 2015.
28. IFPI n.d. See also Kabanda 2016d.
29. Plumer 2012.
30. See also Kabanda 2016d and 2016e.
31. Intel Corporation 2013.
32. Collier 2007, 60–61.
33. World Bank 2016, 5.
34. Kimura et al. 2011, 343–344.
35. Kim 2014 (video), 47:40.
36. World Bank 2016, 5. See also Kabanda 2014b, 61–62.
37. Putumayo n.d.
38. Kabanda 2016d, 14–15.
39. Kabanda 2014b, 63.
40. Achebe 2012, 104.
41. Economist 2015a.
42. Economist 2015a.
43. Economist 2015a.
44. Economist 2015a.
45. Economist 2015a.
46. Economist 2015a.
47. See Mortimer et al. 2010, 6. The artists' cut may vary from country to country and also from situation to situation. Nonetheless, understanding how this works might inform policy formation or equip artists with information that could be useful in negotiations. Regarding other secondary opportunities, artists usually get paid to endorse a company or a product – and they can also use their following to promote their own cross-industry investments. Also, many artists perform for "secondary events" like private shows and earn side income that way (Boluk 2015). Although famous artists normally enjoy such opportunities, less-known artists are not entirely closed off (Kabanda 2016d, 7–8).
48. See Rohter 2012.

49. Rohter 2012.
50. American Visa Bureau 2012.
51. Rohter 2012; see also American Visa Bureau 2012 and Watanabe 2010.
52. American Visa Bureau 2012.
53. Watanabe 2010.
54. American Visa Bureau 2012.
55. Rohter 2012.
56. I am grateful to Joel P. Trachtman, my former professor in legal and institutional aspects of international trade, for bringing Ogbechie's story my attention.
57. University of California, Santa Barbara n.d.
58. Okwunodu Ogbechie 2007.
59. Okwunodu Ogbechie 2007.
60. USCIS 2017.
61. US Department of Labor 2009.
62. See also Kabanda 2014b, 44–45.
63. Trachtman 2009, 7.
64. Trachtman 2009, 7.
65. Trachtman 2009, 72.
66. Trachtman 2009, 72.
67. Pearlman 2009
68. Robinson 2013, Back cover.
69. Robinson 2017.
70. Pearlman 2009.
71. It must be noted though that this behavior is not limited to artists; it also happens in other sectors.
72. Whaley 2013.
73. Whaley 2013.
74. See Kabanda 2016d and Erickson 2015.
75. For such a thing to be worked out, bilateral or plurilateral or even multilateral agreements may have to be negotiated. These may be similar to the US Free Trade Agreements with countries like Chile and Singapore that include "provisions allowing for temporary entry of business persons, traders, investors and intra company transferees" (Trachtman 2009, 230). Trachtman came up with an illustrative draft agreement on labor migration. "[It] is provided merely to indicate the types of provisions that might be negotiated by states if they were to determine to enter into

a multilateral 'General Agreement on Labor Immigration'" (Trachtman 2009, 347). Article 5.1.1.3 on Occupational Group Commitments provides as follows: "Vertical occupational group commitments relate to immigrants who are categorized within a particular occupational group. Wherever possible, each member shall utilize the ISCO 2008 [International Standard Classification of Occupations 2008], as a basis for its occupational group commitments. Each member shall publish a set of definitions of each occupational group, showing how its definitions differ from relevant ISCO 2008 definitions" (Trachtman 2009, 349).

76. Whaley 2013.
77. Collier 2007, 55.
78. Even if more developing countries may have joined this process by now, progress here is slow.
79. Sauvé 2003, 171–172.
80. Sauvé 2003, 171–172.

6 ON CULTURAL TOURISM

1. UN 2015, 24.
2. WTTC 2015a.
3. Becker 2013, 2, 8.
4. Achebe 2012, 1.
5. Rugwabiza 2012. See also Kabanda 2016b.
6. Rugwabiza 2012.
7. Achebe 2012, 1.
8. Achebe 2012, 1–2.
9. S. Johnson 2016, 91.
10. Achebe 2012, 56.
11. WTO n.d. "The General Agreement on Trade in Services (GATS)." For specific technical language see source or Box 4.1 in Chapter 4.
12. Buchholz 2007, 17.
13. WTTC 2015a.
14. Creative Tourism Network n.d.
15. Achebe 2012, 56.
16. See Casellas et al. 2012; Sasajima 2015; and Kaysen 2016.
17. Creative Tourism Network n.d.
18. Blair A. Ruble, e-mail message to author, March 31, 2017.
19. Throsby 2010, 16.

20. African Economic Outlook 2012, 99.
21. Throsby 2010, 131.
22. Nigeria High Commission, London n.d.
23. Nigeria High Commission, London n.d.
24. Kahneman 2011, 302–304.
25. FutureBrand n.d. "2011–2012 Country Brand Index," 53.
26. Throsby 2010, 131–132.
27. Throsby 2010, 133–134.
28. Kishtainy et al. 2012, 312.
29. Kaul 2009, 6.
30. "Narrowly defined," according to Toni Morrison, globalization "means the free movement of capital and the rapid distribution of data and products operating within a politically neutral environment shaped by multinational corporate demands. Its larger connotations, however, are less innocent, encompassing as they do, not only the demonization of embargoed states or the trivialization-cum-negotiation with war lords and corrupt politicians, but also the collapse of nation states under the weight of transnational economics, capital, and labor; the preeminence of Western culture and economy; and the Americanization of the developed and developing world through the penetration of U.S. cultures into the West in fashion, film, music, and cuisine" (Morrison 2017, 96–97).
31. Sen 2000, 240.
32. Carvajal 2015.
33. Carvajal 2015.
34. Becker 2013, 2.
35. Becker 2015.
36. Becker 2013, 2, 8.
37. Becker 2015.
38. Gelles 2015.
39. Becker 2015.
40. Economist 2015b.
41. Sen 2000, 243.
42. Zinsser 1984, 152.
43. Kaul 2009, 150.
44. For more on Chopin and his dance lessons see Goldberg 2013.
45. Melo 2016, 10.
46. James D. Wolfensohn, interview with author, New York, January 14, 2013.

47. Kaplan and Norton 2004, 3–4.
48. Kaplan and Norton 2004, 4.
49. BBC 2013.
50. European Council on Tourism and Trade 2013.
51. WTTC 2015b, 1.
52. Sen 2000, 241–242.
53. Davis 1988, 20, 15.
54. Nelson 2014.
55. One could argue that since nations engage in negotiating contracts, power play may also come in here. Countries with a weak image may have less bargaining power than those with a strong image. This could also be the case regarding citizens or firms in such countries. The work of Nobel-economists Oliver Hart and Bengt Holmström on contact theory, though not directly related, may come in here. (See The Royal Swedish Academy of Sciences 2016.)
56. World Bank 2014a. The homicides were "6.9 per 100,000 people in Haiti versus 52 for Jamaica, 35 for Trinidad, 28 for the Bahamas and 24 for Dominican Republic."
57. World Bank 2014a. In "2012, 4.3 million tourists visited the Dominican Republic, 2 million Jamaica and 1.3 million the Bahamas."
58. World Bank 2014a.
59. Wiener 2016, 248–249.
60. Gibson and Connell 2005, 72.
61. Gibson and Connell 2005, 72. As an aside, although there is nothing wrong with using a Mozart sound track in a movie about, say, Haiti, in this case playing Haiti's own music may paint a more supportive picture.
62. World Bank 2014b, 23.

7 THE UNSETTLED QUESTION OF WOMEN IN THE PERFORMING ARTS

1. UN 2015, 22.
2. Geiger and Kent 2015.
3. Fennell 2014, 1: 14.
4. See Kantor and Twohey 2017.
5. World Bank 2011.
6. Nandana Sen, email message to author, June 29, 2016. Indeed, in Mihir Bose's book, *Bollywood: A History*, we learn that way before the so-called

Bollywood emerged, India had a flourishing cinema, one that even precedes Hollywood. There is a feeling among some that this sobriquet is wrapped in a Western "mental trap." "Bollywood" the complaint goes, "demeans something truly Indian." The term "proves that Indians can only define even their most precious products by borrowing Western terms" (Bose 2006, 10). From an African perspective, I have heard similar complaints about Nigeria's Nollywood.

7. DI International Business Development 2012, 2.
8. Ghosh 2013.
9. Analogy by World Bank colleague Shiva Makki.
10. Nandana Sen, email message to author, June 29, 2016.
11. Tere 2012, 4.
12. Nandana Sen, email message to author, June 29, 2016.
13. Varma 2014.
14. Nandana Sen, email message to author, June 29, 2016.
15. Tulshyan 2013.
16. Tere 2012, 6.
17. Nooristani 2013.
18. Nooristani 2013.
19. Nandana Sen, email message to author, June 29, 2016. See also N. Sen 2013b.
20. N. Sen 2013b and 2013a.
21. Joseph 2014, 75.
22. Drèze and Sen 2013, 226.
23. Tulshyan 2014.
24. Tulshyan 2014. Even concerning Hollywood this is the case. As the journalist and author Maureen Dowd concludes, Fixing Hollywood's gender problem in not only important for women in Hollywood; "it's also important for women and girls everywhere." For such industries, as the film director and screenwriter Leigh Janiak observes, influence culture (Dowd 2015).
25. Basáñez 2016, 166. See also Joseph 2014, 75.
26. One could say that there is a structural correlation between acting and the awards, but that is a topic for another day. In fact, does this even account for the voting gap of 77 percent men and 23 percent women in the Academy that chooses who gets an Oscar?
27. Smith et al. 2014.
28. UN Women 2014.
29. Smith et al. 2014, 24.

30. Ross 2014, 44.
31. UNESCO 2014, 37, 28.
32. Fennell 2014, 1: 14.
33. Sen 2000 191.
34. UNESCO 2014, 37.
35. Jennings 2013.
36. For more on this, see Library of Congress n.d.
37. Gates 2007, 1.
38. Gates 2007, 1, 4.
39. Weiner 2016, 240.
40. Goldin and Rouse 1997.
41. Goldin and Rouse 1997.
42. White 2014.
43. Levintova 2013.
44. White 2014. See also Kabanda 2015e.
45. Women's Studies at James Madison University. See also Kabanda 2015e.
46. Drèze and Sen 2013, 224.
47. Yunus 2007, 54–55.
48. Kittredge 2015.
49. Yunus 2007, 55.
50. Basu 2010, x.
51. Rodrik 2015, 11; original emphasis.
52. Rodrik 2015, 11.
53. Rodrik 2015, 11.
54. Yunus 2007, 55.
55. Tere 2012, 6, 8.
56. Basu 2015, 1.
57. Akerlof and Kranton 2010, 85.
58. D. Basu 2013.
59. Smith n.d. [1759], 44.
60. Smith n.d. [1759], 40.

8 THE ARTS IN MENTAL HEALTH, SOCIAL HEALING, AND URBAN RENEWAL

1. WHO 2013, 7–8.
2. WHO 2013, 8.
3. *Sweet Dreams* 2012.

4. Ingoma Nshya n.d.
5. Musinguzi 2017.
6. *Sweet Dreams* 2012.
7. Sen 2006, 174.
8. Forges et al. 1999, 215.
9. De Botton and Armstrong 2016, 25.
10. Mankiw 2011.
11. WHO 2013, 38.
12. Margaret Chan 2013, 05.
13. WHO 2013, 08.
14. WHO 2013, 08.
15. Kigozi et al. 2010.
16. Carey 2015.
17. Christ 2013.
18. Bleckner, a painter, was the first fine artist to be named a UN goodwill ambassador.
19. Kennedy 2009.
20. Kennedy 2009.
21. Kigozi et al. 2010.
22. Throsby 2010, 29.
23. Brueggemann 2010, 1.
24. NJPAC n.d.a.
25. NJPAC n.d.b.
26. Sullivan 1987.
27. Conversation with NJPAC President and CEO John Schreiber and Vice President for Arts Education Alison Scott-Williams (2016).
28. NJPAC n.d.b.
29. Sullivan 1987.
30. Jacobs 2007.
31. Jacobs 2007.
32. Wulfhorst 2015.
33. Wulfhorst 2015.
34. Wulfhorst 2015.
35. Wulfhorst 2015.
36. NJPAC n.d.b.
37. UN 2013, 69.
38. Williams, Chazkel, and Mendonça 2016, xv–xvi, 1.

39. Neate and Platt 2010.
40. Quincy Jones 2010, i.
41. Neate and Platt 2010, back cover.
42. Neate and Plate 2010, 20–22.
43. DocumentaryStorm n.d.
44. Neate and Platt 2010, 22.
45. Neate and Platt 2010, 23.
46. Veloso 2010, xvi.
47. Neate and Platt 2010, 23–24.
48. Neate and Platt 2010, 24.
49. Neate and Platt 2010, 24–25.
50. Neate and Platt 2010, 25.
51. TripAdvisor n.d.
52. UNESCO, 2012.
53. Fierberg and Manfred 2015.
54. Throsby 2010, 29.
55. EIU 2016, 2.
56. EIU 2016, 2.
57. EIU 2016, 2–4.
58. See Mulitalo-Lauta and Menon 2006 and Kalmanowitz et al. 2012.
59. Kalmanowitz et al. 2012, 46.
60. Kalmanowitz et al. 2012, 46–47.
61. See Gosh 1998.
62. Tiwari 2012.
63. Fujiwara, Kudrna, and Dolan 2014, 9.
64. WHO 2013, 07.
65. WHO 2013, 17.
66. FundaMentalSDG n.d.
67. UN 2015, 20.
68. WHO 2013, 17.

9 CREATIVE DATA COLLECTION

1. Harford 2015.
2. Jerven 2013, back cover. The larger problem is not limited to Africa. But few studies examine the acute data deficiencies in Africa (Jerven 2013, 1). Yet the continent tends to receive an avalanche of poverty finger-pointing.
3. UniqueTracks 2014.

4. Preamble adapted from Kabanda 2016c.
5. Acocella 2015.
6. Nabokov 1989, 21.
7. Deaton 2010, 14. See also Jerven 2013, 31.
8. Jerven 2013, 1, 36, 9. See also OECD 2001, 11.
9. Jerven 2013, 94.
10. Wilson 1998, 298.
11. Borgman 2016, 4.
12. Borgman 2016, 17, 28.
13. Davies 2017.
14. Weingarten 2007. See also Kabanda 2014b.
15. Weingarten 2007. See also Kabanda 2014b.
16. Jurgensen 2014. See also Contrera 2014.
17. Basu 2011, 75.
18. Hansen 1995.
19. Hansen 1995.
20. Hansen 1995.
21. The emerging research on the arts and subjective wellbeing measures is worthy of attention. Consider *Artful Living*, a paper published by the Curb Center for Art, Enterprise, and Public Policy at Vanderbilt University. Steven J. Tepper and others explore the "thesis that the arts are essential to a high quality of life." Here is their conclusion: "Overall, we find strong support that artistic practice is associated with higher levels of life satisfaction, a more positive self-image, less anxiety about change, a more tolerant and open approach to diverse others, and, in some cases, less focus on materialistic values and the acquisition of goods" (Tepper et al. 2014, 6). Along the same lines, Carol Graham and others have this to say in a Brookings working paper: "In general, our results provide moderate support for well-being being positively associated with arts consumption and production. As we do not have over-time data on the same people, we cannot say anything about the direction of causality. So the effects might run from the arts to well-being, but they could also run in the opposite direction, with happier people more likely to participate in the arts. For example, some of our earlier work suggests that the happiest respondents care less about income and full-time employment than the average, but care more about learning and creativity" (Graham et al. 2014, 8; see also Iyengar 2014).These reports are exploratory and more research is needed in

this area. And we should not forget that, regardless of the measurements, those who advocate for celebrating art for art's sake are not out of their minds. But if such measurements can induce more support for culture in development then they are not a futile exercise.

22. Throsby 2010, ix.
23. World Bank 2014b, 26.
24. UN 2010, 142.
25. Thompson 2011. Sparviero 2015.
26. Lev and Gu 2016.
27. Fridson 2016.
28. Fridson 2016.
29. Diane Coyle, email message to author, April 3, 2017.
30. World Bank 2014b, 27.
31. See Borgman 2016, 71 and 79, for example.
32. "Statistical Handbook of Japan 2017" (Statistics Bureau, Ministry of Internal Affairs and Communications) www.stat.go.jp/english/data/handbook/pdf/2017all.pdf#page=198.
33. The Declaration goes on to say: "We consider that in the face of mounting challenges such as population growth, urbanization, environmental degradation, disasters, climate change, increasing inequalities and persisting poverty, there is an urgent need for new approaches, to be defined and measured in a way which accounts for the broader picture of human progress and which emphasize harmony among peoples and between humans and nature, equity, dignity, well-being and sustainability.

    These new approaches should fully acknowledge the role of culture as a system of values and a resource and framework to build truly sustainable development, the need to draw from the experiences of past generations, and the recognition of culture as part of the global and local commons as well as a wellspring for creativity and renewal" (UNESCO 2015b).
34. UNESCO 2015a.
35. UNESCO 2015a.
36. UNESCO 2015a.
37. World Bank 2013.
38. OECD n.d.
39. Lamy 2011.
40. Sturgeon 2015.

41. IDB 2014.
42. IDB 2014. The database is available at bit.ly/Americas2013CIDatabase.
43. UNSD n.d.
44. Kabanda 2016g, 4. Diane Coyle, email message to author, August 18, 2016.
45. Diane Coyle, email message to author, April 3, 2017.
46. OECD 2001. The United Nations developed the term Satellite Account "to measure the size of economic sectors that are not defined as industries in national accounts. Tourism, for example, is an amalgam of industries such as transportation, accommodation, food and beverage services, recreation and entertainment and travel agencies" (UNWTO n.d., 1; see also Kabanda 2014b, 51–52; Kabanda 2016g, 11).
47. Coyle 2014, 138. Climate change is a perfect example regarding the efficacy of satellite accounts. "Some countries have been publishing ... 'satellite accounts' on the environment for a number of years." Yet "it is hard to identify any direct influence they have had on economic policy debates" (Coyle 2014, 138; Kabanda 2016g, 11).
48. These concepts are adapted from Franz, Laimer, and Manente n.d.
49. YouTube n.d.
50. *Economist* 2013a.
51. See also Kabanda 2014b and 2016d.
52. Borgman 2016, 3–4.
53. See Kabanda 2016g, especially 6–9.
54. Kabanda 2016g, 8–9. Also see Lamy 2011.
55. This idea is also discussed in Kabanda 2016g.
56. See Throsby 2010, especially 52. Some countries may also use such exchanges to exert influence, be it political or otherwise (Kabanda 2016g, 10).
57. This saying is often attributed to Einstein, but it has been assigned to the sociologist William Bruce Cameron among others. It appears in Cameron's 1963 paper called "Informal Sociology: A Casual Introduction to Sociological Thinking." See Novak 2014 and O'Toole 2010.
58. Leontief 1992, 144–145.
59. Jerven 2013, 115.
60. Robinson 2013, 18.

FINALE

1. Arden 2003, front cover.
2. This saying and its variants have been attributed to many people, including Dennis Gabor, Ilya Prigogine, Alan Kay, Steven Lisberger, Peter Drucker, Forrest C. Shaklee, and Anonymous (O'Toole 2012). See also Petersen 2013.
3. Azami 2012; Rasul 2012.
4. Convenience is not deficient by default, but sometimes it leads to such attitudes as "faster is always better," and unrealistic goal setting – see *Goals Gone Wild* by Lisa D. Ordóñez et al. As we noted earlier in this book – and again, this is especially important concerning people's lives and such momentous issues as development – "[a] team comprising poets, artists, anthropologists, psychologists, neuroscientists and philosophers, for example, will undoubtedly come up with more leftfield and psychologically rich ideas than a cohort of overworked MBA consultants," or economists, or artists, or development experts for that matter, "all schooled in similar patterns of thinking." As if to echo Steve Jobs and others, Ewen Haldane makes that point clear. Nevertheless, although sometimes "constructive impatience" is necessary (Sen 2000, 11), he goes on to add: "having a diverse team alone won't help unless we also focus on slowing down. The most original ideas require long periods of solitary reflection, allowing our minds the freedom to mull over amorphous hunches and explore areas adjacent to the immediate challenge" (Haldane 2017). This thought cannot but take us back to Shira Baror and Moshe Bar's findings on original and creative thinking discussed in Chapter 1. (See also Isaacson 2017, especially pages 521–522.) More immediately, however, it challenges us to note that many original ideas are unlikely to make an appointment to meet us at a convenient time.
5. Obama 2006, 48.
6. Wilson 1998, 298.
7. Buchholz, 2007, 1.
8. Weiner 2016, 269. Walter Isaacson, who has written biographies on the theme exploring "how the ability to make connections across disciplines – arts and sciences, humanities and technology – is a key to innovation, imagination, and genius," also notes: "Albert Einstein, when he was stymied in his pursuit of his theory of relativity, would pull out his violin and play Mozart, which helped him reconnect with the harmonies of the cosmos" (Isaacson 2017, 2–3).

9. Of course, many organizations strive to do better. But as a few colleagues at the World Bank have complained, the process of doing things differently is often more or less like putting old wine in a new bottle.
10. See "Attitude Over Latitude," Buchholz 2007, xvii–xviii.

ANNEXES

1. "The purpose of this study," according to the authors, "was to examine the prevalence and nature of female characters in popular films from 11 countries around the world. One unifying theme was apparent: female characters are not equal and they are not aspirational in this sample of global films." These facts from the study illustrate this theme (Smith et al. 2014, 24).

Glossary of Selected Musical Terms

Coda (Italian: tail) "A piece of music at the end of a longer piece of music, usually separate from the basic structure. The coda is often more technically difficult than the rest of the piece." *Source: Cambridge Dictionary* n.d.a.

Deceptive cadence "A musical cadence in which the dominant resolves to a harmony other than the tonic – called also false cadence, interrupted cadence, suspended cadence." It is deceptive to the listener in that instead of resolving to the tonic as it normally does, the dominant resolves somewhere else. For example, in a major key, instead of landing on the tonic (I), the dominant chord (V) ends up resolving on the superdominant (VI), creating suspense to the ear. *Sources: Merriam-Webster* n.d.; *On Music Dictionary* 2016a.

Finale "The close or termination of something: such as the last section of an instrumental musical composition" – for example, the symphony's finale. *Source: Merriam-Webster* 2017a.

Fugue "A form of composition popular in, but not restricted to, the Baroque era, in which a theme or subject is introduced by one voice, and is imitated by other voices in

	succession. Usually only the first few notes of the subject are imitated exactly, then each voice deviates slightly until the next time it enters again with the subject. Generally the voices overlap and weave in and out of each other [in Counterpoint,] forming a continuous, tapestry-like texture." *Source: On Music Dictionary* 2016b.
Leitmotif (German: leading motif)	"A recurring motif in a composition (usually an opera) which represents a specific person, idea, or emotion. This term was first applied to the operas of Richard Wagner." *Source: On Music Dictionary* 2013.
Movement	A "section of a more extended work that is more or less complete in itself. Occasionally movements are linked together, either through the choice of a final inconclusive chord or by a linking note." For example, consider the "first and second movement of Mendelssohn's Violin Concerto" in E minor. Op. 64. *Source: Naxos* n.d.a.
Overture	"An introductory movement for orchestra intended to introduce an opera, oratorio, or other dramatic vocal composition by presenting themes to be heard later in the composition. Also, an independent composition for orchestra; in this case, it is called a 'concert overture.'" *Source: On Music Dictionary* 2016c.
Prelude	1. "An introductory performance, action, or event preceding and preparing for the principal or a more important matter." 2a.

"A musical section or movement introducing the theme or chief subject (as of a fugue or suite) or serving as an introduction to an opera or oratorio." 2b. "An opening voluntary." 2c. "A separate concert piece usually for piano or orchestra and based entirely on a short motif." *Source: Merriam-Webster* 2017b.

Rondo (= French: *rondeau*) A form of composition that "involves the use of a recurrent theme between a series of varied episodes." *Source: Naxos*. b. n.d.

Suite An "instrumental piece consisting of several shorter pieces." For example, "the Baroque suite generally contains a series of dance movements, in particular the *allemande, courante, sarabande* and *gigue*. Later suites of all kinds exist, some formed from extracts of a larger work—an opera, ballet or incidental music." *Source: Naxos* n.d.c.

Symphony "A long piece of music usually in four parts and played by an orchestra (= large group playing different instruments)." *Source: Cambridge Dictionary* n.d.b.

Theme and variations "A style of composition that first presents a basic theme and then develops and alters that theme in successive statements." *Source: On Music Dictionary*. 2016d.

References

Abrams, Amah-Rose. 2016. "Brazilian Government Reinstates Culture Ministry in Political U-Turn." *Artnet*, May 25. Accessed November 28, 2017. https://news.artnet.com/art-world/brazilian-government-reinstates-culture-ministry-political-u-turn-504302.

Achebe, Chinua. 2012. *There Was a Country: A Personal History of Biafra*. New York: Penguin Books.

Acocella, Joan. 2015. "I Can't Go On! What's Behind Stagefright?" *New Yorker*, August 3. Accessed October 29, 2015. www.newyorker.com/magazine/2015/08/03/i-cant-go-on.

Adams, Henry. 2011. "A Tribute to a Great Artist: Steve Jobs." *Smithsonian*, October 5. Accessed November 28, 2017. www.smithsonianmag.com/arts-culture/a-tribute-to-a-great-artist-steve-jobs-99783256/?no-ist.

African Economic Outlook. 2012. *Special Theme: Promoting Youth Employment*. Tunis, Paris, New York, and Addis Ababa: AFDB, OECD, UNDP, and UNECA. Accessed November 28, 2017. www.africaneconomicoutlook.org/sites/default/files/content-pdf/AEO2012_EN.pdf.

AFDB (African Development Bank Group). 2014. "When It Comes to Innovation, Africans Must Believe in Their Own Knowledge," November 4. Accessed November 28, 2017. www.afdb.org/en/news-and-events/when-it-comes-to-innovation-africans-must-believe-in-their-own-knowledge-13719/.

African Musicians Profiles. n.d. "Manu Dibango." Accessed November 28, 2017. www.africanmusiciansprofiles.com/manudibango.htm.

Akerlof, George A. and Rachel E. Kranton. 2010. *Identity Economics: How Our Identities Shape Our Work, Wages, and Well-Being*. Princeton: Princeton University Press.

Algan, Yann and Pierre Cahuc. 2007. "Social Attitudes and Economic Development: An Epidemiological Approach." *Vox*, October 2. Accessed November 28, 2017. www.voxeu.org/article/trust-and-economic-development.

Algan, Yann, Pierre Cahuc, and Andrei Shleifer. 2013. "Teaching Practices and Social Capital." *American Economic Journal: Applied Economics* 5, no. 3: 189–210.

Allen, Brian. n.d. "Special Topic: Value Added as a Measurement of Trade." United States International Trade Commission. Accessed November 28, 2017. www.usitc.gov/special_topic_value_added_measurement_trade.htm.

Almino, Elisa Wouk 2016. "Brazilian Artists Protest Interim President's Dissolution of Ministry of Culture." *Hyperallergic*. May 19. Accessed November 28, 2017. http://hyperallergic.com/299779/brazilian-artists-protest-interim-presidents-dissolution-of-ministry-of-culture/.

American Museum of Natural History. n.d. "Milstein Hall of Ocean Life." Accessed November 28, 2017. www.amnh.org/exhibitions/permanent-exhibitions/biodiversity-and-environmental-halls/milstein-hall-of-ocean-life.

American Visa Bureau. 2012. "No Celebrity Treatment in US Visa Rules." April 11. Accessed January 5, 2018. www.visabureau.com/america/news/11-04-2012/no-celebrity-treatment-in-us-visa-rules.aspx.

Annan, Kofi A. 2013. "Foreword." In *Equity in Extractives Africa Progress Report 2013: Stewarding Africa's Natural Resources for All*. Geneva: The Africa Progress Panel. Accessed May 10, 2014. www.africaprogresspanel.org/wp-content/uploads/2013/08/2013_APR_Equity_in_Extractives_25062013_ENG_HR.pdf.

Arden, Paul. 2003. *It's Not How Good You Are, It's How Good You Want to Be: The World's Best Selling Book*. London: Phaidon Press.

ARIPO (African Regional Intellectual Property Organization). n.d. "Copyright." Accessed November 28, 2017. www.aripo.org/services/copyright.

Asia-Europe Foundation. 2010. "Danish Center for Culture and Development (CKU)." culture360.asef.org. September 03. Accessed December 28, 2017. http://culture360.asef.org/resources/danish-center-culture-and-development-cku.

Azami, Dawood. 2012. "Taliban poetry and the lone fighter." *BBC Magazine*, 10 July. Accessed November 28, 2017. www.bbc.com/news/world-asia-17905361.

Baily, John. 2001. "The Censorship of Music in Afghanistan." *The Revolutionary Association of the Women of Afghanistan*, April 24. Accessed November 28, 2017. www.rawa.org/music.htm.

Ball, Matthew (aka Boluk, Liam). 2015. "Less Money, Mo' Music and Lots of Problems: A Look at the Music Biz." *REDEF*, July 28. Accessed November 28, 2017. http://redef.com/original/less-money-mo-music-lots-of-problems-the-past-present-and-future-of-the-music-biz.

Bar, Moshe. 2016. "Think Less, Think Better." *New York Times*, June 17. Accessed November 28, 2017. www.nytimes.com/2016/06/19/opinion/sunday/think-less-think-better.html.

Baror, Shira and Moshe Bar. 2016. "Associative Activation and Its Relation to Exploration and Exploitation in the Brain." *Psychological Science* 27, no. 6 (April 27): 776–789. Accessed November 28, 2017. http://journals.sagepub.com/doi/pdf/10.1177/0956797616634487.

Basáñez, Miguel E. 2016. *A World of Three Cultures: Honor, Achievement and Joy*. New York: Oxford University Press.

Basu, Diksha. 2013. "Failure in Bollywood." *New York Times*, July 26. Accessed November 28, 2017. https://india.blogs.nytimes.com/2013/07/26/failure-in-bollywood/#more-67683.

Basu, Kaushik. 2010. *Beyond the Invisible Hand*. Princeton: Princeton University Press.

2011. *An Economist's Miscellany*. New Delhi: Oxford University Press.

2015. "Foreword." In *Women, Business and the Law 2016: Getting to Equal*. Washington, DC: World Bank. doi:10.1596/978-1-4648-0677-3. Accessed October 6, 2015. http://wbl.worldbank.org/~/media/WBG/WBL/Documents/Reports/2016/Women-Business-and-the-Law-2016.pdf.

Bayly, Chistopher A. 2004. *The Birth of the Modern World 1780–1914: Global Connections and Comparisons*. Oxford: Blackwell Publishing.

BBC. 2010. "Finland Makes Broadband a 'Legal Right.'" July 1. Accessed June 12, 2014. www.bbc.com/news/10461048.

2013. "Music Tourism 'Boosts UK's Economy by £2.2bn a Year.'" October 11. Accessed May 22, 2014. www.bbc.co.uk/newsbeat/24496893.

BEA (Bureau of Economic Analysis). 2013. "BEA Expands Coverage of Intellectual Property Products." Accessed September 3, 2015. www.bea.gov/national/pdf/flyer_bea_expands_coverage_of_intellectual.pdf.

2013. "National Income and Product Accounts Gross Domestic Product, Second Quarter 2013 (Advance Estimate); Comprehensive Revision: 1929 through 1st Quarter 2013." July 31. Accessed November 28, 2017. http://bea.gov/newsreleases/national/gdp/2013/gdp2q13_adv.htm.

2017. "Arts and Culture Grow for Third Straight Year." April 19. Accessed November 28, 2017. www.bea.gov/newsreleases/general/acpsa/acpsanewsrelease.htm.

Becker, Elizabeth. 2013. *Overbooked: The Exploding Business of Travel and Tourism*. New York: Simon and Schuster.

2015. "The Revolt against Tourism." *New York Times*, July 17. Accessed November 28, 2017. www.nytimes.com/2015/07/19/opinion/sunday/the-revolt-against-tourism.html.

Berman, Harold J. and Samir N. Saliba. 2009. *The Nature and Functions of Law*. 7th edn. New York: Foundation Press.

Borgman, Christine L. 2016. *Big Data, Little Data, No Data: Scholarship in the Networked World*. Cambridge: MIT Press.

Bose, Mihir. 2006. *Bollywood: A History*. Stroud, UK: Tempus Publishing.

Bourdieu, Pierre. 1983. "Forms of Capital." In Handbook of Theory and Research for the Sociology of Education, ed. J. C. Richards. New York: Greenwood Press.

Bowlingalone.com. n.d. "About the Book." Accessed November 28, 2017. http://bowlingalone.com.

British Council. n.d. "Creative Economy, Brazil." Accessed November 29, 2017. http://creativeeconomy.britishcouncil.org/places/brazil/.

Brody, Jane E. 2017. "The Surprising Effects of Loneliness on Health." *New York Times*, December 11. Accessed December 7, 2018. www.nytimes.com/2017/12/11/well/mind/how-loneliness-affects-our-health.html.

Brooks, Katherine. 2015. "This Dance Project Is Out to Prove Climate Change Is an Issue We Can't Ignore." *Huffington Post*, March 25. Accessed November 29, 2017. www.huffingtonpost.com/2015/03/25/on-the-nature-of-things_n_6939826.html.

Brueggemann, John. 2010. *Rich, Free, and Miserable: The Failure of Success in America*. Lanham, MD: Rowman & Littlefield Publishers, Inc.

Brzeski, Patrick. 2016. "Wanda Chairman Reveals Ambitious Plan to Invest Billions in 'All Six' Hollywood Studios." *Hollywood Reporter*, November 2. Accessed November 29, 2017. www.hollywoodreporter.com/features/wanda-chairman-wang-jianlin-plans-invest-billions-hollywood-942854.

Buchholz, Todd G. 2007. *New Ideas from Dead Economists: An Introduction to Modern Economic Thought*. Revised and Updated edn. New York: Plume.

Burnett III, James H. 2013. "Young Musicians Get Lessons in the Law." *Boston Globe*, December 25. Accessed June 9, 2014. www.bostonglobe.com/arts/2013/12/25/young-musicians-get-crash-course-copyright-law/MH4DeNLLpLajLAM84PvSTO/story.html.

Caballero, Mara Cristina. 2004. "Academic Turns City into a Social Experiment." *Harvard Gazette*, March 11. Accessed November 29, 2017. https://news.harvard.edu/gazette/story/2004/03/academic-turns-city-into-a-social-experiment/ .

Callen, Tim. 2012. "Gross Domestic Product: An Economy's All." *Finance and Development*, updated: March 28. Accessed August 1, 2016. www.imf.org/external/pubs/ft/fandd/basics/gdp.htm.

Cambridge Dictionary. n.d.a. "Coda." Accessed January 1, 2018. https://dictionary.cambridge.org/us/dictionary/english/coda.

n.d.b. "Symphony." Accessed January 1, 2018. https://dictionary.cambridge.org/us/dictionary/english/symphony.

Carey, Benedict. 2015. "The Chains of Mental Illness in West Africa." *International New York Times*, October 11. Accessed October 18, 2015. www.nytimes.com/2015/10/12/health/the-chains-of-mental-illness-in-west-africa.html.

Carson, Rachel. 2002. *Silent Spring*. 40th Anniversary edn. New York: Mariner Books. (Orig. publ. 1962.)

Carvajal, Doreen. 2015. "In Tourist Destinations, a Picture of Excess." *New York Times*, July 11. Accessed April 8, 2016. www.nytimes.com/2015/07/12/world/europe/selfie-vacation-damage-majorca-paris-ibiza-rome.html.

Casellas, Antònia, Esteve Dot-Jutgla, and Montserrat Pallares-Barbera. 2012. "Artists, Cultural Gentrification and Public Policy." *Urbani izziv* 23, no. s1: s104-s114. Accessed November 29, 2017. http://urbani-izziv.uirs.si/Portals/uizziv/papers/urbani-izziv-en-2012-23-supplement-1-010.pdf.

Center for American Progress. 2008. "Governor Mike Huckabee: How Music Education Can Build a Better America." September 10. Accessed January 4, 2018. www.americanprogress.org/events/2008/09/10/16683/governor-mike-huckabee-how-music-education-can-build-a-better-america/.

Center for Copyright Information. n.d. "Copyright Alert System FAQS." Accessed June 9, 2014. www.copyrightinformation.org/resources-faq/copyright-alert-system-faqs/.

Chan, Margaret. 2013. Foreword. In *Mental Health Action Plan 2013–2020*. Geneva: WHO. Accessed November 29, 2017. http://apps.who.int/iris/bitstream/10665/89966/1/9789241506021_eng.pdf#page=7.

Christ, Scott. 2013. "20 Surprising, Science-Backed Health Benefits of Music." *Greatist*, December 12. Accessed October 18, 2015. http://greatist.com/happiness/unexpected-health-benefits-music.

CBS News. 2013. "Price of Success: Will the Recycled Orchestra Last?" November 17. Accessed July 28, 2014. www.cbsnews.com/news/price-of-success-will-the-recycled-orchestra-last/.

CKU (Center for Kultur & Udvikling). n.d. Accessed March 16, 2015. www.cku.dk/; Accessed November 29, 2017. https://issuu.com/cku-centerforkulturogudvikling.

2016. "The Right to Art and Culture 2013–2016 – Danish Experiences with the Power of Art, Culture and Creative Industries in Development Cooperation." Copenhagen. December 17. https://issuu.com/cku-centerforkulturogudvikling/docs/cku_final_report_web.

Coleman, James S. 1988. "Social Capital in the Creation of Human Capital." *American Journal of Sociology* 94. Supplement: Organizations and Institutions:

Sociological and Economic Approaches to the Analysis of Social Structure: S95–S120. Accessed November 29, 2017. www.jstor.org/stable/2780243.

Collier, Paul. 2007. *The Bottom Billion: Why the Poorest Countries are Failing and What Can Be Done about It*. New York: Oxford University Press.

Commission on Intellectual Property Rights. 2002. *Integrating Intellectual Property Rights and Development Policy*. Accessed June 9, 2014. www.iprcommission.org/papers/pdfs/final_report/CIPRfullfinal.pdf.

Contrera, Jessica. 2014. "Joshua Bell Is Playing in the Metro Again. This Time, Maybe You Won't Pass It Up." *Washington Post*, September 23. Accessed December 28, 2015. www.washingtonpost.com/lifestyle/style/joshua-bell-is-playing-in-the-metro-again-this-time-you-can-plan-to-be-there/2014/09/23/7a699e28-4282-11e4-9a15-137aa0153527_story.html.

Cookson, Robert. 2014. "Streaming Is the Answer for Chinese Music Industry." *Financial Times*, May 28. Accessed November 29, 2017. www.ft.com/content/60255bc6-e4c0-11e3-894f-00144feabdc0.

Coyle, Diane. 2014. *GDP: A Brief but Affectionate History*. Princeton: Princeton University Press.

Creative Tourism Network. n.d. "About the Creative Tourism." Accessed April 7, 2016. www.creativetourismnetwork.org/about/.

Davis, Jessica Hoffmann. 2005. *Framing Education as Art: The Octopus Has a Good Day*. New York: Teachers College Press.

Davis, Wade. 2009. *The Wayfinders: Why Ancient Wisdom Matters in the Modern World*. Toronto, ON: House of Anansi Press.

1988. *Passage of Darkness: The Ethnobiology of the Haitian Zombie*. Chapel Hill: The University of North Carolina Press.

Davies, William. 2017. "How Statistics Lost their Power – and Why We Should Fear What Comes Next." *Guardian*, January 19. Accessed November 29, 2017. www.theguardian.com/politics/2017/jan/19/crisis-of-statistics-big-data-democracy.

Deaton, Angus. 2010. "Understanding the Mechanisms of Economic Development." *Journal of Economic Perspectives* 24, no. 3 (Summer): 3–16. Accessed November 29, 2017. www.princeton.edu/~deaton/downloads/Understanding_the_Mechanisms_of_Economic_Development_Aug2010.pdf.

2013. *The Great Escape: Health, Wealth, and the Origins of Inequality*. Princeton: Princeton University Press.

De Botton, Alain, and John Armstrong. 2016. *Art as Therapy*. Reprint. London: Phaidon Press Limited.

De Laat, Joost. 2010. "Economic Cost of Roma Exclusion." Policy Note. *Human Development Sector Unit*. World Bank: Washington, DC. Accessed April 8,

2014. http://siteresources.worldbank.org/EXTROMA/Resources/Economic_Costs_Roma_Exclusion_Note_Final.pdf.

Diop, Makhtar. 2013. Meeting attended by author, March 1. World Bank, Washington, DC.

DI International Business Development. 2012. "The Indian Film Industry." DIBD India, September 25. Accessed June 5, 2014. http://di.dk/SiteCollectionDocuments/DIBD/sektoranalyser/The%20Indian%20Bollywood%20Industry_2013.pdf.

DocumentaryStorm. n.d. "Favela Rising." Accessed October 24, 2015. http://documentarystorm.com/favela-rising.

Dowd, Maureen. 2015. "The Women of Hollywood Speak Out." *New York Times Magazine*, November 20. Accessed December 26, 2017. www.nytimes.com/2015/11/22/magazine/the-women-of-hollywood-speak-out.html.

Drèze, Jean, and Amartya Sen. 2013. *An Uncertain Glory: India and Its Contradictions*. Princeton: Princeton University Press.

Duggan, Jennifer. 2013. "Climate Change Art Exhibition Opens in Beijing." *Guardian*, May 28. Accessed July 2, 2014. www.theguardian.com/environment/chinas-choice/2013/may/25/climate-change-art-exhibition-beijing.

Economist. 2013a. "Counting the Change." August 17. Accessed May 18, 2014. www.economist.com/news/business/21583687-media-companies-took-battering-internet-cash-digital-sources-last.

2013b. "Paraguay's New President: Cartes Plays His Cards." December 18. Accessed November 29, 2017. www.economist.com/news/americas/21591867-trickle-down-economics-one-south-americas-poorest-countries-cartes-plays-his-cards.

2014. "The Music Industry: Beliebing in Streaming." March 22. Accessed June 17, 2014. www.economist.com/news/business/21599350-record-bosses-now-hope-online-streaming-could-become-big-enough-business-arrest-their.

2015a. "Let Me Hear Your Khoomei Ringing Out." November 7. Accessed November 18, 2015. www.economist.com/news/europe/21677991-sergei-shoigus-childhood-home-not-your-average-russian-region-let-me-hear-your-khoomei-ringing.

2015b. "On the Road Again." November 21. Accessed February 15, 2018. www.economist.com/news/business-and-finance/21678740-reports-death-business-traveller-are-greatly-exaggerated.

EIU (Economist Intelligence Unit). 2016. *Mental Health and Integration: Provision for Supporting People with Mental Illness: A Comparison of 15 Asia Pacific Countries*. London. Accessed November 29, 2017. www.eiuperspectives.economist.com/sites/default/files/Mental_health_and_integration.pdf.

Ehrlich, Ben. 2015. "The Neuroscience of Art: What Are the Sources of Creativity and Innovation?" Salzburg Global Seminar. Accessed November 29, 2017. www.salzburgglobal.org/fileadmin/user_upload/Documents/2010-2019/2015/Session_547/SalzburgGlobal_Report_547_FINAL_lo_res.pdf.

Ehrlich, Paul R. and Anne H. Ehrlich. 2010. "The Culture Gap and Its Needed Closures." *International Journal of Environmental Studies* 67 (August 4). Accessed November 26, 2017. http://mahb.stanford.edu/wp-content/uploads/2011/08/3-2010_preAHE_Culture-gap-and-its-needed-closures.pdf.

"Enigmax." 2009. "The Pirate Bay Trial: The Official Verdict–Guilty." *TorrentFreak*, April 17. Accessed November 29, 2017. https://torrentfreak.com/the-pirate-bay-trial-the-verdict-090417/.

Erickson, Kevin. 2015. "The Data Journalism That Wasn't." *FutureBlog*, August 21. Accessed November 29, 2017. https://futureofmusic.org/blog/2015/08/21/data-journalism-wasnt.

Ernesto. 2015. "Pirate Bay Founder Builds the Ultimate Piracy Machine." TorrentFreak, December 19. Accessed November 29, 2017. https://torrentfreak.com/pirate-bay-founder-builds-the-ultimate-piracy-machine-151219/.

European Commission. 2015. "Selected Publications on the Inclusion/integration of Refugees and Migrants in European Societies through Culture and Arts." Library and e-Resources, November. Accessed November 29, 2017. http://ec.europa.eu/libraries/doc/inclusion_refugees_and_immigrants_by_culture_arts.pdf.

European Council on Tourism and Trade. 2013. "Laos Is Selected as World Best Tourist Destination for 2013." May 3. Accessed May 23, 2014. http://ectt.webs.com/apps/blog/show/26126702-laos-is-selected-as-world-best-tourist-destination-for-2013.

Faris, Stephan. 2013. "Can a Tribe Sue for Copyright? The Maasai Want Royalties for Use of Their Name." Bloomberg Business, October 24. Accessed November 10, 2015. www.bloomberg.com/bw/articles/2013-10-24/africas-maasai-tribe-seek-royalties-for-commercial-use-of-their-name.

Fennell, Shailaja and Onno Ruhl. 2014. "Does Education Drive Economic Growth?" (video). Conference, Salwan Media OG14 Uniting Knowledge Communities Conference, Imperial Hotel, New Delhi, India, February 7–8, 2014. Accessed November 29, 2017. www.oneglobeforum.com/video/2014/dr-shailaja-fennell-does-education-drive-economic-growth.

Fierberg, Emma (producer) and Tony Manfred (original reporting). 2015. "A 2016 Rio Olympics Water Venue Is Full of Human Waste and Teeming with Viruses—Here's a Video of What It Looks Like." *Business Insider*, August 5, video courtesy of Associated Press. Accessed October 24, 2015. www.businessinsider.com/rio-de-janeiro-waters-pollution-olympics-2015-7.

Finger, J. Michael. 2004. "Introduction and Overview." In *Poor People's Knowledge: Promoting Intellectual Property in Developing Countries*, ed. J. Michael Finger and Philip Schuler. Washington, DC: World Bank. Accessed November 29, 2017. www.griequity.com/resources/industryandissues/IntellectualProperty/PoorPeoplesKnowledge.pdf.

and Philip Schuler, ed. 2004. *Poor People's Knowledge: Promoting Intellectual Property in Developing Countries*. Washington, DC: World Bank.

Fitzgibbon, Will. 2017. "Paradise Papers Research Raises Questions Over Glencore's $440m Congo Discount." The International Consortium of Investigative Journalists. December 14. Accessed January 7, 2018. www.icij.org/investigations/paradise-papers/paradise-papers-research-raises-questions-glencores-440m-congo-discount/.

Florida, Richard. 2013. "More Losers Than Winners in America's New Economic Geography." *CityLab/Atlantic*, January 20. Accessed April 11, 2016. www.citylab.com/work/2013/01/more-losers-winners-americas-new-economic-geography/4465/.

Forges, Alison des, Timothy Longman, Michele Wagner, Kirsti Lattu, Eric Gillet, Catherine Choquet, Trish Huddelston, and Jemera Rone. 1999. *Leave None to Tell the Story: Genocide in Rwanda*. New York: Human Rights Watch. Accessed October 24, 2015. www.hrw.org/reports/pdfs/r/rwanda/rwanda993.pdf.

Fowler, Betsy J. 2004. "Preventing Counterfeit Craft Designs." *Poor People's Knowledge: Promoting Intellectual Property in Developing Countries*, ed. J. Michael Finger and Philip Schuler. Washington, DC.

Franz, Alfred, Peter Laimer, and Mara Manente. n.d. "European Implementation Manual on Tourism Satellite Accounts." European Commission. Accessed May 14, 2014. http://ec.europa.eu/eurostat/ramon/statmanuals/files/TSA_EIM_EN.pdf.

Franz, Jared. 2008. "The Economics of Ideas: Theory and Evidence." diss., University of Illinois at Chicago. Google Books.

Fraser, Nick. 2008. "John Maynard Keynes: Can the Great Economist Save the World?" *The Independent*, November 8. Accessed April 17, 2014. www.independent.co.uk/news/business/analysis-and-features/john-maynard-keynes-can-the-great-economist-save-the-world-994416.html.

Fridson, Martin S. 2016. "The End of Accounting and the Path Forward for Investors and Managers (a Review)." Financial Analysts Journal 11, no. 1: 1. Accessed April 17, 2017. www.cfapubs.org/doi/full/10.2469/br.v11.n1.13.

Fuentes, Agustin. 2017. *The Creative Spark: How Imagination Made Humans Exceptional.* New York: Dutton.

Fujiwara, Daniel, Laura Kudrna, and Paul Dolan. 2014. *Quantifying and Valuing the Wellbeing Impacts of Culture and Sport.* London: UK Department for Culture, Media & Sport. Accessed January 11, 2016. www.gov.uk/government/uploads/system/uploads/attachment_data/file/304899/Quantifying_and_valuing_the_wellbeing_impacts_of_sport_and_culture.pdf.

FundaMentalSDG. n.d. "Home." Accessed October 24, 2015. www.fundamentalsdg.org/.

FutureBrand. n.d. "2011–2012 Country Brand Index." Accessed November 29, 2017. www.ontit.it/opencms/export/sites/default/ont/it/documenti/files/ONT_2011-11-29_02777.pdf.

n.d. "2012–2013 Country Brand Index." Accessed November 29, 2017. https://mouriz.files.wordpress.com/2013/02/cbi-futurebrand-2012-13.pdf.

Galloway, Stephen. 2012. "Who Says Piracy Costs the U.S. $58 Billion a Year?" *Hollywood Reporter*, May 12. Accessed June 9, 2014. www.hollywoodreporter.com/news/piracy-costs-megaupload-kim-dotcom-318374.

Gálvez-Nogales, Eva. 2010. "Agro-Based Clusters in Developing Countries: Staying Competitive in a Globalized Economy." Agricultural Management, Marketing and Finance Occasional Paper 25, Food and Agriculture Organization of the United Nations, Rome. Accessed, November 2, 2012. www.fao.org/docrep/012/i1560e/i1560e00.htm.

Gardner, Howard. 1999. "The Happy Meeting of Multiple Intelligences and the Arts." *Harvard Education Letter* 15, no. 6. November/December. Accessed November 14, 2015. http://hepg.org/hel-home/issues/15_6/helarticle/the-happy-meeting-of-multiple-intelligences-and-th.

Gates, Eugene. 2007. "Fanny Mendelssohn Hensel: A Life of Music Within Domestic Limits." *The Kapralova Society Journal* 5, no. 2 (Fall): 1, 4. Accessed January 12, 2017. www.kapralova.org/journal9.pdf.

Geiger, Abigail and Lauren Kent. 2015. "Number of Women Leaders around the World Has Grown, but They're Still a Small Group." PewReaserchCenter, July 30. Accessed January 10, 2017. www.pewresearch.org/fact-tank/2015/07/30/about-one-in-ten-of-to days-world-leaders-are-women/.

Gelles, David. 2015. "Unilever Finds That Shrinking Its Footprint Is a Giant Task." *New York Times*, November 21. Accessed December 29, 2015. www.nytimes.com/2015/11/22/business/unilever-finds-that-shrinking-its-footprint-is-a-giant-task.html.

Gibson, Chris and John Connell. 2005. *Music and Tourism: On the Road Again.* Clevedon, UK: Channel View Publications.

Ghosh, Palash. 2013. "Bollywood at 100: How Big Is India's Mammoth Film Industry?" *International Business Times*, May 3. Accessed June 5, 2014. www.ibtimes.com/bollywood-100-how-big-indias-mammoth-film-industry-1236299.

Goldberg, Halina. 2013. *Music in Chopin's Warsaw*. Reprint edn. Oxford: Oxford University Press.

Goldblatt, Patricia. 2006. "How John Dewey's Theories Underpin Art and Art Education." *Education and Culture* 22, no. 1: 17–34. Accessed November 29, 2017. http://muse.jhu.edu/journals/education_and_culture/v022/22.1goldblatt.pdf.

Goldin, Claudia, and Cecilia Rouse. 1997. "Orchestrating Impartiality: The Impact of 'Blind' Auditions on Female Musicians." Working Paper 5903, National Bureau of Economic Research, Cambridge, MA. Accessed 26 March 2015. www.nber.org/papers/w5903.

Gollin, Michael A. 2008. *Driving Innovation: Intellectual Property Strategies for a Dynamic World*. New York: Cambridge University Press.

Gosh, Amitav. 1998. *Dancing in Cambodia, at Large in Burma*. New Delhi: Ravi Dayal Publisher.

Graham, Carol, Soumya Chattopadhyay, and Jai Roberto Lakhanpal. 2014. *Using New Metrics to Assess the Role of the Arts in Well-Being: Some Initial Results from the Economics of Happiness*. Washington, DC: The Brookings Institution. March. Accessed January 29, 2017. www.arts.gov/sites/default/files/Brookings-Final-Report.pdf.

Haecker, Allyss Angela. 2012. "Post-Apartheid South African Choral Music: An Analysis of Integrated Musical Styles with Specific Examples by Contemporary South African Composers." DMA (Doctor of Musical Arts) thesis, University of Iowa. Accessed May 11, 2017. http://ir.uiowa.edu/cgi/viewcontent.cgi?article=3462&context=etd.

Haldane, Ewen. 2017. "Is It Time for a Slow Innovation Movement?" *The Drum*, August 15. Accessed November 29, 2017. www.thedrum.com/opinion/2017/08/15/it-time-slow-innovation-movement.

Hansen, Trine Bille. 1995. "Measuring the Value of Culture." *The European Journal of Cultural Policy* 1, no. 2: 309–322. Accessed March 28, 2016. www.tandfonline.com/doi/abs/10.1080/10286639509357988.

Harford, Tim. 2015. "The Pillars of Tax Wisdom." *FT Magazine*, November 20. Accessed December 1, 2015. www.ft.com/intl/cms/s/0/4fee3138-8d6b-11e5-a549-b89a1dfede9b.html.

Harper, Garrett, Chris Cotton, and Zandra Benefield. 2013. *Nashville Music Industry: Impact, Contribution and Cluster Analysis*. Nashville: Nashville

Area Chamber of Commerce. Accessed January 7, 2017. www.nashville.gov/Portals/0/SiteContent/MayorsOffice/EcDev/docs/NashvilleMusicIndustrySt udy.pdf.

Harris, Bryan. 2017. "South Korean President Park Geun-hye Ousted in Bribery Scandal." *Financial Times*, March 9. Accessed November 29, 2017. www.ft .com/content/34152354-0529-11e7-ace0-1ce02ef0def9.

Heilbroner, Robert L. 1971. "Introduction." In *Is Economics Relevant?: Reader in Political Economics*, ed. Robert L. Heilbroner and Arthur M. Ford. Pacific Palisades, CA.: Goodyear Pub. Co.

Helft, Miguel. 2014. "How Music Education Influenced Larry Page." *Fortune*, November 18. Accessed November 29, 2017. http://fortune.com/2014/11/18/ larry-page-music-education/.

Hiskey, Daven. 2011. "Post-It Notes Were Invented by Accident." Today I Found Out, November 9. Accessed May 15, 2017. www.todayifoundout.com/index .php/2011/11/post-it-notes-were-invented-by-accident.

History. 1998. "Georgia Governor Zell Miller Proposes Writing 'The Mozart Effect' into Law." January 13. Accessed May 20, 2014. www.history.com/this-day-in-hi story/georgia-governor-zell-miller-proposes-writing-the-mozart-effect-into-law.

Holland, Emily. 2017. "The Government's Role in Combating Loneliness." *Wall Street Journal*, September 12. Accessed January 7, 2018.

Holt-Lunstad, Julianne and Timothy B. Smith. 2016. "Loneliness and Social Isolation as Risk Factors for CVD: Implications for Evidence-Based Patient Care and Scientific Inquiry." *Heart* 102, no. 13 (April): 987–989. Accessed January 7, 2018. http://dx.doi.org/10.1136/heartjnl-2015-309242.

Huizenga, Tom. 2013. "Can Yo-Yo Ma Fix the Arts?" NPR, April 9. Accessed November 29, 2017. www.npr.org/sections/deceptivecadence/19192013/04/0 9/176681242/can-yo-yo-ma-fix-the-arts.

Human Rights Watch. 2013. "World Report 2013: Mali." Accessed May 1, 2014. www.hrw.org/world-report/2013/country-chapters/mali?page=1.

ICIJ (International Consortium of Investigative Journalists). 2017. "Paradise Papers: Secrets of The Global Elite." November 5. Accessed December 1, 2017. www .icij.org/investigations/paradise-papers/.

IDB (Inter-American Development Bank). 2014. "OAS, IDB, and British Council Present the Study 'The Economic Impact of the Creative Industries in the Americas.'" January 16. Accessed May 16, 2014. www.iadb.org/en/news/news-re leases/2014-01-16/economic-impact-of-the-creative-industries-study,10735. html.

IFPI (International Federation of the Phonographic Industry). n.d. "Tackling Music Piracy." Accessed July 21, 2015. www.ifpi.org/music-piracy.php.

2012. "Key Facts and Figures." *Digital Music Report*, 2012. Accessed September 19, 2012. www.ifpi.org/content/library/DMR2012_key_facts_and_figures.pdf.

2015. "IFPI Digital Music Report 2015: Charting the Path to Sustainable Growth." Accessed June 19, 2015. www.ifpi.org/downloads/Digital-Music-Report-2015.pdf.

2016. "Global Music Report 2016: State of the Industry." Accessed November 29, 2017. www.ifpi.org/downloads/GMR2016.pdf.

Imagine 2020. n.d. Accessed November 25, 2017. www.transforma.org.pt/en/?/projetos/imagine-2020.

Imasogie, Osagie and Thaddeus J. Kobylarz. 2013."Yes, Lady Gaga's Songs Contribute to GDP." *Wall Street Journal*, May 27. Accessed September 3, 2015. www.wsj.com/articles/SB10001424127887324767004578491452865597808.

Indo Asian News Service. 2012. "Mental Disorders Double in Taiwan." November 16. Accessed November 29, 2017. www.yahoo.com/news/mental-disorders-double-taiwan-173536614.html.

Ingersoll, Katie and John Carnwath. 2015. "A New Way to Think about Intrinsic vs. Instrumental Benefits of the Arts." *Createquity*, March 13. Accessed November 29, 2017. http://createquity.com/2015/03/a-new-way-to-think-about-intrinsic-vs-instrumental-benefits-of-the-arts/.

Ingham, Tim. 2015. "Independent Labels Trounce UMG, Sony and Warner in US Market Shares." *Music Business Worldwide*, July 29. Accessed February 18, 2016. www.musicbusinessworldwide.com/independent-label-us-market-share-trounces-universal-sony-warner/.

Ingoma Nshya. n.d. "Our History." Accessed November 29, 2017. www.ingomanshya.org/our-history.html.

Innovation Nashville. n.d. Accessed November 29, 2017. www.eventbrite.com/o/innovation-nashville-1034151741.

Intel Corporation. 2013. "Women and the Web: Bridging the Internet Gap and Creating New Global Opportunities in Low and Middle-Income Countries." Santa Clara, CA. Accessed March 19, 2015. www.intel.com/content/www/us/en/technology-in-education/women-in-the-web.html.

Investopedia n.d.a. "Gross Domestic Product–GDP." Accessed April 29, 2017. www.investopedia.com/terms/g/gdp.asp.

n.d.b. "Trade in Value Added (TiVA)." Accessed August 13, 2017. www.investopedia.com/terms/t/trade-value-added-tiva.asp.

iRoko. n.d. "About Us." Accessed August 27, 2017. http://iroko.ng/about/.

2015. "iROKO Launches Worldwide Content Distribution and Licensing Division, IROKO Global." Press Release. Accessed November 16, 2015.

http://iroko.ng/iroko-launches-worldwide-content-distribution-and-licensing-division-iroko-global/.

iRoko Partners. n.d. Accessed November 29, 2017. http://iroko.ng/.

Isaacson, Walter. 2011. *Steve Jobs*. New York: Simon & Schuster.

2017. *Leonardo da Vinci*. New York: Simon & Schuster.

Iyengar, Sunil and Ayanna Hudson. 2014. "Who Knew? Arts Education Fuels the Economy." *Chronicle of Higher Education*, March 10. Accessed May 28, 2014. http://chronicle.com/article/Who-Knew-Arts-Education-Fuels/145217/.

Iyengar, Sunil. 2014. "Taking Note: The Arts and Subjective Well-Being Measurement." *Art Works Blog*, June 5. Accessed January 29, 2017. www.arts.gov/art-works/2014/taking-note-arts-and-subjective-well-being-measurement.

Jacobs, Andrew. 2007. "Not Hot Just Yet, but Newark Is Starting to Percolate." *New York Times*, May 6. Accessed October 24, 2015. www.nytimes.com/2007/05/06/nyregion/06newark.html.

Jana Sanskriti Centre for Theatre of the Oppressed. n.d.a. "About Us." Accessed July 26, 2014. www.janasanskriti.org/aboutus.html.

n.d.b. *Annual Report 2000–2001*. West Bengal: Jana Sanskriti. Accessed December 31, 2017. www.janasanskriti.org/colorannuarrep.pdf.

Jennings, Luke. 2013. "Sexism in Dance: Where Are All the Female Choreographers?" *Guardian*, April 28. Accessed November 29, 2017. www.theguardian.com/stage/2013/apr/28/women-choreographers-glass-ceiling.

Jensen, Robert and Emily Oster. 2009. "The Power of TV: Cable Television and Women's Status in India." *Quarterly Journal of Economics* 124, no. 3: 1057–94.

Jerven, Morten. 2013. *Poor Numbers: How We Are Misled by African Development Statistics and What to Do about It.* Ithaca: Cornell University Press.

Jewell, Catherine. 2016. "Digital Pioneer, Jaron Lanier, on the Dangers of "Free" Online Culture." *WIPO Magazine*, April. Accessed November 29, 2017. www.wipo.int/wipo_magazine/en/2016/02/article_0001.html .

Johnson, Beau. n.d. "An Introduction to Colleges & Universities in Nashville." Accessed October 8, 2012. http://nashvilleeducation.com/resources/an-introduction-to-colleges-universities-in-nashville.

Johnson, Steven. 2016. *Wonderland: How Play Made the Modern World*. New York: Riverhead Books.

2017. "How Play Shapes the World" *1A* WAMU 88 and NPR. Hosted by Joshua Johnson. January 25. Accessed November 29, 2017. https://the1a.org/shows/2017-01-25/how-play-shapes-the-world.

Johnson, Tim. 2017. "Why Mathematics Has Not Been Effective in Economics." *Magic, Maths and Money: The Relationship between Science and*

Finance (blog), July 27. Accessed December 1, 2017. http://magic-maths-money.blogspot.com/2017/07/why-mathematics-has-not-been-effective.html.

Jones, Quincy. 2010. Praise for Culture Is Our Weapon: Making Music and Changing Lives in Rio de Janeiro.. New York: Penguin Group. (Orig. publ. 2006.)

Joseph, Ammu. 2014. "Action, reaction, introspection, rectification." In *Media and Gender: A Scholarly Agenda for the Global Alliance on Media and Gender*, ed. Aimée Vega Montie, 74–78. Paris: UNESCO and IAMCR (International Association for Media and Communication Researchers). Accessed November 29, 2017. http://unesdoc.unesco.org/images/0022/002283/228399e.pdf.

Juma, Calestous. 2011. *The New Harvest: Agricultural Innovation in Africa*. 1st edn. New York: Oxford University Press.

Jung, Liege Gonzalez. 2016. "Why Winning Back the Ministry of Culture May Have Been a Loss for Brazil's Artists." *Artsy.net*, June 9. Accessed April 29, 2017. www.artsy.net/article/artsy-editorial-why-having-a-ministry-of-culture-could-hurt-the-arts-in-brazil.

Jurgensen, John. 2014. "Joshua Bell on Playing for the President, and in the Subway." *Speakeasy* (blog), *Wall Street Journal*, October 14. Accessed December 28, 2015. http://blogs.wsj.com/speakeasy/2014/10/14/joshua-bell-on-playing-for-the-president-and-in-the-subway/.

Kabanda, Patrick. 2007. "Music as Social Action in Southern Africa." Accessed December 4, 2011. http://musikaba.net/projects/category/botswana-southafrica-swaziland/.

2013. "'Where Culture Leads, Trade Follows': A Framework for Developing Uganda's Music as International Trade in Services." Master's thesis, The Fletcher School of Law and Diplomacy, Tufts University, Medford, Massachusetts.

2014a. "An Untapped Economy: Africa's Creative Sector." *World Policy Journal*, February 19. Accessed November 29, 2017. www.worldpolicy.org/blog/2014/02/19/untapped-economy-africas-creative-sector.

2014b. "The Creative Wealth of Nations: How the Performing Arts Can Advance Development and Human Progress." Policy Research working paper; no. WPS 7118. Washington, DC: World Bank Group. Accessed November 29, 2017. http://documents.worldbank.org/curated/en/512131468147578042/The-creative-wealth-of-nations-how-the-performing-arts-can-advance-development-and-human-progress.

2015a. "Development as Music: Using Africa's Creative Wealth to Improve Lives across the Continent." *Nasikiliza* (blog). World Bank, June 6. Accessed November 29, 2017. http://blogs.worldbank.org/nasikiliza/development-as-music-using-africas-creative-wealth-to-improve-lives-across-the-continent.

2015b. "Haiti's Economic Imperative." Letter to the Editor. *International New York Times*, January 20. Accessed June 4, 2015. www.nytimes.com/2015/01/20/opinion/haitis-economic-imperative.html?_r=0.

2015c. "Mozart Seduces the World Bank and the IMF." *Let's Talk Development* (blog). WorldBank, April 1. Accessed November 29, 2017. http://blogs.worldbank.org/developmenttalk/mozart-seduces-world-bank-and-imf.

2015d. "The Road Not Shared: Turning to the Arts to Help Increase Pedestrian Safety." *Let's Talk Development* (blog). World Bank, September 22. Accessed November 29, 2017. http://blogs.worldbank.org/developmenttalk/road-not-shared-turning-arts-help-increase-pedestrian-safety.

2015e. "Work as Art: Links between Creative Work and Human Development." Background Paper. Human Development Report 2015. New York: UNDP. Accessed November 29, 2017. http://hdr.undp.org/sites/default/files/kabanda_hdr_2015_final.pdf.

2016a. "Creative Natives in the Digital Age: How Digital Technology has Revolutionized Creative Work." Policy Research working paper; no. WPS 7683. Washington, DC: World Bank Group. Accessed April 29, 2017. http://documents.worldbank.org/curated/en/214511467992816485/Creative-natives-in-the-digital-age-how-digital-technology-has-revolutionized-creative-work.

2016b. "Creative Trade for Human Development." Policy Research working paper; no. WPS 7684. Washington, DC: World Bank Group. Accessed April 29, 2017. http://documents.worldbank.org/curated/en/432811468194960078/Creative-trade-for-human-development.

2016c. "Introducing a Cultural Trade Index." *Let's Talk Development* (blog). World Bank, November 29. Accessed April 29, 2017. http://blogs.worldbank.org/developmenttalk/introducing-cultural-trade-index.

2016d. "Music for Development in the Digital Age." Background Paper. World Development Report 2016: Digital Dividends. World Bank, Washington, DC. Accessed April 29, 2017. http://pubdocs.worldbank.org/pubdocs/publicdoc/2016/3/923101459255847647/WDR16-BP-Music-for-Development-Kabanda.pdf.

2016e. "Music Going for a Song." *Finance and Development*, September. Accessed November 29, 2017. www.imf.org/external/pubs/ft/fandd/2016/09/kabanda.htm.

2016f. "The Arts, Africa and Economic Development: the problem of Intellectual Property Rights. In Cultural Economies and Cultural Activism." Ed. Jonathan P. Vickery. Special issue, *Journal of Law, Social Justice and Global Development* 16, no. 1 (May 1). Accessed November 29, 2017. www2.warwick.ac.uk/fac/soc/law/elj/lgd/2016-1/patrick_finalfinal.pdf.

2016g. "The Cultural Trade Index: An Introduction." Policy Research working paper; no. WPS 7871. Washington, DC: World Bank Group. http://documents.worldbank.org/curated/en/593131477313199422/The-cultural-trade-index-an-introduction.

2016h. "El mundo nos da basura, y nosotros les devolvemos música." *Kreatópolis* (blog). Inter-American Development Bank, August 26. Accessed November 29, 2017. https://blogs.iadb.org/kreatopolis/2016/08/26/el-mundo-nos-da-basura-y-nosotros-le-devolvemos-musica/.

Kahneman, Daniel. 2011. *Thinking, Fast and Slow.* New York: Farrar, Straus and Giroux.

Kalmanowitz, Debra, Jordan S. Potash, and Siu Mei Chan, editors. 2012. *Art Therapy in Asia: To the Bone or Wrapped in Silk.* London: Jessica Kingsley Publishers.

Kantor, Jodi and Megan Twohey. 2017. "Harvey Weinstein Paid Off Sexual Harassment Accusers for Decades." *New York Times,* October 5, 2017. Accessed December 1, 2017. www.nytimes.com/2017/10/05/us/harvey-weinstein-harassment-allegations.html.

Kaplan, Robert S. and David P. Norton. 2004. *Strategy Maps: Converting Intangible Assets into Tangible Outcomes.* Boston: Harvard Business Publishing.

Karp, Hannah and Alistair Barr. 2014. "Apple Buys Beats for $3 Billion, Tapping Tastemakers to Regain Music Mojo." *Wall Street Journal,* May 28. Accessed November 29, 2017. www.wsj.com/articles/apple-to-buy-beats-1401308971.

Kaul, Adam R. 2009. *Turning the Tune: Traditional Music, Tourism, and Social Change in an Irish Village.* New York: Berghahn Books.

Kaysen, Ronda. 2016. "Artists and Their Muse: Gentrification." *New York Times,* December 2. Accessed November 29, 2017. www.nytimes.com/2016/12/02/realestate/artists-and-their-muse-gentrification.html.

Kelaher, Edward T. 2017. Welcome remarks, the Potomac Chapter of the American Guild of Organists in conjunction with the District of Columbia and Northern Virginia Chapters. Epiphany Evensong and Annual Twelfth Night Dinner. All Saints Church, Chevy Chase, MD. January 9.

Kennedy, Randy. 2009. "For Child Soldiers, a Chance to Wield Brushes, Not Arms." *New York Times,* April 28. Accessed March 27, 2016. www.nytimes.com/2009/04/29/arts/design/29blec.html.

Kent, Lauren. 2015. "Number of Women Leaders around the World Has Grown, but They're Still a Small Group." PewReaserchCenter, July 30. Accessed January 10, 2017. www.pewresearch.org/fact-tank/2015/07/30/about-one-in-ten-of-todays-world-leaders-are-women/.

Kigozi, Fred, Joshua Ssebunnya, Dorothy Kizza, Sara Cooper, Sheila Ndyanabangi, and the Mental Health and Poverty Project. 2010. "An Overview of Uganda's Mental Health Care System: Results from an Assessment Using the WHO's Assessment Instrument for Mental Health Systems." *International Journal of Mental Health*, January 20. Accessed October 14, 2015. www.ijmhs.com/content/4/1/1.

Kim, Donald D., Erich H. Strassner, and David B. Wasshausen. 2014. "Industry Economic Accounts Results of the Comprehensive Revision Revised Statistics for 191997–2012." *BEA*, February. Accessed May 5, 2017. www.bea.gov/scb/pdf/2014/02%20February/0214_industry%20economic%20accounts.pdf.

Kim, Jim Yong. 2014. "Voice and Agency: Empowering Women and Girls for Shared Prosperity. Featuring the Hon. Hillary Rodham Clinton." Video, May 14. Accessed July 25, 2014. http://live.worldbank.org/voice-and-agency-empowering-women-hillary-rodham-clinton.

Kimura, Kaoru, Duncan Wambogo Omole, and Mark Williams. 2011. "ICT in Sub-Saharan Africa: Success Stories." In *Yes Success Stories from a Dynamic Continent* ed. Chuhan-Pole and Manka S. Angwafo. Washington, DC: World Bank. Accessed July 8. 2014. http://siteresources.worldbank.org/AFRICAEXT/Resources/258643-1271798012256/ICT-19.pdf.

Kishtainy, Niall (Consultant editor), George Abbot, John Farndon, Frank Kennedy, James Meadway, Christopher Wallace, and Marcus Weeks. 2012. *The Economics Book (Big Ideas Simply Explained)*. New York: DK Publishing.

Kittredge, Clare. 2015. "The Physical Side of Stress." Everyday Health, January 23. Accessed October 12, 2015. www.everydayhealth.com/womens-health/physical-side-of-stress.aspx.

Kolbert, Elizabeth. 2014. "Save the Elephants." *New Yorker*, July 7. Accessed July 7, 2014. www.newyorker.com/talk/comment/2014/07/07/140707taco_talk_kolbert.

Kokas, Aynne. 2017. *Hollywood Made in China*. Oakland, CA: University of California Press.

Kramer, Wolf. 2015. Letter to the Editor. *Economist*, December 19. Accessed January 18, 2016. www.economist.com/news/letters/21684108-letters-editor.

Krugman, Paul R. 1993. "What Do Undergrads Need to Know about Trade?" *The American Economic Review* 83, no. 2 (May): 23–26. Accessed February 25, 2017. www.iecofin.uniroma1.it/pdf/Krugman.pdf.

2013. "The New Growth Fizzle." *The Conscience of a Liberal* (blog). *New York Times*, August 18. Accessed December 29, 2016. http://krugman.blogs.nytimes.com/2013/08/18/the-new-growth-fizzle/?_r=2.

2015. "People Aren't Androids." *The Conscience of a Liberal* (blog), *New York Times*, February 21. Accessed March 26, 2017. http://krugman.blogs.nytimes.com/2015/02/21/people-arent-androids/.

La Ferrara, Eliana, Alberto Chong, and Suzanne Duryea. 2012. "Soap Operas and Fertility: Evidence from Brazil." *American Economic Journal: Applied Economics* 4, no. 4: 1–31.

Lallanilla, Marc. 2013. "5 Intriguing Facts About the Roma." *Live Science*, October 23. Accessed November 30, 2017. www.livescience.com/40652-facts-about-roma-romani-gypsies.html.

Lamy, Pascal. 2011. "'Made in China' Tells Us Little about Global Trade." *Financial Times*, January 24. Accessed June 2, 2017. www.ft.com/content/4d37374c-27fd-11e0-8abc-00144feab49a.

Landfill Harmonic. n.d. Accessed July 28, 2014. www.landfillharmonicmovie.com

Landrieu, Mitchell. 2016. Framing Remarks. In "Creative Placemaking: The Role of Arts in Community Development" (Webcast). Convening. Wilson Center, Washington, DC. December 6. Accessed April 8, 2017. www.wilsoncenter.org/event/creative-placemaking-the-role-arts-community-development.

Larcarte, Julio A. 1984. "Aspects of International Trade and Assistance Relating to the Expansion of Employment in the Developing Countries." In *International Trade and Third World Development*, ed. Pradip K. Ghosh and Dilip Ghosh, 124–51. Westport, CT: Greenwood Press.

Lee, Spike. 2006. "When the Levees Broke: A Requiem in Four Acts." HBO. Accessed April 11, 2017. www.hbo.com/documentaries/when-the-levees-broke-a-requiem-in-four-acts/synopsis.html.

Lee, Yong-Sook and Ying-Chian Tee. 2009. "Reprising the Role of the Developmental State in Cluster Development: The Biomedical Industry in Singapore." *Singapore Journal of Tropical Geography* 30, no. 1 (March): 86–97. Accessed April 11, 2017. http://dx.doi.org/10.1111/j.1467-9493.2008.00359.x.

Lehrer, Jonah. 2011. "Steve Jobs: 'Technology Alone Is Not Enough.'" *New Yorker*, October 7. Accessed April 11, 2017. www.newyorker.com/news/news-desk/steve-jobs-technology-alone-is-not-enough.

Leontief, Wassily. 1992. "The Present State of Economic Science." *Adam Smith's Legacy: His Place in the Development of Modern Economics*, ed. Michael Fry. London: Routledge.

Lester, Simon and Bryan Mercurio, with Arwel Davies and Kala Leitner. 2008. *World Trade Law: Text, Materials and Commentary*. Oxford: Hart Publishing.

Lev, Baruch and Feng Gu. 2016. *The End of Accounting and the Path Forward for Investors and Managers*. Wiley Finance Series. Hoboken, NJ: John Wiley & Sons, Inc.

Levintova, Hannah. 2013. "Here's Why You Seldom See Women Leading a Symphony." *Mother Jones*, September 23. Accessed March 26, 2015. www.motherjones.com/media/2013/09/women-conductors-gap-charts-marin-alsop-proms.

Library of Congress. n.d. "Felix Mendelssohn: Reviving the Works of J.S. Bach." Accessed December 26, 2017. https://www.loc.gov/item/ihas.200156436/.

Lihs, Harriet. 2009. *Appreciating Dance: A Guide to the World's Liveliest Art*. 4th edn. Hightstown, NJ: Princeton Book Company.

Lipman, Joanne. 2013. "Is Music the Key to Success?" *New York Times*, October 12. Accessed November 30, 2017. www.nytimes.com/2013/10/13/opinion/sunday/is-music-the-key-to-success.html.

2014. "A Musical Fix for American Schools." *Wall Street Journal*, October 10. Accessed November 30, 2017. www.wsj.com/articles/a-musical-fix-for-american-schools-1412954652.

Livio, Mario. 2009. "When It Comes to the Economy, Math Isn't Magic." NPR, March 3. Accessed April 21, 2017. www.npr.org/2011/07/29/101389401/when-it-comes-to-the-economy-math-isnt-magic.

2015. "Mysteries of an Expanding Universe." Conversation with Krista Tippet, On Being. NPR, June 18. Accessed April 21, 2017 https://onbeing.org/programs/mario-livio-mysteries-of-an-exp anding-universe/.

Lohr, Steve. 2002. "New Economy: The Intellectual Property Debate Takes a Page from 19th-Century America." *New York Times*, October 14. Accessed November 25, 2011. www.nytimes.com/2002/10/14/business/new-economy-intellectual-property-debate-takes-page-19th-century-america.html.

Luke, Clair and Michael Igoe. 2015. "Bill Easterly's take on the SDGs." *Devex Newswire*, March 4. Accessed April 11, 2017. www.devex.com/news/bill-easterly-s-take-on-the-sdgs-85621.

McCarthy, Niall. 2014. "Women Earn Less than Men in Hollywood." *Statista*, August 5. Accessed November 28, 2017. www.statista.com/chart/2533/women-earn-less-than-men-in-hollywood/.

2015. "Gender Inequality Rife at the Oscars." *Statista*, February 23. Accessed April 14, 2016. www.statista.com/chart/3254/gender-inequality-rife-at-the-oscars/.

MacGillis, Alec. 2007. "Candidate: Former Arkansas Governor Mike Huckabee Proposal: Focus on Arts and Music Education." *Washington Post*, August 29. Accessed April 8, 2012. www.washingtonpost.com/wp-dyn/content/article/2007/08/28/AR2007082801711.html.

Mackay, Mairi. 2009. "Nollywood Loses Half of Film Profits to Piracy, Say Producers." *CNN*, June 24. Accessed June 9, 2014. www.cnn.com/2009/SHOWBIZ/Movies/06/24/nollywood.piracy/.

Millennium Alliance for Humanity and Biosphere (MAHB). n.d. "MAHB Changes Its Name." Accessed March 24, 2016. http://mahb.stanford.edu/welcome/mahb-changes- its-name/.

Mankiw, N. Gregory. 2011. *Principles of Economics*. 6th edn. Mason, OH: Cengage Learning.

Mansfield, Edwin and Gary W. Yohe. 2003. *Microeconomics: Theory and Applications*. 11th edn. New York: W. W. Norton & Company.

Márquez, Iván Duque and Felipe Buitrago Restrepo. 2013. *The Orange Economy: An Infinite Opportunity*. Inter-American Development Bank. Accessed November 30, 2017. http://publications.iadb.org/handle/11319/3659?locale-attribute=en.

Maurer, Andreas and F. Ted Tschang. 2011. *An Exploratory Framework for Measuring Services Value-Added*. Singapore: The Pacific Economic Cooperation. Accessed May 15, 2014. www.pecc.org/resources/trade-and-investment-1/1683-an-exploratory-framework-for-measuring-services-value-added-paper/file.

May, Christopher and Susan K. Sell. 2005. *Intellectual Property Rights: A Critical History*. Ipolitics. Boulder, CO: Lynne Rienner Publishers.

McKinley, Jesse. 2013. "Colleges Help Ithaca Thrive in a Region of Struggles." *New York Times*, August 4. Accessed November 30, 2017. www.nytimes.com/2013/08/05/nyregion/with-education-as-economic-engine-ithaca-thrives-in-struggling-region.html.

Meeks-Owens, Chandler. 2013. Comment on "Can a Tribe Sue for Copyright? The Maasai Want Royalties for Use of Their Name." *Bloomberg Business*, October 24. Accessed November 30, 2017. www.bloomberg.com/news/articles/2013-10-24/africas-maasai-tribe-seek-royalties-for-commercial-use-of-their-name.

Mehr, Samuel A., Adena Schachner, Rachel C. Katz, and Elizabeth S. Spelke. 2013. "Two Randomized Trials Provide No Consistent Evidence for Nonmusical Cognitive Benefits of Brief Preschool Music Enrichment." *PLOS ONE*, December 11. Accessed November 30, 2017. http://journals.plos.org/plosone/article?id=10.1371/journal.pone.0082007.

Melo, James. 2016. *Program Notes: Frédéric Chopin*. North Bethesda, MD: The National Philharmonic at Strathmore.

Merges, Robert P. 2011. *Justifying Intellectual Property*. Cambridge, MA: Harvard University Press.

Merges, Robert P., Peter S. Menell, and Mark A. Lemley. 2012. *Intellectual Property in the New Technological Age*. 6th edn. New York: Wolters Kluwer Law & Business.

Merriam-Webster. n.d. "Deceptive Cadence." Accessed January 1, 2018. www.merriam-webster.com/dictionary/deceptive%20cadence.

2017a. "Finale." Updated on December 25. Accessed January 1, 2018. www.merriam-webster.com/dictionary/finale.

2017b. "Prelude." Updated on December 19. Accessed January 1, 2018. www.merriam-webster.com/dictionary/prelude.

Milanović, Branko. 2015a. "Junk the Phrase 'Human Capital.'" *Aljazeera America*, February 13. Accessed March 29, 2017. http://america.aljazeera.com/opinions/2015/2/junk-the-phrase-human-capital.html.

2015b. "On 'Human Capital' One More Time." *Globalinequality*, February 19. Accessed March 29, 2017. http://glineq.blogspot.com/2015/02/on-human-capital-one-more-time.html.

Mockus, Antanas. 2015. "The Art of Changing a City." *New York Times*, July 16. Accessed November 30, 2017. www.nytimes.com/2015/07/17/opinion/the-art-of-changing-a-city.html?_r=0.

Moffatt, Mike. 2015. "An Introduction to Endogenous Growth Models." *About.com*, November 16. Accessed December 29, 2016. http://economics.about.com/cs/economicsglossary/g/endogenous_g.htm.

Morrison, Toni. 2017. *The Origin of Others (The Charles Eliot Norton Lectures)*. Cambridge, MA: Harvard University Press.

Mortimer, Julie Holland, Chris Nosko, and Alan Sorensen. 2010. "Supply Responses to Digital Distribution: Recorded Music and Live Performances." *Information Economics and Policy*, 24, no. 1: 6. Accessed June 8, 2015. www2.bc.edu/julie-mortimer-2/concerts_01oct2010.pdf.

Moudio, Rebecca. 2013. "Nigeria's Film Industry: A Potential Gold Mine?" *Africa Renewal*, 24–25 May. Accessed December 22, 2015. www.un.org/africarenewal/sites/www.un.org.africarenewal/files/Africa-Renewal-May-2013-en.pdf.

Mulitalo-Lauta, Pa'u Tafaogalupe and Karin Menon. 2006. "Art Therapy and Pacific Island Peoples in New Zealand: A Preliminary Observation and Evaluation from a Pacific Island Perspective." *Social Work Review* (Autumn): 22–30. Accessed April 15, 2017. http://anzasw.nz/wp-content/uploads/Tu-Mau-Issue-18-Autumn-06-Article-Mulitalo-Lauta-and-Menon.pdf.

Musinguzi, Bamuturaki. 2010. "No Royalty in Music Industry." *EastAfrican Magazine*, June 14. Accessed November 27, 2011. www.theeastafrican.co.ke/magazine/No+royalty+in+music+industry/-/434746/937536/-/mo1h4k/-/index.html.

2017. Women Drumming Away the Trauma of Genocide. *The East African*, February 18. Accessed March 4, 2017. www.theeastafrican.co.ke/magazine/

Women-drumming-away-the-trauma-of-genocide/434746-3817664-19drcz/index.html.

My Hero. n.d. "Hummingbird [excerpt from *Dirt! The Movie*]." Accessed November 28, 2017. www.myhero.com/film_dirt.

Nabokov, Vladimir. 1989. *Speak, Memory: An Autobiography Revisited*. Reissue edn. New York: Vintage.

Nashville Area Chamber of Commerce. n.d. "Colleges & Universities." Accessed November 30, 2017. www.nashvillechamber.com/explore/live/schools/colleges-universities.

Nashville Convention & Visitors Corp. n.d. "The Story of Music City." Accessed November 30, 2017. www.visitmusiccity.com/music/aboutmusiccity/storyofmusiccity.

Nashville.gov. Mayor's Office. 2013. "Nashville's Music Industry." Accessed January 7, 2017. www.nashville.gov/Mayors-Office/Economic-and-Community-Development/Music-City-Music-Council/Music-Industry.aspx.

Naxos. n.d.a. "Movement." Accessed January 1, 2018. www.naxos.com/mainsite/NewDesign/fglossary.files/bglossary.files/Movement.htm.

n.d.b. "Rondo." Accessed January 1, 2018. www.naxos.com/mainsite/NewDesign/fglossary.files/bglossary.files/Rondo.htm.

n.d.a. "Suite." Accessed January 1, 2018. www.naxos.com/mainsite/NewDesign/fglossary.files/bglossary.files/Suite.htm.

Ndaba, Obadias. 2014. "Africa Is Richer Than You Think." *Huffington Post*, April 29. Accessed July 14, 2017. www.huffingtonpost.com/obadias-ndaba/africa-is-richer-than-you_b_5223129.html.

Neate, Patrick and Damian Platt. 2010. *Culture Is Our Weapon: Making Music and Changing Lives in Rio de Janeiro*. New York: Penguin Group. (Orig. publ. 2006.)

Nelson, Dean. 2014. "In Haiti, Beauty That Plays Hard to Get (To)." *New York Times*, February 13. Accessed November 30, 2017. www.nytimes.com/2014/02/16/travel/in-haiti-beauty-that-plays-hard-to-get-to.html.

Newsweek. 2007. "The Gospel According to Mike Huckabee." October 10. Accessed January 4, 2018. www.newsweek.com/gospel-according-mike-huckabee-103607.

Nigeria High Commission London. n.d. "Culture and Tourism." UK. Accessed March 3, 2017. www.nigeriahc.org.uk/culture-tourism#fiscal.

NJPAC (New Jersey Performing Arts Center). n.d.a. "About NJPAC." Accessed March 11, 2017. www.njpac.org/about-njpac.

n.d.b. "History." Accessed March 11, 2017. www.njpac.org/about-njpac/history.

Nobelprize.org. n.d.a. "The Nobel Peace Prize 2004." Nobel Media AB 2014. Accessed November 26, 2017. www.nobelprize.org/nobel_prizes/peace/laureates/2004/.

n.d.b. "Wangari Maathai– Facts." Nobel Media AB 2014. Accessed November 26, 2017. www.nobelprize.org/nobel_prizes/peace/laureates/2004/maathai-facts.html.

Nooristani, Humira. 2013. "The Bollywood Effect: Women and Film in South Asia." *Foreign Policy*, April 11. Accessed October 6, 2015. http://foreignpolicy.com/2013/04/11/the-bollywood-effect-women-and-film-in-south-asia/.

Nordland, Rod. 2015. "After Taliban Attack in Kabul, a Music Teacher Keeps Playing." *New York Times*, December 30. Accessed May 5, 2017. www.nytimes.com/2015/12/31/world/asia/after-taliban-attack-in-kabul-a-music-teacher-keeps-playing.html.

Novak, Matt. 2014. "Nine Albert Einstein Quotes That Are Totally Fake." *Paleofuture* (blog). *Gizmodo*, March 14. Accessed December 29, 2017. https://paleofuture.gizmodo.com/9-albert-einstein-quotes-that-are-totally-fake-1543806477.

NPR (National Public Radio). 2014. "An Idea that Stuck: How a Hymnal Bookmark Helped Inspire the Post-It Note." July 26. Accessed November 30, 2017. www.npr.org/2014/07/26/335402996/an-idea-that-stuck-how-a-hymnal-bookmark-helped-inspire-the-post-it-note.

Nsehe, Mfonobong. 2011. "Hollywood, Meet Nollywood." *Forbes*, April 19. Accessed November 30, 2017. www.forbes.com/sites/mfonobongnsehe/2011/04/19/hollywood-meet-nollywood/#7d07c67a5d7a.

Nye Jr., Joseph S. 2006. "Think Again: Soft Power." *Foreign Policy*, February 23. Accessed May 2, 2014. www.foreignpolicy.com/articles/2006/02/22/think_again_soft_power.

2008. *The Powers to Lead*. New York: Oxford University Press.

O., T. 2012. "Angels in Lagos." *Economist*, October 28. Accessed March 9, 2013. www.economist.com/blogs/baobab/2012/10/nigerias-entrepreneurs.

Obama, Barack. 2006. *The Audacity of Hope: Thoughts on Reclaiming the American Dream*. New York: Crown Publishers.

OECD-WTO (Organisation for Economic Co-Operation and Development-World Trade Organization). n.d. *Trade in Value-Added: Concepts, Methodologies and Challenges*. Paris: OECD. Accessed February 13, 2017. www.oecd.org/sti/ind/49894138.pdf.

OECD. n.d. "Trade in Value Added" Accessed November 30, 2017. www.oecd.org/trade/measuringtradeinvalue-addedanoecd-wtojointinitiative.htm.

2001. "Glossary of Statistical Accounts, Satellite Accounts." September 25. Last updated March 13, 2003. Accessed November 30, 2017. http://stats.oecd.org/glossary/detail.asp?ID=2385.

2002. "Measurement of the Non-Observed Economy: A Handbook." Paris. Accessed November 30, 2017. www.oecd.org/std/na/1963116.pdf.

OECD and UN. 2011. *Economic Diversification in Africa: A Review of Selected Countries*. OECD Publishing. Accessed November 30, 2017. www.oecd.org/countries/tunisia/46148761.pdf.

Ogbechie, Sylvester Okwunodu. 2007. "Borders and Access (or Lack of Access) to Transnational Spaces." *AACHRONYM: Global African Arts, Art-Equity and Cultural Patrimony*, October 11. Accessed April 16, 2013. http://aachronym.blogspot.com/2007/10/borders-and-access-or-lack-of-access-to.html.

Ohridska-Olson, R. and S. Ivanov. 2010. "Creative Tourism Business Model and Its Application in Bulgaria." Proceedings of the Black Sea Tourism Forum "Cultural Tourism – the Future of Bulgaria," September 23–25, Varna, Bulgaria, 23–39.

Okeowo, Alexis. 2015. "Handel in Kinshasa; An Unlikely Orchestra Wins the World's Attention." *New Yorker*, November 9. Accessed December 2, 2015. www.newyorker.com/magazine/2015/11/09/handel-in-kinshasa.

Olian Jr., Irwin A. 1974. "International Copyright and the Needs of Developing Countries: The Awakening at Stockholm and Paris." *Cornell International Law Journal* 7, no. 2: 88–112.

Omanufeme, Steve. 2016. "Runaway Success." *Finance and Development*, June. Accessed February 19, 2017. www.imf.org/external/pubs/ft/fandd/2016/06/omanufeme.htm.

On Music Dictionary. 2013."Leitmotif." Last Updated February 14. Accessed January 1, 2018. https://dictionary.onmusic.org/terms/1975-leitmotif.

2016a. "Deceptive Cadence." Last Updated May 23. Accessed January 1, 2018. https://dictionary.onmusic.org/terms/1034-deceptive_cadence.

2016b. "Fugue." Last Updated May 25. Accessed January 1, 2018. https://dictionary.onmusic.org/terms/1519-fugue.

2016c. "Overture." Last Updated June 6. Accessed January 1, 2018. https://dictionary.onmusic.org/terms/2460-overture.

2016d. "Theme and Variations." Last Updated May 7. Accessed January 1, 2018. https://dictionary.onmusic.org/terms/3553-theme_and_variations

Onishi, Norimitsu. 2016. "Nigeria's Booming Film Industry Redefines African Life." *New York Times*, February 18. Accessed April 9, 2016. www.nytimes.com/2016/02/19/world/africa/with-a-boom-before-the-cameras-nigeria-redefines-african-life.html?login=email&_r=0.

Ordóñez, Lisa D., Maurice E. Schweitzer, Adam D. Galinsky and Max H. Bazerman. 2009. *Goals Gone Wild: The Systematic Side Effects of Over-Prescribing Goal Setting Working Paper 09–083*. Boston: Harvard Business School. Working Paper 09–083. Accessed August 16, 2017. www.hbs.edu/faculty/Publication%20Files/09-083.pdf.

O'S, J. 2014. "How Nigeria's Economy Grew by 89 Percent Overnight." *Economist Explains*, April 7. January 10, 2017. www.economist.com/blogs/economist-explains/2014/04/economist-explains-2.

O'Toole, Garson. 2010. "Not Everything That Counts Can Be Counted." Quote Investigator. May 26. Last Updated December 28, 2016. Accessed December 29, 2017. https://quoteinvestigator.com/2010/05/26/everything-counts-einstein/.

2012. "We Cannot Predict the Future, but We Can Invent It." Quote Investigator. September 27. (Update History: The 2008 citation for Lincoln was added on April 14, 2016.) Accessed March 26, 2017. http://quoteinvestigator.com/2012/09/27/invent-the-future/.

Palca, Joe. 2015. "Climate Scientist Tries Arts to Stir Hearts Regarding Earth's Fate." *NPR*, February 16. Accessed May 5, 2017. www.npr.org/2015/02/16/386064582/climate-scientist-tries-arts-to-stir-hearts-regarding-earths-fate.

PBS (Public Broadcasting Service). 2009. *Dirt! The Movie*. Accessed April 11, 2017. www.pbs.org/independentlens/dirt-the-movie/film.html.

Pearlman, Edward. 2009. "CEFTA – Cultural Exchange Free Trade Agreement." iPetitions. March 27. Accessed January 6, 2018. www.ipetitions.com/petition/cefta/.

Penna, Frank J., Monique Thormann, and J. Michael Finger. 2004. "The Africa Music Project." In *Poor People's Knowledge: Promoting Intellectual Property in Developing Countries*, ed. J. Michael Finger and Philip Schuler. Washington, DC: World Bank. Accessed November 30, 2017. www.griequity.com/resources/industryandissues/IntellectualProperty/PoorPeoplesKnowledge.pdf.

Pérez-Peña, Richard. 2014. "College Classes Use Arts to Brace for Climate Change." *New York Times*, March 31. Accessed November 30, 2017. www.nytimes.com/2014/04/01/education/using-the-arts-to-teach-how-to-prepare-for-climate-crisis.html?_r=0.

Peters, Gerhard and John T. Woolley. 2007. "Mike Huckabee: Press Release – Mike Huckabee Triumphs at Republican Presidential Debate." *The American Presidency Project*. December 13. Accessed January 4, 2018. www.presidency.ucsb.edu/ws/index.php?pid=93377.

Petersen, Rob. 2013. "The Best Way to Predict the Future Is to Create It. 12 Reasons Why." *BarnRaisers*, December 22. Accessed March 26, 2017. http://barnraisersllc.com/2013/12/12-reasons-predict-future-create/.

Pham, Alex. 2009. "Napster Founder Shawn Fanning's Newest Brainchild." *Los Angeles Times*, April 25. Accessed November 18, 2015. http://articles.latimes.com/2009/apr/25/business/fi-fanning25.

Plumer, Brad. 2012. "SOPA [Stop Online Piracy Act]: How Much Does Online Piracy Really Cost the Economy?" *Washington Post*, January 5. Accessed June 14, 2015. www.washingtonpost.com/blogs/ezra-klein/post/how-much-does-online-piracy-really-cost-the-economy/2012/01/05/gIQAXknNdP_blog.html.

Polgreen, Lydia. 2015. "A Music-Sharing Network for the Unconnected." *New York Times Magazine*, December 2. Accessed June 24, 2015. www.nytimes.com/2015/06/07/magazine/a-music-sharing-network-for-the-unconnected.html.

Pollard, Jane, Cheryl McEwan, and Alex Hughes, eds. 2011. *Postcolonial Economies*. London: Zed Books.

Public Citizen. n.d. "Public Citizen's Lori Wallach and EU Trade Commissioner Pascal Lamy Sound Off on GATS." citizen.org. Accessed December 28, 2017. www.citizen.org/our-work/globalization-and-trade/public-citizens-lori-wallach-and-eu-trade-commissioner#PC_News.

Putnam, Robert D. n.d. "Better Together: The Arts and Social Capital." Saguaro Seminar on Civic Engagement in America. John F. Kennedy School of Government, Harvard University. Accessed April 5, 2017. www.creativecity.ca/database/files/library/better_together.pdf.

2001. *Bowling Alone: The Collapse and Revival of American Community*. New York: Touchstone Books by Simon & Schuster.

Putnam, Robert D. with Robert Leonardi and Raffaella Y. Nonett. 1993. *Making Democracy Work: Civic Traditions in Modern Italy*. Princeton: Princeton University Press.

Putumayo. n.d. "About Putumayo World Music." Accessed February 27, 2017. www.putumayo.com/history/.

Radio Free Europe/Radio Liberty. 2009. "British Ethnomusicologist: 'It Isn't Actually Correct to Say Taliban Have Banned Music.'" June 22. Accessed March 29, 2017. www.rferl.org/content/British_Ethnomusicologist_Discusses_Talibans_Campaign_Against_Musicians/1753865.html.

Raghavan, Sudarsan. 2012. "In Northern Mali, Music Silenced as Islamists Drive Out Artists." *Washington Post*, November 30. Accessed April 21, 2014. www

.washingtonpost.com/world/in-northern-mali-music-silenced-as-islamists-drive-out-artists/2012/11/30/110ea016-300c-11e2-af17-67abba0676e2_story.html.

Raines, Patrick and LaTanya Brown. 2006. "The Economic Impact of the Music Industry in the Nashville-Davidson-Murfreesboro." *Nashville Area Chamber of Commerce*, January. Accessed November 2, 2012. http://secure.nashvillechamber.com/president/musicindustryimpactstudy.pdf.

Rasul, Nadia. 2012. "Taliban Poetry: Yes, They Write Poems, and They're Surprisingly Diverse." *Atlantic*, June 11. Accessed March 26, 2017. www.theatlantic.com/international/archive/2012/06/taliban-poetry-yes-they-write-poems-and-theyre-surprisingly-diverse/258304/.

Ratha, Dilip and Patrick Kabanda. 2015. "African Art Needs to Come Home – and This Is Why." *Guardian*, October 21. Accessed March 29, 2017. www.theguardian.com/global-development-professionals-network/2015/oct/21/african-art-needs-to-come-home-and-this-is-why.

Read, Leonard E. 1999. "I, Pencil: My Family Tree as told to Leonard E. Read." Irvington-on-Hudson, NY: The Foundation for Economic Education, Inc. Library of Economics and Liberty. (Orig. Pub. 1958).Accessed December 31, 2016. www.econlib.org/library/Essays/rdPncl1.html.

Resource Matters. 2017. *Deciphering the $440 Million Discount for Glencore's DR Congo Mines*. November. Accessed January 7, 2018. https://resourcematters.org/wp-content/uploads/2017/11/Resource-Matters-The-440-million-discount-2017-11-29-FINAL-1.pdf.

Reuters. 2016. "Brazil President Reinstates Culture Ministry after Artists Protest." May 22. Accessed December 1, 2017. www.reuters.com/article/us-brazil-politics/brazil-president-reinstates-culture-ministry-after-artists-protest-idUSKCN0YD0TX.

Robinson, Ken. 2001. *Out of Our Minds: Learning to Be Creative*. 1st edn. Chichester, UK: Capstone.

Robinson, Marilynne. 2013. *When I Was a Child I Read Books: Essays*. New York: Picador.

2017. "What Are We Doing Here?" *New York Review of Books*. November 9. Accessed January 6, 2018. www.nybooks.com/articles/2017/11/09/what-are-we-doing-here/.

Rodale, Maria. 2009. "The End of GDP: A New Economic Model Closer to Nature." *Huffington Post*, September 28. (Updated November 17, 2011.) Accessed December 1, 2017. www.huffingtonpost.com/maria-rodale/the-end-of-gdp-a-new-econ_b_302129.html.

Rodrik, Dani. 2015. *Economics Rules: The Rights and Wrongs of the Dismal Science*. New York: W. W. Norton & Company.

Rohter, Larry. 2012. "U.S. Visa Rules Deprive Stages of Performers." *New York Times*, April 11. Accessed March 15, 2013. www.nytimes.com/2012/04/11/arts/us-visa-rules-frustrate-foreign-performers.html.

Romer, Paul M. 1994. "The Origins of Endogenous Growth." *Journal of Economic Perspectives* 8, no. 1 (Winter): 3–22. Accessed December 29, 2016. www.aeaweb.org/articles?id=10.1257/jep.8.1.3.

Root-Bernstein, Robert S. and Michèle M. Root-Bernstein. 2001. *Sparks of Genius: The Thirteen Thinking Tools of the World's Most Creative People.* New York: Mariner Books.

Ross, Karen. 2014. "Women in Decision-Making Structures in Media." In *Media and Gender: A Scholarly Agenda for the Global Alliance on Media and Gender*, ed. Aimée Vega Montie, 44–48. Paris: UNESCO in cooperation with IAMCR (International Association for Media and Communication Researchers). Accessed April 1, 2017. http://unesdoc.unesco.org/images/0022/002283/228399e.pdf.

Rothman, Joshua. 2015. "Was Steve Jobs an Artist?" *New Yorker*. October 14. Accessed January 7, 2018. www.newyorker.com/culture/cultural-comment/was-steve-jobs-an-artist.

Ruble, Blair A. 2017. *The Muse of Urban Delirium: How the Performing Arts Paradoxically Transform Conflict-Ridden Cities Into Centers of Cultural Innovation*. Washington, DC: New Academia Publishing, LLC.

Rugwabiza, Valentine. 2012. "'Africa Should Trade More with Africa to Secure Future Growth.'" *WTO*, Accessed March 5, 2015. www.wto.org/english/news_e/news12_e/ddg_12apr12_e.htm.

SAMRO (Southern African Music Rights Organisation). n.d. "Company Profile." Accessed February 26, 2017. www.samro.org.za/about.

2015. *Integrated Report 2015*. Accessed February 26, 2017. www.samro.org.za/sites/default/files/Samro_IR_9175_FULL%20IR_4Nov_WEB_FINAL%20REPORT.pdf.

Sanghani, Radhika. 2015. "Patricia Arquette Oscars Speech: Jennifer Lawrence Owes Her a Big Drink." *Telegraph*, February 23. Accessed April 14, 2016. www.telegraph.co.uk/women/womens-life/11429367/Patricia-Arquette-Oscars-speech-Jennifer-Lawrence-owes-her-a-drink.html.

Sanneh, Kelefa. 2009. "Michael Jackson." *New Yorker*, July 6 and 13. Accessed November 10, 2015. www.newyorker.com/magazine/2009/07/06/michael-jackson.

Sasajima, Hideaki. 2015. "Cultural Aspects of Artist-led Gentrification in SoHo between the 1950s and 1970s: A Field Analysis of the Agglomeration Processes of Art Venues." Paper presented at the RC21 International Conference on "The

Ideal City: Between Myth and Reality. Representations, Policies, Contradictions and Challenges for Tomorrow's Urban Life," Urbino, Italy. August 27–29. Accessed April 8, 2017. www.rc21.org/en/wp-content/uploads/2015/08/000-Sasajima.pdf.

Sauvé, Pierre. 2003. "Labor Mobility and the WTO: Liberalizing Temporary Movement." In *Global Economic Prospects 2004: Realizing the Development Promise of Doha*. Washington, DC: World Bank. Accessed December 1, 2017. http://siteresources.worldbank.org/INTRGEP2004/Resources/gep2004fulltext.pdf.

Schreiber, John and Alison Scott-Williams. 2016. Conference call. Washington, DC. October 25.

Schultz, Theodore W. 1992. "Adam Smith and Human Capital." In *Adam Smith's Legacy: His Place in the Development of Modern Economics*, ed. Michael Fry. London: Routledge.

Scott, Allen J. 1997. "The Cultural Economy of Cities." *International Journal of Urban and Regional Research* 21, no. 2: 323–339. Accessed March 31, 2017. http://onlinelibrary.wiley.com/doi/10.1111/1468-2427.00075/epdf.

2004. *On Hollywood: The Place, the Industry*. Princeton: Princeton University Press.

Seabrook, John. 2012. "Factory Girls: Cultural Technology and the Making of K-Pop." *New Yorker*, October 8. Accessed July 14, 2014. www.newyorker.com/magazine/2012/10/08/factory-girls-2.

Sen, Amartya. 2000. *Development as Freedom*. New York: Anchor Books.

2001. "Preface." In *Workshop on the Development of the Music Industry in Africa*. Development Economics Research Group on International Trade. June 20–21. Washington, DC: World Bank. Accessed November 18, 2011. http://siteresources.worldbank.org/INTCEERD/Resources/CWI_music_industry_in_Africa_synopsis.pdf.

2004. "*How Does Culture Matter?*" In *Culture and Public Action*, ed. Vijayendra Rao and Michael Walton. Stanford: Stanford University Press.

2006. *Identity and Violence: The Illusion of Destiny*. New York: W. W. Norton & Company.

2012. "What's the Use of Economics?" Lecture, Penthouse, Harvard Student Organization Center at Hilles, Harvard University, Cambridge, MA, December 1.

2013. "Our Past and Our Future." Opening Keynote Speech, World Culture Forum, Bali International Conventional Centre, Nusa Dua, Bali, Indonesia, November 25. Accessed April 18, 2014. http://wcf.inclusivemuseum.org/files/2013/12/Prof-Amartya_Sen_Speech_World-Culture-Forum_Bali.pdf.

Sen, Nandana 2013a. "'Gender Sensitivity Is a Matter of Life and Death . . . All of Us Are Accountable.'" *Indian Express*, February 19. Accessed January 13, 2017. http://archive.indianexpress.com/news/-gender-sensitivity-is-a-matter-of-life-and-death. . .-all-of-us-are-accountable-/1076012/.

2013b. "Pass by on the Sidewalk, without Looking." *Outlook*, March 25. Accessed January 20, 2017. www.outlookindia.com/magazine/story/pass-by-on-the-sidewalk-without-looking/284355.

Smith, Adam. 1994. *The Wealth of Nations*, ed. Edwin Cannan. New York: Modern Library. (Orig. publ. 1776.)

n.d. *The Theory of Moral Sentiments*. Whitefish, MT: Kessinger Legacy Reprints. (Orig. publ. circa 1759.)

Smith, Mark. K. 2000–2009. "Social Capital." *The Encyclopedia of Informal Education (Infed)*. Accessed January 4, 2016. http://infed.org/mobi/social-capital/.

2002, 2008. "Howard Gardner and Multiple Intelligences." *Infed*. Accessed October 15, 2014. www.infed.org/mobi/howard-gardner-multiple-intelligences-and-education.

Smith, Stacy L., Marc Choueiti, and Katherine Pieper, with assistance from Yu-Ting Liu and Christine Song. 2014. *Gender Bias without Borders: An Investigation of Female Characters in Popular Films Across 11 Countries*. Geena Davis Institute on Gender in Media. Accessed October 6, 2015. http://seejane.org/wp-content/uploads/gender-bias-without-borders-full-report.pdf.

Sparviero, Sergio. 2015. "Hollywood Creative Accounting: The Success Rate of Major Motion Pictures." *Media Industries Journal* 2, no. 1. Accessed February 2, 2017. www.mediaindustriesjournal.org/index.php/mij/article/download/40/173.

Statistics Bureau, Ministry of Internal Affairs and Communications, Japan. "Statistical Handbook of Japan 2017." 2017. Accessed September 25, 2017. www.stat.go.jp/english/data/handbook/pdf/2017all.pdf#page=187.

Stewart, Jude. 2017. "Boredom Is Good for You." *Atlantic*. June. Accessed January 4, 2018. www.theatlantic.com/magazine/archive/2017/06/make-time-for-boredom/524514.

Stiglitz. Joseph E. 2009. "The World Development Report: Development Theory and Policy." In *Development Economics through the Decades: A Critical Look at 30 Years of the World Development Report*. Washington, DC: World Bank. Accessed December 1, 2017. https://openknowledge.worldbank.org/bitstream/handle/10986/2586/47108.pdf?sequence=1.

Sturgeon, Timothy. 2015. "Trade in Value Added Indicators: What They Are, What They Aren't, and Where They're Headed." *Vox*, May 20. Accessed February 13, 2017. http://voxeu.org/article/trade-value-added-indicators-caveat-emptor.

Sui, Cindy. 2016. "Taiwan Steps up Efforts to Improve Mental Health Care." *BBC*, February 19. Accessed December 1, 2017. www.bbc.com/news/world-asia-35610064.

Sullivan, Joseph F. 1987. "Kean Is Planning Arts Center for Newark With 8,000 Seats." *New York Times*, July 23. Accessed October 16, 2015. www.nytimes.com/1987/07/23/nyregion/kean-is-planning-arts-center-for-newark-with-8000-seats.html.

Swanson, Ana. 2015. "The Oscars in Six Charts and Maps." Wonkblog, *Washington Post*, February 22. Accessed October 5, 2015. www.washingtonpost.com/news/wonkblog/wp/2015/02/22/the-oscars-in-six-charts-and-maps/.

Sweet Dreams. 2012. "About the Film." Accessed March 4, 2017. www.sweetdreamsrwanda.com/film/.

Takingrootfilm.com. 2015. "The Story." *Taking Root: The Vision of Wangari Maathai*. Accessed March 15, 2017. http://takingrootfilm.com/story.htm.

Tamkivi, Sten. 2014. "Lessons from the World's Most Tech-Savvy Government." *Atlantic*, January 24. Accessed November 11, 2015. www.theatlantic.com/international/archive/2014/01/lessons-from-the-worlds-most-tech-savvy-government/283341/.

Tere, Nidhi Shendurnikar. 2012. "Gender Reflections in Mainstream Hindi Cinema." *Global Media Journal (Indian Edition/ISSN 2249 – 5835)* 3, no. 1 (June): 1–9. Accessed January 13, 2017. www.caluniv.ac.in/global-mdia-journal/Students'%20Research/SR4%20NIDHI.pdf.

The Crossroads Project, n.d. "Concept." Accessed November 25, 2017. www.thecrossroadsproject.org/performance.html#concept.

The Green Belt Movement n.d.a. "Be a Hummingbird." Accessed November 28, 2017. www.greenbeltmovement.org/get-involved/be-a-hummingbird.

n.d.b. "Who We Are." Accessed November 26, 2017. www.greenbeltmovement.org/who-we-are.

The New Orleans Jazz & Heritage Foundation, Inc. n.d. "About Us." Accessed November 25, 2017. https://www.jazzandheritage.org/about-us.

The New Orleans Jazz & Heritage Foundation, Inc. 2013. "Second-Life Recycling." October 7. Accessed November 25, 2017. www.jazzandheritage.org/news/second-life-recycling.

The Royal Swedish Academy of Sciences. 2016. "Contract Theory." *The Prize in Economic Sciences* 2016. Stockholm. Accessed April 20, 2017. www.nobelprize.org/nobel_prizes/economic-sciences/laureates/2016/popular-economicsciences2016.pdf.

This Is Nollywood. n.d. Accessed November 27, 2011. www.thisisnollywood.com/film.htm.

Thompson, Derek. 2011. "How Hollywood Accounting Can Make a $450 Million Movie 'Unprofitable.'" *Atlantic*, September 14. Accessed February 2, 2016. www.theatlantic.com/business/archive/2011/09/how-hollywood-accounting-can-make-a-450-million-movie-unprofitable/245134/.

Thompson, Lyndon.2013. "Profiting from trade in value added." *OECD Observer*. 295, Q2 2013. September 1. Accessed February 15, 2017. http://m.oecdobserver.org/news/fullstory.php/aid/4121/Profiting_from_trade_in_value_added.html.

Throsby, David. 2001. *Economics and Culture*. Cambridge, UK: Cambridge University Press.

2010. *The Economics of Cultural Policy*. Cambridge, UK: Cambridge University Press.

Tichy, Noel M. and Warren G. Bennis. 2007. *Judgment: How Winning Leaders Make Great Calls*. New York: Penguin Group.

Tierney, John. 2015. "The Reign of Recycling." *New York Times*, October 3. Accessed August 16, 2017. www.nytimes.com/2015/10/04/opinion/sunday/the-reign-of-recycling.html.

Timberg, Scott. 2015. *Culture Crash: The Killing of the Creative Class*. New Haven: Yale University Press.

Times of India. 2010. "Piracy Cost Bollywood $959m: Report." March 20. Accessed June 9, 2014. http://timesofindia.indiatimes.com/india/Piracy-cost-Bollywood-959m-Report/articleshow/5703165.cms.

TIPA (Taiwan Intellectual Property Training Academy). n.d. "About TIPA." Accessed June 9, 2014. www.tipa.org.tw/ep1.asp.

Tepper, Steven J. with contributions from Blake Sisk, Ryan Johnson, Leah Vanderwerp, Genevieve Gale, and Min Gao. 2014. *Artful Living: Examining the Relationship between Artistic Practice and Subjective Wellbeing Across Three National Surveys*. Nashville, Tennessee: The Curb Center for Art, Enterprise, and Public Policy at Vanderbilt University. Accessed January 29, 2017. www.arts.gov/sites/default/files/Research-Art-Works-Vanderbilt.pdf.

Tiwari, Shubha. 2012. "Review of *Dancing in Cambodia, At Large in Burma*." *Boloji*, May 17. Accessed April 11, 2017. www.boloji.com/index.cfm?md=Content&sd=Articles&ArticleID=12249.

Trachtman, Joel P. 2009. *The International Law of Economic Migration: Toward the Fourth Freedom*. Kalamazoo, MI: W.E. Upjohn Institute.

TripAdvisor. n.d. "Rio de Janeiro, RJ." Overview. Accessed March 11, 2017. www.tripadvisor.com/Tourism-g303506-Rio_de_Janeiro_State_of_Rio_de_Janeiro-Vacations.html.

Tulshyan, Ruchika. 2013. "Rape Every 20 Minutes for the World's Largest Democracy?" *Forbes*, January 2. Accessed December 1, 2017. www.forbes.com/sites/worldviews/2013/01/02/rape-every-20-minutes-for-the-worlds-largest-democracy/#634f0dd24734.

2014. "How Bollywood Is Failing the Women of India." *Forbes*, April 19. Accessed December 1, 2017. www.forbes.com/sites/ruchikatulshyan/2014/04/19/how-bollywood-is-failing-the-women-of-india/#2842df4b3345.

UN. 2010. *Creative Economy Report 2010: A Feasible Development Option*. UNDP and UNCTAD. Accessed March 28, 2016. http://unctad.org/en/Docs/ditctab20103_en.pdf.

2013. *Creative Economy Report 2013 Special Edition: Widening Local Development Pathways*. New York and Paris: UNDP/UNESCO. Accessed April 10, 2014. www.unesco.org/culture/pdf/creative-economy-report-2013.pdf.

2015. "Transforming Our World: the 2030 Agenda for Sustainable Development." (A/RES/70/1). Sustainable Development Knowledge Platform. Accessed December 18, 2016. https://sustainabledevelopment.un.org/content/documents/21252030%20Agenda%20for%20Sustainable%20Development%20web.pdf.

UNCTADstat. (United Nations Conference on Trade and Development Statistics). 2014. "Data Center." Accessed September 1, 2016. http://unctadstat.unctad.org/EN/.

UNEP (United Nations Environment Programme), CITES (Convention on International Trade in Endangered Species), IUCN (International Union for Conservation of Nature), and TRAFFIC (TRAFFIC.org). 2013. "Elephants in the Dust—The African Elephant Crisis." Accessed December 1, 2017. www.cites.org/sites/default/files/common/resources/pub/Elephants_in_the_dust.pdf.

UNESCO (United Nations Education, Scientific, and Cultural Organization). 2001. "UNESCO Universal Declaration on Cultural Diversity." November 2. Accessed December 1, 2017. http://portal.unesco.org/en/ev.php-URL_ID=13179&URL_DO=DO_TOPIC&URL_SECTION=201.html.

2009. "Nollywood Rivals Bollywood in Film/Video Production," May 5. Accessed April 4, 2016. www.unesco.org/new/en/media-services/single-view/news/nollywood_rivals_bollywood_in_filmvideo_production/.

2012. "Rio de Janeiro: Carioca Landscapes between the Mountain and the Sea." World Heritage List. Accessed March 11, 2017. http://whc.unesco.org/en/list/1100.

2014. *UNESCO Priority Gender Equality Action Plan 2014–2021*. Paris. Accessed April 1, 2017. http://unesdoc.unesco.org/images/0022/002272/227222e.pdf.

2015a. "Cultural Employment. Measuring How Culture Contributes to Economic Development." Accessed May 7, 2014. www.uis.unesco.org/culture/Pages/cultural-employment.aspx.

2015b. Hangzhou International Congress. "Culture: Key to Sustainable Development." Accessed October 30, 2015. www.unesco.org/fileadmin/MULTIMEDIA/HQ/CLT/images/FinalHangzhouDeclaration20130517.pdf.

UNESCO, World Commission on Culture and Development. 1996. *Our Creative Diversity*. Paris: UNESCO. Accessed April 11, 2016. http://unesdoc.unesco.org/images/0010/001055/105586e.pdf.

UNSD (United Nations Statistics Division). n.d. "The System of National Accounts (SNA)" Accessed May 8, 2017. http://unstats.un.org/unsd/nationalaccount/sna.asp.

UN Women. 2014. "Press Release: Global Film Industry Perpetuates Discrimination against Women." September 22. Accessed October 6, 2015. www.unwomen.org/en/news/stories/2014/9/geena-davis-study-press-release.

UNWTO (The United Nations World Tourism Organization). n.d. "Basic Concepts of the Tourism Satellite Account (TSA)." Accessed August 22, 2016. http://statistics.unwto.org/sites/all/files/docpdf/concepts.pdf.

UniqueTracks. 2014. "Witty Response to Craigslist Ad Asking Musicians to Play for Free," August 30. Accessed September 3, 2015. www.uniquetracks-blog.com/uniquetracks-is-currently-closed-for-renovation/.

University of California, Santa Barbara. n.d. "Sylvester Okwunodu Ogbechie." Department of History of Art & Architecture. Accessed February 28, 2017. www.arthistory.ucsb.edu/people/sylvester-okwunodu-ogbechie.

University of Wisconsin-Madison, Group 2. 2009. "Nollywood: Osuofia in London." Hybridity in West African Popular Culture, July 7. "Case Studies in West African Popular Culture." Accessed December 22, 2015. http://africa.wisc.edu/hybrid/2009/07/07/nollywood-osuofia-in-london/.

US Department of Labor. 2009. "Work Authorization for Non-U.S. Citizens: Temporary Agricultural Workers (H-2A Visas)." Updated: September. Accessed February 27, 2017. www.dol.gov/compliance/guide/taw.htm.

USCIS (U.S. Citizenship and Immigration Services). 2017. "O-1 Visa: Individuals with Extraordinary Ability or Achievement." Last Reviewed/Updated January 5. Accessed February 27, 2017. www.uscis.gov/working-united-states/temporary-workers/o-1-visa-individuals-extraordinary-ability-or-achievement.

United States History. n.d. "History of Hollywood, California." Accessed February 26, 2017. www.u-s-history.com/pages/h3871.html.

Varma, Subodh. 2014. "'It's Not a Fair Deal for Women in Bollywood.'" *Times of India*, September 24. Accessed April 1, 2017. http://timesofindia.indiatimes.com/india/Its-not-a-fair-deal-for-women-in-Bollywood/articleshow/43279806.cms.

Veloso, Caetano. 2010. Foreword. In *Culture Is Our Weapon: Making Music and Changing Lives in Rio de Janeiro*. New York: Penguin Group. (Orig. publ. 2006.)

Voon, Tania. 2007. *Cultural Products and the World Trade Organization*. Cambridge, UK: Cambridge University Press.

Wanda Group n.d.a. "Cultural Tourism Planning and Research Institute." Accessed December 30, 2017. www.wanda-group.com/businesses/culture/research_institute/.

n.d.b. "Group Profile." Accessed December 30, 2017. www.wanda-group.com/corporate/.

Watanabe, Teresa. 2010. "Immigration Agency Working to Fix Visa Denials to Artists, Others." *Los Angeles Times*, August 10. Accessed January 5, 2018. http://articles.latimes.com/2010/aug/10/local/la-me-workvisa-20100810.

WWCD (Webster's World of Cultural Democracy). n.d. "What Is 'Cultural Democracy'"? Accessed April 18, 2017. www.wwcd.org/cddef.html.

Weingarten, Gene. 2007. "Pearls before Breakfast." *Washington Post*, April 8. Accessed June 16, 2014. www.washingtonpost.com/wp-dyn/content/article/2007/04/04/AR2007040401721.html.

Weiner, Eric. 2016. *The Geography of Genius: Lessons from the World's Most Creative Places*. Reprint edn. New York: Simon & Schuster.

Weinstein, Jack Russell. 2007. "Adam Smith's Philosophy of Education." *The Adam Smith Review*, 3: 51–157. Accessed December 31, 2016. https://pdfs.semanticscholar.org/cab2/88d21502d287562d204f626b0d73e0eabf39.pdf.

Whaley, Floyd. 2013. "Powering the Philippine Economy with Elvis and Zeppelin." *New York Times*, January 31. Accessed November 30, 2017. www.nytimes.com/2013/02/01/business/global/powering-the-philippine-economy-with-elvis-and-zeppelin.html.

White, Michael. 2014. "In a Battle of the Batons, a Barely Visible Alchemy; Elim Chan's Flick Conducting Prize Is Rare Win for a Woman." *New York Times*, December 10. Accessed November 30, 2017. www.nytimes.com/2014/12/11/arts/music/elim-chans-flick-conducting-prize-is-rare-win-for-a-woman.html.

Women's Studies at James Madison University (Wikispace). n.d. "The Degradation of Women in Music." Accessed March 30, 2015. http://womensstudiesjmu.wikispaces.com/The+Degradation+of+Women+in+Music.

World Bank. n.d.a. "Afghanistan." Accessed May 5, 2017. www.worldbank.org/en/country/afghanistan

n.d.b. "Cultural Heritage: An Asset for Urban Development and Poverty Reduction." Washington, DC. Accessed April 28, 2014. http://siteresources.worldbank.org/INTCHD/Resources/430063-1250192845352/CHandslums_Oct.pdf.

n.d.c. "Mali." Accessed April 19, 2014. www.worldbank.org/en/country/mali.

2001. "Workshop on the Development of the Music Industry in Africa." Development Economics Research Group on International Trade. June 20–21. Accessed May 9, 2014. http://siteresources.worldbank.org/INTCEERD/Resources/CWI_music_industry_in_Africa_synopsis.pdf.

2011. "World Development Report 2012: Gender Equality and Development." Washington, DC: World Bank. Accessed November 30, 2017. https://siteresources.worldbank.org/INTWDR2012/Resources/7778105-1299699968583/7786210-1315936222006/Complete-Report.pdf.

2013. "Inclusion Matters: The Foundation for Shared Prosperity." Washington, DC: World Bank. doi:10.1596/978–1-4648–0010-8. Accessed April 7, 2014. http://documents.worldbank.org/curated/en/114561468154469371/Inclusion-matters-the-foundation-for-shared-prosperity.

2013. "WTO, World Bank to Develop Services Trade Database." August 6. Accessed July 25, 2014. www.worldbank.org/en/news/press-release/2013/08/06/wto-world-bank-to-develop-services-trade-database.

2014a. "The Republic of Haiti. Cultural Heritage Preservation and Tourism Sector Support Project." Report No: PAD610. Accessed May 22, 2014. http://documents.worldbank.org/curated/en/360221468251118158/pdf/PAD6100P1446140B00PUBLIC050101400SD.pdf.

2014b. "The World Bank Group Strategy." Washington, DC: World Bank Group. Accessed April 22, 2014. https://openknowledge.worldbank.org/bitstream/handle/10986/16095/32824_ebook.pdf?sequence=5.

2015. "World Development Report 2015: Mind, Society, and Behavior." Washington, DC: World Bank. doi:10.1596/978–1-4648–0342-0. Accessed November 30, 2017. http://documents.worldbank.org/curated/en/645741468339541646/pdf/928630WDR0978100Box385358B00PUBLIC0.pdf.

2016. "World Development Report 2016: Digital Dividends." Washington, DC: World Bank. doi:10.1596/978-1-4648-0671-1. Accessed November 30, 2017. http://documents.worldbank.org/curated/en/896971468194972881/pdf/102725-PUB-Replacement-PUBLIC.pdf.

WHO (World Health Organization). 2013. "Mental Health Action Plan 2013–2020." Geneva: WHO. Accessed October 15, 2015. www.who.int/mental_health/publications/action_plan/en/.

World Policy Journal. 2011. "This Land Is Your Land: A Conversation with Hernando de Soto." Summer. Accessed April 23, 2014. www.worldpolicy.org/journal/summer2011/this-land-is-your-land.

WIPO (World Intellectual Property Organization). n.d. "What Is Intellectual Property?" Accessed February 19, 2018. www.wipo.int/about-ip/en/.

2008. "WIPO Intellectual Property Handbook: Policy." Accessed November 6, 2015. www.wipo.int/edocs/pubdocs/en/intproperty/489/wipo_pub_489.pdf.

2013. "Teaching Intellectual Property (IP) in Countries in Transition." Accessed April 3, 2017. www.wipo.int/edocs/pubdocs/en/wipo_pub_transition_7.pdf.

2014. "WIPO Studies on the Economic Contribution of the Copyright Industries." Accessed January 11. 2018. www.wipo.int/export/sites/www/copyright/en/performance/pdf/economic_contribution_analysis_2014.pdf.

2015. "Guide on Surveying the Economic Contribution of Copyright Industries." Revised edn. Geneva. Publication No. 893 E. Accessed February 21, 2017. www.wipo.int/edocs/pubdocs/en/copyright/893/wipo_pub_893.pdf.

WTO (World Trade Organization). n.d. "The General Agreement on Trade in Services (GATS): Objectives, Coverage and Disciplines." Accessed April 23, 2014. www.wto.org/english/tratop_e/serv_e/gatsqa_e.htm.

n.d.a. "WTO Legal Texts." Accessed November 29, 2011. www.wto.org/english/docs_e/legal_e/legal_e.htm#TRIPs.

n.d.b. "Services: Rules for Growth and Investment." Accessed February 26, 2017. www.wto.org/english/thewto_e/whatis_e/tif_e/agrm6_e.htm.

n.d.c. "Services Trade. " Accessed February 26, 2017. www.wto.org/english/tratop_e/serv_e/serv_e.htm.

n.d.d. "What Is the WTO?" Accessed February 26, 2017. www.wto.org/english/thewto_e/whatis_e/whatis_e.htm.

2017. "TRIPS Agreement (as amended on 23 January 2017)." PART I General Provisions and Basic Principles. Accessed December 28, 2017. https://www.wto.org/english/docs_e/legal_e/31bis_trips_01_e.htm.

Williams, Daryle, Amy Chazkel, and Paulo Knauss de Mendonça, eds. 2016. *The Rio de Janeiro Reader: History, Culture, Politics*. Durham, NC: Duke University Press.

Wilson, Edward Osborne. 1998. *Consilience: The Unity of Knowledge*. New York: Alfred A. Knopf, Inc.

2017. *The Origins of Creativity*. New York: Liveright.

WTTC (World Travel & Tourism Council). 2015a. "Travel and Tourism Economic Impact 2015: World." London. Accessed October 10, 2016.www.wttc.org/-/media/files/reports/economic%20impact%20research/regional%202015/world2015.pdf.

2015b. "Travel and Tourism Economic Impact 2015: Laos." London. Accessed April 14, 2017. www.wttc.org/-/media/files/reports/economic%20impact%20research/countries%202015/laos2015.pdf.

2015c. "Travel & Tourism Economic Impact 2015: Nigeria." London. Accessed April 14, 2017. www.wttc.org/-/media/files/reports/economic%20impact%20research/countries%202015/nigeria2015.pdf.

2017. "Economic Impact 2017 – March 2017." Accessed October 3, 2017. www.wttc.org/-/media/files/reports/economic-impact-research/countries-2017/nigeria2017.pdf#page=5.

WQXR. 2013. "After the 'Mozart Effect': Music's Real Impact on the Brain." November 6. Accessed November 30, 2017. www.wqxr.org/story/after-mozart-effect-music-impact-brain/.

Wulfhorst, Ellen. 2015. "New Jersey's Largest City Is a Mess." *Business Insider*, June 25. Accessed October 24, 2015. www.businessinsider.com/r-mayor-faces-complexities-of-poverty-crime-in-reviving-njs-largest-city-2015-6.

Xiao, An. 2013. "Mental Health and Healing through the Lens of Taiwan's History." *Hyperallergic*, October 28. Accessed April 11, 2017. http://hyperallergic.com/88453/mental-health-and-healing-through-the-lens-of-taiwans-history/.

YouTube. n.d. "Statistics." Accessed October 30, 2015. www.youtube.com/yt/press/statistics.html.

Yunus, Muhammad, with Karl Weber. 2007. *Creating a World without Poverty: Social Business and the Future of Capitalism*. New York: PublicAffairs.

Yusuf, Shahid, with Angus Deaton, Kemal Derviş, William Easterly, Takatoshi Ito, and Joseph E. Stiglitz. 2009. *Development Economics through the Decades: A Critical Look at 30 Years of the World Development Report*. Washington, DC:

World Bank. Accessed November 30, 2017. https://openknowledge.worldbank.org/bitstream/handle/10986/2586/47108.pdf?sequence=1&isAllowed=y.

Zinsser, William. 1984. *Willie and Dwike: An American Profile.* New York: Harper & Row.

Zucman, Gabriel. 2015. *The Hidden Wealth of Nations: the Scourge of Tax Havens.* Chicago: University of Chicago Press.

Index